About This Book

What can you achieve with this

This book is a guide for internal and external learning profes.........want to add performance consulting to their scope of services. It has tools, stories, and guidelines for becoming a consultant, operating more like a consultant in deference to a training specialist, and positioning yourself as a consultant with clients.

Why is the topic important?

This book was written because trainers are recognizing the need to apply the principles of performance improvement in their work. Training can help people be more effective in the workplace; however, alone it rarely produces the desired long-term results. Learning professionals are realizing that they need to improve their skills at working with clients to identify actual barriers to performance and participating in the design of a more expanded suite of solutions. At the same time, clients and consumers are recognizing that training by itself rarely leads to sustained performance. They want professionals to collaborate with them in uncovering and removing barriers to workplace performance.

How is this book organized?

This book is in two parts. Part One is about how to become a performance improvement consultant. Part Two describes the methods and tools for analyzing performance needs, determining work requirements, identifying solutions beyond training, and measuring people performance. There are five chapters in each part, and each chapter contains stories, guidelines, tools, techniques, and checklists you can use to engage clients in the process of becoming a performance consultant, uncovering needs, collaborating with other experts, and recommending solutions beyond training.

About Pfeiffer

Pfeiffer serves the professional development and hands-on resource needs of training and human resource practitioners and gives them products to do their jobs better. We deliver proven ideas and solutions from experts in HR development and HR management, and we offer effective and customizable tools to improve workplace performance. From novice to seasoned professional, Pfeiffer is the source you can trust to make yourself and your organization more successful.

Essential Knowledge Pfeiffer produces insightful, practical, and comprehensive materials on topics that matter the most to training and HR professionals. Our Essential Knowledge resources translate the expertise of seasoned professionals into practical, how-to guidance on critical workplace issues and problems. These resources are supported by case studies, worksheets, and job aids and are frequently supplemented with CD-ROMs, websites, and other means of making the content easier to read, understand, and use.

Essential Tools Pfeiffer's Essential Tools resources save time and expense by offering proven, ready-to-use materials—including exercises, activities, games, instruments, and assessments—for use during a training or team-learning event. These resources are frequently offered in looseleaf or CD-ROM format to facilitate copying and customization of the material.

Pfeiffer also recognizes the remarkable power of new technologies in expanding the reach and effectiveness of training. While e-hype has often created whizbang solutions in search of a problem, we are dedicated to bringing convenience and enhancements to proven training solutions. All our e-tools comply with rigorous functionality standards. The most appropriate technology wrapped around essential content yields the perfect solution for today's on-the-go trainers and human resource professionals.

The Performance
Consultant's Fieldbook

The Performance Consultant's Fieldbook

Tools and Techniques for Improving Organizations and People

SECOND EDITION

Judith Hale

Pfeiffer
A Wiley Imprint
www.pfeiffer.com

Published by Pfeiffer
An Imprint of Wiley.
989 Market Street, San Francisco, CA 94103-1741
www.pfeiffer.com

For additional copies/bulk purchases of this book in the U.S. please contact 800-274-4434.

Pfeiffer books and products are available through most bookstores. To contact Pfeiffer directly call our Customer Care Department within the U.S. at 800-274-4434, outside the U.S. at 317-572-3985, fax 317-572-4002, or visit www.pfeiffer.com.

Pfeiffer also publishes its books in a variety of electronic formats. Some content that appears in print may not be available in electronic books.

Library of Congress Cataloging-in-Publication Data

Hale, Judith A.
  The performance consultant's fieldbook: tools and techniques for improving organizations and people/Judith Hale.—2nd ed.
      p. cm.
  Includes bibliographical references and index.
  ISBN-13: 978-0-7879-8534-9 (paper/cd)
  ISBN-10: 0-7879-8534-1 (paper/cd)
1. Business consultants—Handbooks, manuals, etc. 2. Employees—Rating of—Handbooks, manuals, etc. 3. Performance standards—Handbooks, manuals, etc. 4. Performance technology—Handbooks, manuals, etc. I. Title.
  HD69.C6H35 2007
  658.3'124—dc22
                              2006019147

Acquiring Editor: Matt Davis
Director of Development: Kathleen Dolan Davies
Production Editor: Rachel Anderson

Editor: Bev Miller
Manufacturing Supervisor: Becky Carreño
Editorial Assistant: Julie Rodriguez

Interior Design: Joseph Piliero
Illustrations: Lotus Art

Printed in the United States of America
Printing 10 9 8 7 6 5 4 3 2

Contents

Figures / **xi**

CD-ROM Contents / **xv**

Preface / **xvii**

Introduction / **xxi**

PART ONE **Making the Transition / 1**

1. Performance Consulting / **3**

2. The Transition / **33**

3. Costs / **57**

4. Credibility and Influence / **79**

5. Sustaining Change / **103**

PART TWO **Performance Consulting / 113**

6. Environment and Norms / **115**

7. Needs Assessment and Cause Analysis / **137**

8. Interventions / **169**

9. Measuring Results / **199**

10. Measuring People Performance / **217**

Index / **243**

About the Author / **265**

How to Use the CD-ROM / **267**

Figures

1.1   The Expert-Facilitator Continuum / **6**

1.2   The Critic-Doer-Spectator Continuum / **7**

1.3   Example of an Operational Definition of Performance Consulting / **10**

1.4   The ASTD's HRD Roles That Relate to Performance Consulting / **11**

1.5   The ASTD's HRD Competencies That Relate to
Performance Consulting / **11**

1.6   ISPI's HPT Standards / **13**

1.7   Operational Definition Worksheet / **15**

1.8   Operational Definition of Mike's Expectations / **17**

1.9   The Consulting Process / **20**

1.10   Mike's Consulting Process / **25**

1.11   The Finance Team's Process / **27**

1.12   Vision and Mission for This Fieldbook / **28**

1.13   The Finance Team's Vision and Mission Statements / **29**

1.14   My List of Consulting Competencies / **31**

2.1   My Consulting Process Standards / **37**

2.2   Mike's Expectations for Consulting Proficiency / **40**

2.3   Product Portfolio Worksheet 1 / **43**

2.4   Product Portfolio Worksheet 2 / **44**

2.5   Deborah's Portfolio of Current Products and Services / **48**

2.6 Deborah's New Products and Services / **50**

3.1 Major Cost Classifications / **59**

3.2 Manufacturers' Major Cost Components / **60**

3.3 Cost of Sales / **61**

3.4 Cost of Services / **61**

3.5 Cost of Running the Business / **61**

3.6 Examples of Costs / **63**

3.7 Components of Price / **64**

3.8 A Formula for Valuing Time / **65**

3.9 Process or Task Performance Worksheet / **72**

4.1 Evaluating Your Personal Power Base / **85**

4.2 Qualifying Survey for Clients' Readiness and Maturity / **97**

4.3 If-Then Table: Developing a Strategy from the Survey Results / **99**

5.1 Logic Chain: From Need to Measured Results / **105**

5.2 A Logic Chain for Reducing Stress: Need, Solution, Measures of Success / **107**

5.3 Logic Chain Template / **108**

6.1 The Zone of Competence / **117**

6.2 Contextual Job Description / **123**

6.3 Job Description for International Product Managers / **125**

6.4 Elements of a Social System / **127**

6.5 Deborah's Job Description / **133**

7.1 Scorecard Job Aid / **140**

7.2 Scorecard Worksheet / **141**

7.3 The Hierarchy / **146**

7.4 The Hierarchy Job Aid / **148**

7.5 The Hierarchy Worksheet / **152**

7.6 How to Control Bias / **162**

8.1 Interventions at the Individual, Work Group, Department, and Division Levels / **175**

8.2 The Families of Interventions / **176**

8.3 Interventions Job Aid: Information-Focused Interventions / **178**

8.4 Interventions Job Aid: Consequences-Focused Interventions / **180**

8.5   Interventions Job Aid: Design-Focused Interventions / **184**

8.6   Interventions Job Aid: Capacity- and
Capability-Focused Interventions / **186**

8.7   Interventions Job Aid: Action-Focused Interventions / **189**

8.8   Interventions Job Aid: Congruency-Focused Interventions / **192**

8.9   The Hierarchy-Interventions Matrix / **194**

9.1   When Measurement Occurs and Why / **205**

9.2   Measures, Criteria, and Metrics Scorecard / **209**

9.3   Examples of Evidence / **210**

9.4   Evidence Worksheet / **211**

10.1   Reasons and Criteria for Evaluating Performance / **221**

10.2   Directions for the NGT / **222**

10.3   Guidelines for Creating People Performance Worksheets / **222**

10.4   Performance Criteria for the Sales Managers / **223**

10.5   Quantitative Measures Summary Worksheet / **224**

10.6   Qualitative Measures Summary Worksheet / **225**

10.7   Dimensions of a Job / **227**

10.8   Examples of Measures for Job Dimensions / **228**

10.9   Job Evaluation Job Aid / **229**

10.10 The Finance Group's Measures / **236**

10.11 Merit Review Criteria / **240**

CD-ROM Contents

1. **Performance Consulting**

   Figure 1.7 Operational Definition Worksheet

2. **The Transition**

   Figure 2.3 Product Portfolio Worksheet 1
   Figure 2.4 Product Portfolio Worksheet 2

3. **Costs**

   Figure 3.8 A Formula for Valuing Time
   Figure 3.9 Process or Task Performance Worksheet

4. **Credibility and Influence**

   Figure 4.1 Evaluating Your Personal Power Base
   Figure 4.2 Qualifying Survey for Clients' Readiness and Maturity
   Figure 4.3 If-Then Table: Developing a Strategy from the Survey Results

5. **Sustaining Change**

   Figure 5.3 Logic Chain Template

6. **Environment and Norms**

   Figure 6.2 Contextual Job Description

7. **Needs Assessment and Cause Analysis**

   Figure 7.1 Scorecard Job Aid
   Figure 7.2 Scorecard Worksheet

Figure 7.4 The Hierarchy Job Aid

Figure 7.5 The Hierarchy Worksheet

8. Interventions

Figure 8.3 Interventions Job Aid: Information-Focused Interventions

Figure 8.4 Interventions Job Aid: Consequences-Focused Interventions

Figure 8.5 Interventions Job Aid: Design-Focused Interventions

Figure 8.6 Interventions Job Aid: Capacity- and Capability-Focused Interventions

Figure 8.7 Interventions Job Aid: Action-Focused Interventions

Figure 8.8 Interventions Job Aid: Congruency-Focused Interventions

9. Measuring Results

Figure 9.4 Evidence Worksheet

10. Measuring People Performance

Figure 10.2 Directions for the NGT

Figure 10.3 Guidelines for Creating People Performance Worksheets

Figure 10.7 Dimensions of a Job

Figure 10.8 Examples of Measures for Job Dimensions

Figure 10.9 Job Evaluation Job Aid

Figure 10.11 Merit Review Criteria

Preface

This fieldbook tells my story about performance consulting—what it is, why it is important, and how it can contribute to improving performance. Before starting the book, I took the time to read what others had said on performance consulting. Most of the other books stress why performance consulting is important, but they do not provide the tools consultants need to make it work. Some describe models for analyzing performance problems, but they do not explain how to use those models. They are silent on how to establish credibility with clients and how to build a business case for change. I wanted this fieldbook to give you tools and techniques to get relevant information so that you and your clients can make more informed decisions. Every story in this fieldbook is true, and every tool and technique has been tried and proven effective.

In some ways, the fieldbook is autobiographical. The ideas and approach to consulting presented here have evolved over the twenty-five years I have worked with all types of organizations in both the private and public sectors. The fieldbook has also been shaped by my experiences before I even became a consultant, from charting stock market transactions for my dad as a teenager to my education in theater management and my later experiences as a social worker and college instructor.

During college, I began to integrate ideas about what it takes for a business to perform economically with what people require to perform efficiently and effectively. My master's research was on theater management. As a social worker with a large caseload, I learned about the inhumanity, ignorance, and impotence of our social welfare system and how much power a few caring people can wield and how much hope they can bring. While on faculty at a large city college (where I witnessed seven strikes and many of most of my students were either deposed gang leaders or mature working adults), I learned how an education system that is designed to make sure inequality and ignorance stay with us in abundance cannot stop people who want to learn. When I was starting out in business, I joined the faculty of the Insurance School of Chicago, where I learned the concepts of loss control, exposure, hazards, and risk assessment. Later in my association with the American Arbitration Association and the Chicago Chapter of the Industrial Relations Research Association, I developed an appreciation for discovery, evidence, and how to honor disparate views.

What came out of these and other experiences was my consulting firm, Hale Associates, which I named after my father. The company logo is three overlapping circles that stand for integrity, ingenuity, and intelligence. Integrity is about honor, honesty, stewardship, and doing the right thing. Ingenuity has to do with getting things done despite limitations. Intelligence comes from having good data; it is not about being intellectually superior.

This fieldbook is inspired by that troika of principles. It discusses:

- Maintaining your integrity by insisting on being fact-based yet accepting other people's points of view

- Using your ingenuity to get good information and to get your clients involved and committed to change

- Applying what you learn to help organizations and people be successful

As consultants, we all bring a wealth of experience and learning to our assignments. What we need are processes, tools, and techniques that help us direct our experiences toward producing meaningful results. This is what I provide with this fieldbook. I hope you enjoy it and find the information it contains useful and enlightening.

AUDIENCE FOR THE BOOK

This fieldbook is intended for trainers, organizational development consultants, and human resource development professionals, who know firsthand the implications of implementing limited solutions to complex organizational problems. It provides processes, tools, and techniques that these professionals can use, whether they operate as internal or external consultants, to expand their role in their clients' organizations. It offers guidance on how to help clients better understand their organization and develop cost-effective programs to improve performance.

ACKNOWLEDGMENTS

A lot of people helped me put the first edition together. Some of those people, along with others, contributed to this edition. I give special thanks to Dave Haskett for his willingness to do a quick turnaround on the material. His comments on cost and measures were invaluable. Seth Carey, Chris Appleton, and Chris Duszinski, of McDonald's Corporation, were especially helpful, asking pointed questions and also serving as excellent models. Keith Hall, of Smith-Kline Beecham, got me to rethink the hierarchy and make it better. It was Dean Larson, of U.S. Steel, who got me to add the intervention on measures. Barbara Gough was kind enough to do a fast read and check my logic on the subjects of cost and the work environment. My brother Steve and friend Linda Gohlke brought a fresh perspective, as both are naive when is comes to performance consulting. Their comments on the hierarchy and interventions encouraged me to divide these topics into smaller segments, making them easier to understand. My friend Rob Foshay made valuable suggestions to the new chapter on sustaining change and the additions to the chapter on interventions, and Mike Reidy, of Union Tank Car, brought insights that only a first-time reader can do,

Many other people offered words of encouragement. Two people were especially helpful: my developmental editor, Joan Kalkut, of Empire Communications, and Carla Williams, a long-time colleague. Joan brought to her job the right combination of tenacity (getting me to keep my story lines straight) and suggestions on how to incorporate the tools and technique into the stories. It was her encouragement that gave me the courage to put forth some of my ideas. Carla Williams, who worked with me for nine years, has seen most of the tools and techniques in action. She knows the stories; more important, she has a logical way of looking at the world. She built the case for putting the chapter on cost in Part One. Her point was that everything comes down to money, so performance consultants must understand the economics of consulting and their client's business. Special credit goes to Matt Holt, Kathleen Dolan-Davies, and Matt Davis of Pfeiffer, who helped me navigate the world of publishing and provided resources that made this book possible.

My thanks go to my mother, who endured my many hours at the computer. It was from her and my dad that I learned about personal integrity and doing what you believe in, and all of my friends and colleagues who have used this fieldbook in their work and continue to offer words of encouragement and gratitude.

August 2006   Judith Hale

Introduction

*T*his fieldbook consists of two parts. Part One explores the process of becoming a performance consultant. Part Two focuses on processes that performance consultants can use to identify barriers to performance, diagnose performance problems, recommend appropriate intervention, and measure results. Each chapter describes processes, tools, and techniques you can use to position yourself as a consultant and provides examples of how to use them. These processes, tools, and techniques are appropriate for both internal and external consultants. The tools are provided on the accompanying CD-ROM so that you can modify them for your own work. At the end of each chapter are suggestions of resources for learning more.

PART ONE: MAKING THE TRANSITION

Part One is about becoming a performance consultant. Chapter One defines performance consulting and describes what distinguishes it from other types of consulting. It discusses four criteria that set performance consultants apart from other consultants and a consulting process that communicates what you do and how you work with clients. The process is designed to help you meet the four criteria of performance consulting. The chapter covers tools and techniques to help you create operational definitions (specifically, of performance consulting) and define and describe your own consulting process.

Chapter Two explains how to move into performance consulting. It contains a detailed transition plan including how to:

- Measure the effectiveness of your consulting process.

- Expand your products and services to include performance consulting.

- Evaluate your current products and services to identify which ones will hinder your transition (because they drain resources) and which ones to leverage to facilitate your transition.

Chapter Three explains how costs are classified and valued. It describes what drives costs and how to manage them. The tools and techniques in this chapter will help you determine your own costs and what drives them. There is a tool you can use to value your own time. You can apply these concepts in your work with clients as well to help them evaluate the cost-effectiveness of their programs and determine the cost of poor performance.

Chapter Four focuses on how to positively shape people's perceptions of you and the value of your services. The tools and techniques in this chapter are designed to help you:

- Get useful information.

- Influence clients' decisions and actions.

- Assess clients' capability and commitment to change.

- Build a strategy for working with clients at different levels of readiness for change.

Chapter Five examines how to sustain change or ensure that programs get fully deployed. The tools and techniques in this chapter are designed to help you initiate conversations with clients about how to track the adoption of new behaviors, dramatize the logic behind funding decisions to identify better metrics, get commitment for ongoing support for programs after sponsors leave, and report results after the launch to confirm the effectiveness of the program.

PART TWO: PERFORMANCE CONSULTING

Part Two is about doing consulting work. Each chapter describes tools and techniques and includes stories illustrating their use.

Chapter Six looks at how the work environment and group norms affect performance. The tools and techniques it offers are designed to:

- Identify and discriminate among changes in the organization, changes in a particular job, and changes in an individual that interfere with performance.

- Recognize how group norms can have a negative effect on performance and what to do to improve performance in such circumstances.

Chapter Seven explains how to diagnose performance problems and identify barriers to performance and offers the tools needed:

- A scorecard you can use to guide discussions about which problems need to be addressed and what will be accepted as evidence of improvement
- A hierarchy to guide you through a comprehensive process of identifying what interferes with performance

Chapter Eight is about selecting and recommending interventions to improve performance or eliminate barriers to performance. The tools presented here include:

- The "families of interventions" job aid.
- An if-then table for selecting interventions.
- A matrix you can use to identify the appropriate combination of interventions based on the cause of a specific performance problem.

Chapter Nine is about measures and criteria. It defines measures, criteria, and metrics; discusses how to select the appropriate measures; and describes how to evaluate an intervention. It includes the following tools:

- A measures, criteria, and metrics table
- Guidelines for selecting measures
- An intervention worksheet for selecting measures for your interventions

Chapter Ten is about measuring people's performance and evaluating jobs. It provides these tools:

- Guidelines for measuring job inputs, processes, outputs, and outcomes
- A "people performance" worksheet for measuring outputs (productivity) and outcomes (results)
- Guidelines for obtaining behavioral anchors to measure people's performance

WHY THE EMPHASIS ON THE USE OF TOOLS?

The tools presented in this fieldbook are important for a number of reasons. They are designed to:

- *Function like job aids.* Job aids encourage consistency. By consistently following a set of guidelines, you will build skill and confidence.
- *Provide criteria for developing and evaluating your processes.* Criteria will help you identify which of your processes you need to improve

- *Provide models you can use to improve your interactions with clients.* Models will help your clients better understand what you do and what they have to do to improve organizational and people performance

- *Help you communicate that you know what you are doing and have processes in place for doing it.* The tools will help you build customer confidence in you and your methods.

- *Give your clients a framework for working with you.* The tools will give clients some indication of what their end state should look like. Knowing what it is you are trying to find out will help them focus their attention on the discussion. Without an end state in view, their attention will be on figuring out where you are going and why.

- *Serve as interim deliverables and working documents.* At the end of your meeting, you and your client will have a document that describes your decisions and thinking. Your client can use that document to communicate what the two of you are doing and why.

- *Support presentations.* Either you or your client can use the tools in presentations to explain what you discovered, what you are going to do about it, and how you will measure your results.

- *Develop the client's skills and educate the client on how to improve performance.* The tools model the thinking processes used in discovery, diagnosis, treatment, and measurement. Using the tools will help clients develop their own ability to identify performance problems, select appropriate interventions, and measure results.

- *Focus the client's attention on the process of identifying and solving problems instead of on individuals or fault finding.* The tools move your discussions to facts not people.

KEY DEFINITIONS

One of the problems facing any new field is the lack of a common language, so here are some working definitions of the terms used in this fieldbook. You will find that they are in harmony with the terms other performance consulting experts use:

- *Assessment:* Finding out what is and is not happening. You engage in assessment to discover what the performance is and where there are opportunities for improvement.

- *Analysis:* Finding out why performance is at the level it is. You engage in analysis so that you can recommend the appropriate intervention or solution to improve performance.

- *Consulting:* The role each of us plays when we engage in assessment, analysis, and recommending interventions.

- *Evaluation:* Placing value on situations, activities, and results. Paying attention to someone's performance means you have judged it worthy of your attention. The term is sometimes used as a synonym for *assessment* and *analysis.*

- *Intervention:* Any purposeful act designed to solve a problem, change behavior, improve performance, increase outputs, and improve outcomes. Examples of interventions are introducing programs, adopting new technology, changing the structure of the organization, redesigning jobs, and training.

- *Measurement:* A subset of evaluation; the process of gathering information and comparing what you discover to some criteria to determine if a gap in performance exists or if there has been improvement.

- *Organization:* An entity that employs people. It can refer to the whole entity or part of it—that is, a company, division, department, function, work unit, or team.

- *Performance:* How well people do work (produce products and services) that is of value to customers and the organization.

- *Performance improvement:* The application of specific interventions to remove barriers to performance and encourage the desired performance.

Part One

Making the Transition

Chapter 1

Performance Consulting

In their desire to improve organizational performance, managers sometimes seek the help of consultants. They may not fully understand the capabilities and biases consultants bring to the assignment, however. The following story illustrates this point.

A large conglomerate hired Mark to head its unit that manufactures and distributes extrusion metals (used to make window frames, louver blades, I-beams for construction, and storm doors). The main plant was in the Midwest, there was a second plant on the East Coast, and a new plant was scheduled to open in Singapore within six months.

The Midwest plant had lost market share over the previous two years. Its on-time delivery record was poor, and turnover among its sales staff was high. The East Coast plant was just meeting its financial goals, and senior management told Mark they were concerned: customer complaints about product quality and missed deliveries were up.

Mark decided to seek the help of a marketing consultant. The consultant recommended a new product image, a new logo, and a new marketing campaign. Mark agreed that a new marketing plan made sense, but he was uncomfortable with the plan because it could take the better part of a year to see results. To see if he could get faster results, Mark sought the advice of a sales consultant. This consultant recommended a sales contest, a new bonus structure, and incentives for achieving sales goals. At about the same time, a senior vice president at corporate headquarters suggested that Mark talk to a management consultant. The consultant suggested reorganizing the business unit around key customer groups, such as construction, institutional buyers, and resellers. Because Mark had been impressed by the successes of the quality assurance department at the company he used to work for, he decided to meet with a quality consultant as well. This consultant offered three significant suggestions: set up cross-functional teams; make each team responsible for a whole process, from receiving orders to delivering finished products; and implement statistical process control techniques for each process.

Mark's U.S. sales manager suggested they hire an organizational development consultant to work with the management team. The goals would be to come up with a new vision and mission for the unit and to improve communication within the team. The Midwest plant manager suggested they hire a training consultant to develop training for sales and production personnel.

Mark received a memo stating that the corporation's architectural firm had been hired to do strategic planning for the entire corporation. One of the anticipated outcomes of the strategic plan was a new model for the plants, since the architectural firm was known for agile designs based on manufacturing principles. A human resource consultant recommended studying causes of turnover, implementing a targeted selection program, and doing an employee morale survey.

On his flight to the Singapore plant, Mark read about the successes of reengineering. He was particularly impressed by the use of sophisticated information systems designed to shorten cycle times. On his return flight, he read another article, this one about performance improvement consulting. It was then that Mark realized that all of the approaches he had been considering had merit. All of the consultants he had hired had started with a solution; however, none of them had begun with an analysis of what was actually causing the poor performance. Instead, they had all assumed that they had the answer.

Mark's experience is not unique. Eager for solutions to their problems, organizations act on the recommendations of experts without first finding out what the problem is. Managers are slowly recognizing the need to take a more fact-based, grounded approach to improving performance however. Changes must leverage real strengths and deal with real weaknesses. This recognition on the part of management presents an opportunity for professionals in training, human resource development (HRD), and other related disciplines to demonstrate how their processes for diagnosing performance problems, selecting appropriate interventions, and measuring results can make a difference. At the same time, professionals in training, HRD, quality assurance, and organizational development (OD) want to shift their role to performance consulting, where they hope to join with management in applying processes designed to find the real barriers to performance. This new role is supported by the National Society for Performance and Instruction when it changed its name to the International Society for Performance Improvement (ISPI) to reflect the new emphasis on improving performance rather than promoting training. In 2001, ISPI published its Human Performance Technology (HPT) standards that define the role and allow practitioners to assess their ability to meet the standards. It now offers a certification, the certified performance technologist (CPT) designation, to practitioners who can demonstrate that they have met the standards in their work. ISPI's conferences, institutes, publications, and certification are aimed at developing a shared understanding of and appreciation for the skills and knowledge required to improve organizational and people performance.

EXPERIENCES FROM THE FIELD: IMPROVING PERFORMANCE

It has been my experience that organizations are fairly erratic about finding ways to improve organizational and people performance. In their search for the optimal size and structure, they buy, merge, and sell whole business units. They centralize functions, only to decentralize them later. They buy new technologies, products, and facilities. They distribute assets across unrelated products, only to consolidate around their name brands later. Organizations reengineer their processes, invest in training, and purchase ready-made programs to develop leadership and managerial skills. To reduce costs, they reduce the number of jobs by downsizing, outsourcing, and moving jobs to other countries. Many of these actions are done in parallel. Some are in conflict, however, and all are solutions in search of a problem.

To get a better understanding of the kinds of programs organizations take on to improve performance, think about the last two to three years in your work life:

- What has your organization done to reduce costs, improve profits, or become more competitive?

- How many times has it reorganized, bought other companies, or been bought by other companies?

- How many times has it centralized functions, only to decentralize them later?

- How many times has your position stayed the same while the people you report to or the department you are assigned to changed?

- How many times have you moved your office? What were the assumptions behind these moves?

- What were some of the initiatives your organization embraced to motivate people, satisfy customers, or be more competitive? Were any of those initiatives based on a serious examination of the company's current state? If so, what evidence did the company use to see if the desired result was achieved? Who did the measuring?

- How successful was the company at implementing changes throughout the organization? Did those changes fulfill the promise of lower costs, higher profits, or competitive advantage? How do you know?

- What role did you play in any of these efforts? What will it take for you to play a more effective role in the future?

WHAT MAKES A PERFORMANCE CONSULTANT?

When I'm asked to explain performance consulting, I point out that performance consultants:

- Are experts in analysis and measurement and provide expert advice, yet also facilitate the client's commitment to taking responsibility for supporting performance

- Play multiple roles

- Are not predisposed toward a particular solution and do not make recommendations until there are data to support them

- Facilitate conversations in ways that keep clients focused on what matters and develop meaningful information and insight

- Focus on outcomes and measured results

Moving Between Expert and Facilitator

I think of consulting as a continuum (see Figure 1.1). At one end is the expert whose job is to give advice. At the opposite end is the facilitator, whose job is to manage the group dynamics.

Experts who are brought in as consultants usually possess education or credentials in a specific professional discipline. As experts, they make definitive statements and express opinions. At this end of the continuum, consulting consists of rendering an opinion and giving advice. The client's attention is focused on the person expressing the opinion: the expert.

Training and HRD professionals think of consulting in terms of the opposite end of the continuum, however. To them, consulting is facilitating. Facilitators rarely give advice, offer opinions, or take a position on a subject; they are perceived as neutral. Their role is to facilitate other people's discovery and commitment to change. So at this end of the continuum, consulting is the

Expert ⟷	Facilitator
Has discipline-specific knowledge	Knows group process
Comes with external status	Can manage group dynamics
Has discipline-specific skills	Has interpersonal skills
Offers opinions	Remains neutral

Figure 1.1. The Expert-Facilitator Continuum

process of guiding people's discovery and bringing them to consensus. The client's attention is focused on what is happening within the group.

Effective performance consultants blend the attributes of an expert with those of a facilitator. They give advice about how to get and interpret the facts and improve organizational and people performance. At the same time, they facilitate the client's commitment to getting facts, measuring results, and supporting performance. The tools and techniques in this fieldbook are designed to help you move back and forth between expert and facilitator. The tools legitimize your opinions but also encourage your clients to come to their own conclusion and retain ownership of the results. The tools and techniques will focus your clients' attention on the processes of discovery, diagnosis, and measurement, not on you.

Playing Multiple Roles

Another continuum can be used to distinguish performance consultants from other types of consultants. This continuum goes from critic to doer to spectator (see Figure 1.2). There are people who criticize, people who do, and people who stand around and watch.

Experts are frequently thought of as critics: they tell you what is right and wrong. Facilitators are similar to spectators: they may stand at the front of the room, but they are on the sidelines of the debate. Doers take responsibility for making things happen: they produce. Performance con-

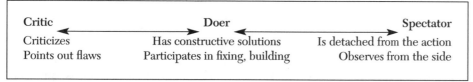

Figure 1.2. The Critic-Doer-Spectator Continuum

sultants play all three roles, depending on the client's needs and what the client wants to accomplish.

Staying Free of Bias

Another thing that distinguishes performance consultants from other consultants is their lack of bias in terms of finding a solution. Other consultants presume that the solution rests in their specialty (which is what Mark came to realize). For example, management consultants assume problems can be solved through better leadership and by changing the organizational structure. Quality consultants assume performance can be improved through cross-functional teams and improved processes. Trainers start with the premise that the solution is training. Performance consultants, however, are not biased toward a specific solution. Instead, our approach is to follow a systematic process to determine what contributes to performance and what impedes it. For example, we don't assume; we find out if:

- People have access to the relevant information, and that information is in an understandable form
- There are consequences that reinforce the desired behaviors and outcomes
- The organizational environment supports the requirements of the job
- People get consistent, clear directions
- Processes are well defined and efficient
- Functions and jobs are designed around key processes
- People have the resources and skills they need to be effective

Facilitating Conversations

To be experts in analysis and measurement, performance consultants must know how to get information beyond just asking questions, observing work in process, and checking documents. They have to know when and how to initiate conversations with management and workers because these conversations build clients' understanding of what is required for people to be effective at their jobs. Conversations also help performance consultants better understand the work environment, including its demands and constraints.

Focusing on Outcomes and Measured Results

As performance consultants, we pay attention to the outcomes or consequences of what is done to improve performance. This means that we measure the outcomes or results of an intervention and assess whether performance has improved as a result of it.

I like to think we challenge our own and other people's thinking. We find out what is really happening so we can bring clarity to situations. We fit pieces together and make sense out of what is going on. This is why it takes special skills to be an effective performance consultant.

DEFINING PERFORMANCE CONSULTING

"Be a leader!" "Be world class!" "Be customer focused!" These are some of the slogans companies use to communicate what they want their employees to do. But if you were to stop people and ask what each of these slogans means, you would probably get many different answers. The same would be true if you were to ask them what performance consulting is all about. If you want to be a performance consultant, you have to be clear about what it means to you.

Once you are clear in your own mind about what a performance consultant is, you can develop a transition plan for yourself, because you will know where you are going.

An operational definition is a technique for understanding any new concept (such as performance consulting). Creating an operational definition for performance consulting will help you, your colleagues, and your clients come to a shared understanding of what performance consulting is; help you clarify what it takes to be a performance consultant; and produce language you can use in your marketing materials.

An operational definition answers three questions: *what, why,* and *how.* When I use an operational definition to clarify a role, I frequently combine it with examples of the typical tasks involved, the required knowledge and skills (sometimes combined as *competencies*), and possible measures of the work performed by people in that job.

In Figure 1.3, an example of an operational definition with a list of typical tasks, performance consulting is defined as a *practice.* You might think of it as a discipline, a role, a process, or something else, however. In this example, the reason for the practice of performance consulting (the *why*) is identified as "to optimize performance." You might come up with a different reason, such as to ensure that everyone has what they need to excel, eliminate barriers to performance, equip management to support performance better, or make sure an investment in training pays off by identifying what has to be in place for people to apply what they learn. The example defines the execution (the *how*) of performance consulting as "the application of proven processes." You might see it in terms of changing your relationship with clients, increasing your scope of services, or shifting from delivery to brokering services. My point is that the label *performance consulting* has to be meaningful to you. It should be based on what your clients and organization require of you, should accurately reflect your role in the organization, and should match the four attributes of being an expert yet a facilitator, playing multiple roles, maintaining a bias-free approach, and focusing on outcomes. Chapter Six provides an example of a job description that integrates all of the elements of an operational definition. Once you have the definition and the typical tasks you perform, you can complete the table by adding what you have to know and be able to do to be effective. In the last column, you can add how your work will be measured.

I also find it helpful to look at what the literature says about performance consulting. This does not mean you have to accept what others say, but you do need to know if your understanding of performance consulting differs from others' understanding, and if so, how. For example, the Department of Labor's *Dictionary of Occupational Titles* describes a consultant as someone who "consults

Figure 1.3. Example of an Operational Definition of Performance Consulting

What: Performance consulting is the practice of taking a disciplined approach to assessing individual and organizational effectiveness, diagnosing causes of human performance problems, and recommending a set of interventions. The approach is based on a body of knowledge about organizational and human performance. The outcome is advice on how to improve organizational and people performance.			
Why: To optimize human and organizational performance.			
How: The application of proven processes.			
Typical tasks:	*Knowledge*	*Skills*	*Expected results*
• Assess individual and organizational performance (performance analysis).			
• Identify factors impeding and contributing to performance (cause analysis).			
• Select, recommend, and evaluate interventions (interventions).			
• Facilitate the implementation of interventions and the adoption of new behaviors (implementation).			
• Facilitate the development and use of measures and evaluation strategies.			

with clients to define a need or problem, conducts studies and surveys to obtain data, and analyzes the data to advise on or recommend a solution." This is the *what*. The definition also states that a consultant "utilize[es] knowledge of theory, principles, or technology of specific discipline or field of specialization." This is the *how*. Finally, it defines the specific activities (the tasks) a consultant engages in (paraphrased here):

- *Consults* with clients to ascertain and define the need or problem area and determines the scope of investigation required to obtain solution

- *Conducts a study or survey* on the need or problem to obtain data required to find a solution

- *Analyzes the data* to determine a solution, such as implementing alternative methods and procedures, changing processing methods and practices, modifying machines or equipment, or redesigning products or services

• *Advises clients* on alternative methods of solving problem or recommends a specific solution

In one study, the American Society for Training and Development (ASTD) identified the roles HRD professionals play in organizations. Four of the roles they identified fall under performance consulting (see Figure 1.4).

Figure 1.4. The ASTD's HRD Roles That Relate to Performance Consulting

Source: The numbers are the same ones used in the ASTD's original list, which appeared in McLagan, P., and Suhadolnik, D., *Models for HRD Practice* (Alexandria, VA: ASTD, 1989). Reprinted by permission.

1. *Researcher:* The role of identifying, developing, or testing new information and translating the information into its implications for improved individual or organization performance

3. *Organization change agent:* The role of influencing and supporting changes in organizational behavior

4. *Needs analyst:* The role of identifying ideal and actual performance and performance conditions and determining causes of discrepancies

10. *Evaluator:* The role of identifying the impact of an intervention on individual or organizational effectiveness

When you review all of the roles, you may come to a different understanding of which ones fit under performance consulting. The ASTD also listed thirty-five HRD competencies. Figure 1.5 lists the ones that I think relate directly to performance consulting.

Figure 1.5. The ASTD's HRD Competencies That Relate to Performance Consulting

Source: The numbers are the same ones used in the ASTD's original list. The competencies appear on page 23 of *The Research Report,* which is part of McLagan, P., and Suhadolnik, D., *Models for HRD Practice* (Alexandria, VA: ASTD, 1989). Reprinted by permission.

TECHNICAL COMPETENCIES: having functional skills and knowledge

3. *Competency identification* (identifying the knowledge and skill requirements of jobs, tasks, and roles) requires skill in identifying inputs and assessing their accuracy and completeness.

7. *Objectives preparation* (preparing clear statements that describe desired outputs) requires skill in identifying the relevant outputs and proposing criteria to measure their attainment.

8. *Performance observation* (tracking and describing behaviors and their effects) requires skill in what drives or causes behaviors.

BUSINESS COMPETENCIES: having a strong management, economics, or administration base

12. *Business understanding* (knowing how the functions of a business work and relate to each other; knowing the economic impact of business decisions) requires tools for identifying how the functions interrelate and the economic impact of those relationships.

13. *Cost-benefit analysis* (assessing alternatives in terms of their financial, psychological, and strategic advantages and disadvantages) requires tools for identifying direct and indirect costs, judging probability, and weighing trade-offs.

continued

Figure 1.5. The ASTD's HRD Competencies That Relate to Performance Consulting, *cont'd.*

15. *Industry understanding* (knowing the key concepts and variables such as critical issues, economic vulnerabilities, measurements, distribution channels, inputs, outputs, and information sources that define an industry or section) is made easier with tools that capture issues and make them public so they can be discussed and the need for better data (versus the folklore) determined.

16. *Organizational behavior understanding* (seeing the organization as having dynamic, political, economic, and social systems with multiple goals; using this larger framework for understanding and influencing events and change) requires organizational models and tools for describing the system components and how they interplay.

17. *Organizational development theories and techniques understanding* (knowing the techniques and methods used in organizational development; understanding their appropriate use) requires models and methods and skill in their use.

18. *Organizational understanding* (knowing the strategy, structure, power networks, financial position, and systems of a specific organization) requires skill in gaining access to information and interpreting that information.

INTERPERSONAL COMPETENCIES: having a strong communication base

22. Feedback (communicating information, opinions, observations, and conclusions so that they are understood and can be acted on) is helped by having techniques for discriminating useful information and assessing acceptance of that information.

23. *Group process skill* (influencing groups so that tasks, relationships, and individual needs are addressed).

24. *Negotiation skill* (securing win-win agreements while successfully representing a special interest in a decision-making process).

26. *Questioning* (gathering information from stimulating insight in individuals and groups through the use of interviews, questionnaires, and other probing methods) requires skill in selecting and using probing methods that reveal information that is relevant and leads to insight.

27. *Relationship building* (establishing relationships and networks across a broad range of people and groups) requires skill and methods to discriminate relevant from irrelevant cultural nuances and select appropriate behavior.

INTELLECTUAL COMPETENCIES: having the knowledge and skill related to thinking and information processing

29. *Data reduction skill* (scanning, synthesizing, and drawing conclusions from data).

30. *Information search skill* (gathering information from printed and other recorded sources; identifying and using information specialists and reference services and aids).

31. *Intellectual versatility* (recognizing, exploring, and using a broad range of ideas and practices; thinking logically and creatively without undue influence from personal biases).

32. *Model-building skill* (conceptualizing and developing theoretical and practical frameworks that describe complete ideas in understandable, usable ways).

33. *Observing skill* (recognizing objectively what is happening in and across situations).

35. *Visioning skill* (projecting trends and visualizing possible and probable futures and their implications).

When you review all thirty-five competencies, you may come to a different conclusion. The important thing is to be clear about:

• What you think performance consulting is

• Why performance consulting is needed

• How performance consultants accomplish what they say they accomplish

• The kinds of things a performance consultant does

• The skills and knowledge required

• How you want your effectiveness measured

ISPI published its HPT standards when it decided to offer a certification (see Figure 1.6). There are ten standards that define the *what* and *how* of performance improvement consulting. The first four standards are the principles on which the CPT designation is based: taking a systemic view, focusing on results, adding value, and partnering with others. The last six describe the systematic process that a competent consultant should follow.

Figure 1.6. ISPI'S HPT Standards

Source: Copyright 2002. Reprinted with permission of the International Society for Performance Improvement.

FOCUSING ON OUTCOMES

*Focusing on outcomes—that is, results—*puts you in a position to question, confirm, and reconfirm that people share the same vision and goals, the job procedures support efficiency, and people have the skills and knowledge they require. You determine what it is you are trying to solve, measure the outcomes or results of an intervention, and assess whether performance has improved as a result. Sometimes you must challenge the assumed answer to a problem or the expected event or activity of an intervention, and focus instead on the accomplishment or business need that is the client's true priority.

TAKING A SYSTEMS VIEW

Taking a systems view is vital, because organizations are complex systems that affect the performance of the individuals who work within them. It is important to distinguish a systems approach from a process model. A *process* contains inputs and outputs and has feedback loops. A *system* implies an interconnected complex of functionally related components. The effectiveness of each unit depends on how it fits into the whole, and the effectiveness of the whole depends on the way each unit functions. A systems approach considers the larger environment that affects processes and other work. The environment includes inputs and, more important, pressures, expectations, constraints, and consequences.

ADDING VALUE

Did you *add value* in the way you worked with the client and your suggested intervention? This is an assessment your client will be asked to make. You can set the stage by offering your clients a process that will help them fully understand the implications of their choices, set appropriate measures, identify barriers and trade-offs, and take control.

---

continued

Figure 1.6. ISPI'S HPT Standards, *cont'd.*

WORKING IN PARTNERSHIP WITH CLIENTS AND OTHER SPECIALISTS

Working in partnership with clients and other specialists—that is, collaboratively means that you involve all stakeholders in the decision making around every phase of the process and involve specialists in their areas of expertise. Working collaboratively means that decisions about goals, next steps to take in the process, and implementation are shared responsibilities. Partnerships are created from listening closely to your client and trusting and respecting each other's knowledge and expertise, so together you can make the best choices about accomplishments, priorities, and solutions.

BEING SYSTEMATIC—NEEDS OR OPPORTUNITY ANALYSIS

Needs or opportunity analysis is about examining the situation at any level (society, organizational, process, or work group) to identify the external and internal pressures affecting it. Based on what you learn, you determine if the situation is worthy of action or further study. The output is a statement describing the current state, the projected future state, and the rationale or business case for action or nonaction.

BEING SYSTEMATIC—CAUSE ANALYSIS

Cause analysis is about determining why a gap in performance or expectations exists. Some causes are obvious; for example, as new employees lack the required skills to do the expected task and therefore the solution must eliminate that gap. The output is a statement of why performance is not happening or will not happen without some intervention.

BEING SYSTEMATIC—DESIGN

Design is about identifying the key attributes of a solution. The output is a communication that describes the features, attributes, and elements of a solution and the resources required to actualize it.

BEING SYSTEMATIC—DEVELOPMENT

Development is about creating some or all of the elements of the solution. It can be done by an individual or a team. The output is a product, process, system, or technology. Examples are training, performance support tools, a new or reengineered process, the redesign of a work space, or a change in compensation or benefits.

BEING SYSTEMATIC—IMPLEMENTATION

Implementation is about deploying the solution and managing the change required to sustain it. The outputs are changes in or adoption of the behaviors that are believed to produce the anticipated results or benefits. This standard is about helping clients adopt new behaviors or use new or different tools. The implementation plan addresses how you or the client will track change, identify and respond to problems, and communicate the results.

BEING SYSTEMATIC—EVALUATION

Evaluation is about measuring the efficiency and effectiveness of what you did, how you did it, and the degree to which the solution produced the desired results so you can compare the cost incurred to the benefits gained. This standard is about identifying and acting on opportunities throughout the systematic process to identify measures and capture data that will help identify needs, adoption, and results.

FIELD TOOLS: THE OPERATIONAL DEFINITION

It is important to be clear about what you mean by performance consulting, because you will probably have to explain it to others. Here are some ideas for developing your own definition. Use the worksheet in Figure 1.7 to record your decisions:

Figure 1.7. Operational Definition Worksheet

What:			
Why:			
How:			
Typical Tasks	**Required Knowledge**	**Required Skills**	**Expected results** Outputs: Outcomes:

1. Whether you are an internal consultant or an independent, external consultant, set up a special planning session.

2. Include staff or colleagues and key customers who support your decision to become a performance consultant or add consulting to your scope of services. Because you already have a relationship with these people, they should have a vested interest in what services you provide.

3. Tell everyone that the agenda is to help you (and those who work with you) define performance consulting.

4. Ask everyone to think about what performance consulting means to them, and bring those thoughts to the meeting.

5. Once you are together, ask the group these questions:

- "What does performance consulting mean to you?"
- "How would my behavior have to change for you to call me a performance consultant?"
- "If I were to produce a brochure listing my products and services, what would I have to list for you to believe I am a performance consultant?"
- "Why would you want me to change from what I do now to performance consulting?"
- "Why would you *not* want me to change from what I do now?"
- "Who would benefit from my becoming a performance consultant [or adding consulting to my scope of services]?"
- "Who might *not* benefit from my becoming a performance consultant?"
- "How would I do my work differently if I were performance consultant?"
- "How would my relationships and interactions with clients be different if I were a performance consultant?"
- "What are the tasks a performance consultant typically does? Which of those tasks are different from what I do now?"
- "What must a performance consultant know to do these tasks? What must I know that I do not know now?"
- "What are the skills a performance consultant must have? Which of these skills are different from the ones I have now?"
- "How might my clients measure the cost benefit of my operating as a performance consultant?"
- "What would I have to have [or buy] to be an effective consultant in terms of resources, skills, client relations, systems, and so on?"

6. Use what you learn to develop an operational definition of performance consulting. Complete as many of the elements (tasks, knowledge, skills, results) as you can.

7. Ask the group to comment on your definition.

8. Modify the definition until you and your group are in agreement as to what a performance consultant is.

The definition should describe the business and explain what you are about, why you are in business, and how you operate or do business. It should begin the process of identifying the work you do, what you have to know, what you have to be able to do, and how your success or effectiveness might be measured.

FIELD NOTES: CLARIFYING EXPECTATIONS

Mike worked for a large global company. The firm referred to itself, its franchisees, its suppliers and distributors, and its international investment partners collectively as "the system." Mike was asked to head up a new shared services department at corporate headquarters. The department's mandate was to institutionalize processes throughout the company, its subsidiaries, and suppliers that would improve the system's overall performance. System performance was measured in terms of consistent low costs, products that met standards, and increased market shares.

The people assigned to Mike's department had previously worked in training and development, logistics, quality assurance, finance, information systems (IS), word processing, and administration. Everyone in the department, including those in word processing and administration, carried the same title: consultant specializing in performance improvement.

Mike wanted his team to operate as internal consultants with expertise in measurement. When describing what he wanted to see from his team, he said things like, "Consultants stay focused, are politically astute, build alliances, shape performance, remain objective, and measure the financial impact of what they do." His team finally insisted that they all work together to better define what this meant. Figure 1.8 shows how they operationally defined Mike's expectations.

Figure 1.8. Operational Definition of Mike's Expectations

> *STAYING FOCUSED* means having the skill, knowledge, and willingness to:
>
> - Discriminate those actions or decisions that will produce the greatest outcomes from those that won't.
> - Act in ways that are more likely to produce the desired outcome in deference to those that won't.
>
> *Why stay focused?* So resources are directed to activities most likely to produce the desired outcome.
>
> *How do we stay focused?* By:
>
> - Directing resources and attention to things that matter
> - Asking hard questions and challenging the relevance of others' actions
> - Saying what is really going on without condemnation
>
> ---
>
> *BEING POLITICALLY ASTUTE* means having the skill, knowledge, and willingness to find out who influences decisions and action.
>
> *Why be politically astute?* So we will be in a position to influence decisions and actions.

continued

Figure 1.8. Operational Definition of Mike's Expectations, *cont'd.*

How do we become politically astute? By:

- Finding out what decision makers attend to and value
- Using that knowledge to establish relationships with them
- Using those relationships to strategically barter information, access, and support without jeopardizing business or professional integrity

---

BUILDING ALLIANCES means having the skills, knowledge, and willingness to:

- Identify when and what types of alliances are appropriate.
- Define the purpose of the alliance and what we expect from it.

Why build alliances? So we can leverage the resources, intelligence, and power of the larger group.

How do we build alliances? By:

- Developing a strategy for entering into the alliance
- Sharing expectations with the other members of the alliance
- Soliciting their expectations of us
- Setting mutual goals
- Developing a plan of action to advance those goals
- Committing to the plan
- Evaluating the usefulness of our business relationship

SHAPING PERFORMANCE means having the skills, knowledge, and willingness to influence what others do and think.

Why shape performance? So others' actions and priorities are aligned with what the organization requires for success today and in the future.

How do we shape performance? By:

- Sharing our expectations and thoughts
- Giving people accurate, timely, and constructive information and feedback
- Responding to others in ways they will perceive as fair
- Modeling the behavior we expect in others
- Seeking win-win solutions
- Maintaining confidences
- Not misrepresenting others' actions
- Honoring our commitments
- Dealing directly with others

Figure 1.8. Operational Definition of Mike's Expectations, *cont'd.*

REMAINING OBJECTIVE means having the skills, knowledge, and willingness to remain detached.

Why be objective? So our judgment is not clouded by the emotions and motives of others.

How do we be objective? By:

- Distinguishing among emotions, interpretations, and facts (evidence), and conclusions
- Not getting caught up in the drama of the moment

MEASURING FINANCIAL IMPACT means having the skills, knowledge, and willingness to assess the financial impact of decisions or actions on the business, business relationships, other departments, other programs, and other projects.

- Assess the financial impact of decisions or actions on the business as a whole, on business relationships, on other departments, and on other programs and projects

Why measure financial impact? So we can recognize and act on opportunities to:

- Optimize the financial impact of beneficial actions and decisions.
- Avoid or minimize the financial impact of negative decisions or actions.

How do we measure financial impacts? By:

- Identifying and interpreting financial data
- Identifying decisions and actions that have financial implications

DEFINING YOUR OWN CONSULTANT PROCESS

This new field of performance consulting can be confusing not only to clients but also to those of us who want to play this role. I've found that documenting my consulting process helps me communicate what I do and how it differs from what other consultants do (see Figure 1.9) It also helps me more accurately estimate the time and resources required to fulfill a client's request, and it helps me explain where my involvement is important but might change, depending on the needs of the client. The phases in which I can add the greatest value are Phases I, II, III, IV, and VII. It is in these phases that I and other performance consultants bring discipline and proven procedures to our work that distinguish us from other types of consultants.

Phase I: Defining the request

Qualify the job.
Qualify the client.
Determine expectations.
Define working protocols.
Define roles, relationships,
  and responsibilities.
Scope out a plan.

Phase II: Fact-finding

Start with hypotheses.
Include all the voices.
Use more than one method.
Look for corroborating evidence.
Apply rigor to control bias.
Consider the environment.

Phase III: Analyzing the findings

Compile the results.
Apply analytical techniques.
Look for significant findings and differences.
Identify the costs.
Find out the consequences on costs, satisfaction,
  image, and so on.
Report the results.

Phase IV: Designing the solution

Describe the audiences (direct and indirect).
Specify the requirements.
Specify the long-term support.
Specify communication and implementation requirements.
Specify the costs and benefits.
Specify other relevant success measures.
Specify the pilot test and rollout plans.
Specify how and who will measure results.

Phase V: Developing the solution

Prepare or secure materials, systems, and other required
  elements.
Prepare collateral and management support materials.
Prepare public relations materials.

Phase VI: Implementing the solution

Set up an implementation team.
Conduct the pilot test.
Debrief the findings.
Launch the rollout.

Phase VII: Measuring the results

Gather the data.
Compare to preestablished measures.
Report the results.

Figure 1.9. The Consulting Process

Phase I: Defining the Request

Phase I is about scoping out the request, the client's expectations, and the nature of the relationship. The outcome of Phase I is enough information to answer these questions:

- *Can I do it?* The request may be outside my area of expertise. I've learned not to try to be all things to all people. Chapters Three, Four, and Five describe in greater detail some of the general skills and knowledge required to be a successful consultant.

- *Do I want to do it?* Every request comes with trade-offs. Some requests, because of their timing, may put other projects at risk. Some requests come with so many constraints attached that they require extra resources just to manage the client and the project. This takes energy away from doing the real work.

- *Do I want to work with these people?* Some people are too busy, distracted, or uncommitted to be involved at the level necessary. Lack of involvement is a red flag, because it reduces the chances that my findings and recommendations will be accepted. Another red flag is being denied access to people who have key information and a stake in what is being proposed. Without the buy-in of the stakeholders, the chances that the project will be successful over the long haul are minimal. Furthermore, lack of acceptance and adoption reflect negatively on the consultant.

- *What is the client's level of sophistication?* Unsophisticated clients increase my costs (by taking more of my time), and I may or may not be able to pass those increased costs on to the client. (Internal consultants have the same problem.) Unsophisticated clients require more coaching and direction, which requires a greater time commitment by the consultant, whether or not the consultant charges the client for it. Chapter Four has a process for qualifying the client.

- *Is there any chance of my making a difference?* Some problems are so complex that a long-range strategy is necessary. Before I accept an assignment, I want to know how long the sponsor and initial project team will stick around and, if they are replaced, whether their replacements will be equally committed to the project. Chapter Five describes some of the environmental issues that contribute to performance problems.

- *How much does the current problem cost?* This information is key to determining the worth of the problem and the worth of the solution. Chapter Three is about determining costs, and Chapters Nine and Ten explain valuing and measuring problems in greater detail.

- *What will it take to complete the subsequent phases?* Before I begin an assignment, I want to find out if I can (or should) do it alone, if I want the client to provide a team, or if I need to involve other professional resources.

- *How much will it cost the client?* Determining this includes calculating my fee (if you are an internal consultant, it includes calculating what your time on the project will cost your organization) and the amount of any other required resources. I use this information to measure the return on investment, or payback.

Phase II: Fact-Finding

Phase II is about getting and validating the facts. What distinguishes performance consultants from other consultants is the rigor and discipline with which they gather data. I always point out to the client that I have documented procedures for assessing needs and for each of my data-gathering tactics, to control bias. How much data gathering I do and what type depends on the information I gain in Phase I.

Phase III: Analyzing the Findings

Phase III is about analyzing the results of the fact-finding phase. Performance consultants purposefully look for corroborating evidence and use descriptive and inferential statistics in their analysis. They stress their use of proven procedures and the discipline they bring to their work.

Phase IV: Designing the Solution

Phase IV is critical to understanding what resources will be required to develop, implement, and provide ongoing support for the solution to the client's problem.

Phase V: Developing the Solution

Phase V is a natural point for turning the project over to the client or another professional with the appropriate expertise. Nonetheless, I always include this phase as part of the process because someone has to do it.

Phase VI: Implementing the Solution

Phase VI is another phase in which the performance consultant may or may not play a role. It depends on the nature of the assignment and what resources the client can dedicate to implementation.

Phase VII: Measuring the Results

Phase VII also distinguishes the performance consultant from other consultants. Performance consultants have to know how to measure what changed or improved as a result of implementing the solution or a program.

Benefits to Defining and Describing the Work

There are a lot of benefits to defining and describing how you do your work. It helps you communicate the scope of your services. It makes it easier for you to negotiate agreements concerning when you do and do not want to be involved. It helps the client understand all that goes into improving performance. It helps you place a value on your services. Just as important, having a well-defined process enables you to determine how effectively and efficiently you do your work by helping you measure the results of it. Only by measuring your results can you continuously improve what you do.

FIELD TECHNIQUES: DEFINING YOUR CONSULTING PROCESS

To define your own consulting process, meet with your team and other colleagues who support you in your desire to be an effective performance consultant. Then follow these steps:

1. Review the literature on performance consulting. Determine if there are any processes you think you might want to adopt or modify to reflect your own vision of how you want to operate.

2. Develop a vision for the role of performance consulting in your organization. Later in this chapter are suggestions on how to develop a vision and mission statement.

3. Describe the process you use now when working with clients.

4. Identify where you want to add to or change your current process so that it will better support your vision.

5. Decide how you want to describe your overall consulting process, such as a flowchart or a list of procedures.

6. Document your consulting process, and share it with supportive clients to get their feedback and confirm that it makes sense to them.

FIELD NOTES: DEFINING THE CONSULTING PROCESS

Mike's vision was for everyone on his staff to operate as internal consultants. As consultants, he wanted them to:

- Develop and consistently follow a consulting process for working with clients

- Develop subprocesses for defining needs, estimating required resources, providing solutions or services, measuring the cost benefit of those solutions or services, and shifting responsibility to their clients for implementing and maintaining the solutions

- Assess their clients' readiness and commitment to implementing the solutions and supporting the change over time

- Measure the results of their solutions or services in terms of cost benefit

- Measure how efficiently and effectively they handled each assignment

- Measure their customers' satisfaction with their services, the results, and the consulting relationship

- Measure the degree to which their solutions are implemented and their clients retain ownership of and accountability for them

- Continually improve their processes

Mike was particularly interested in measuring how well the team's recommendations were implemented and supported over time. To do this, they would first have to assess their clients' capability to support a solution and their commitment to implementing it. In the past, the company had invested significant dollars and human resources in developing good ideas and programs. Implementation of those ideas and programs, however, had been uneven at best. Mike wanted to set up a process that would allow him to separate development accountability from implementation accountability. He and his staff identified the kinds of requests they expected to receive based on their experience:

- Develop procedures for managers to assess suppliers' financial viability and determine appropriate profit margins
- Develop guidelines for managers to use in identifying cost drivers in a supply chain or product line
- Lead or participate in cross-functional teams charged with major initiatives, since their group has expertise in diagnosis (cause analysis) and measurement
- Arrange and coordinate meetings (miniconferences) for senior management, key suppliers, and partners
- Research trends, and do financial analyses
- Prepare presentation materials, and produce reports for limited and worldwide distribution
- Participate in developing specifications for information systems to track and communicate the financial performance of key products and specific markets
- Do needs analyses
- Do cost-benefit studies
- Consult on measurement
- Identify the training needs of supply chain and product managers
- Train managers in financial analysis, decision-making tools, word processing tools, and electronic system tools
- Outsource other training requirements

As admirable and challenging as these assignments might be, they would not improve the performance of the system without a commitment by its managers to implement solutions and measure the results. Mike knew he probably could not change the kinds of things senior management or the other departments asked for, but he could change how his department responded to their requests. With this in mind, Mike and his team decided to define how they would do business. They began by developing an overall consulting process for working with management and the other departments (see Figure 1.10).

Figure 1.10. Mike's Consulting Process

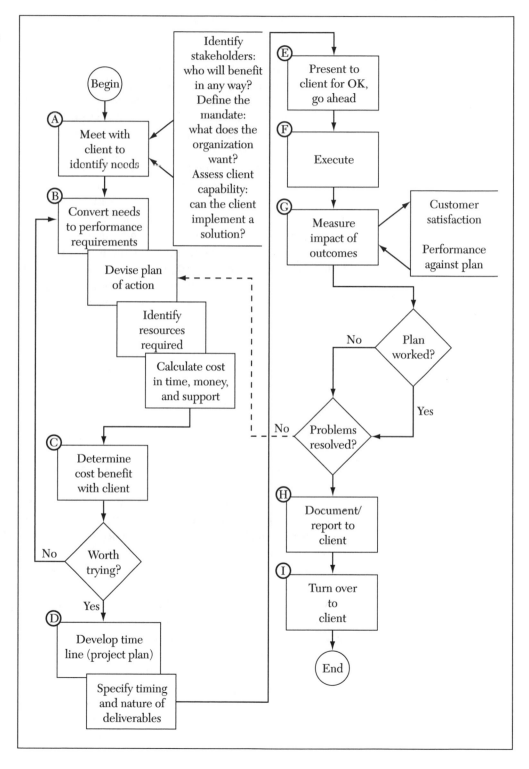

The first activity (labeled A in Figure 1.10) would be to meet with the client to develop an understanding of the client's request. The request could be to solve a problem, develop a product, or provide a service similar to what the team had done in the past. The outcomes of those meetings (B) would be enough information for the team to determine what it would take in terms of resources (time and money) to fulfill the request (that is, the cost) and the client's capability and commitment to following through once the request had been fulfilled. This step would require the team to place some economic value on their time and on any other required resources. The next activity (C) would be to meet with the client to mutually determine whether the potential gain (benefit) would be worth the estimated cost. Together, the consultants and client would determine the worth of the effort, if the client has the resources and commitment to implement or execute what was produced, and how the value of the service or product would be determined after it is rendered or implemented.

Once the client and consultants agree to proceed, the next step (D) would be to develop a more detailed project plan, with a time line, milestones, and deliverables. Again, the client and consultant would either agree to the plan and time line (E) or modify it. The steps under execute (F) might be extensive or simple, depending on the complexity of the request. For Mike and his team, it was the steps in measuring the results (G) and gaining the client's commitment to owning and managing the project (I) that had been missing in the past. These were the two steps that would set his department apart from others brought in to fix problems and make improvements.

The overall process required everyone on Mike's team to become expert at establishing shared expectations with clients, assessing the clients' readiness and willingness to use what is developed, determining the cost of improving (or not improving) performance, planning and managing projects, and measuring the results or outcomes of what happens. These were the required skills to be a consultant in Mike's department.

Each of Mike's subteams—finance, word processing, training, IS, and logistics—refined the overall process to make it more germane to the kinds of requests they might handle. The IS team, for example, added a component under F (execute) for testing new application software and proving its acceptance and value before rolling it out across the system. Finance was the subteam that operated closest to the role of experts. They spent most of their time supplying quick answers. However, they wanted to work on more strategic projects, so they decided to sort requests for their services into one of three categories: help desk; business as usual, or regular reports; and strategic assignments. They then set up different processes for each type of request. This allowed the finance group to track what they did and who they did it for and to develop more efficient procedures for measuring their results (see Figure 1.11).

Having a common process (with variations for specific kinds of requests) resulted in a number of benefits. It gave everyone on the team a better understanding of what the others did and what each could contribute that would be

Figure 1.11. The Finance Team's Process

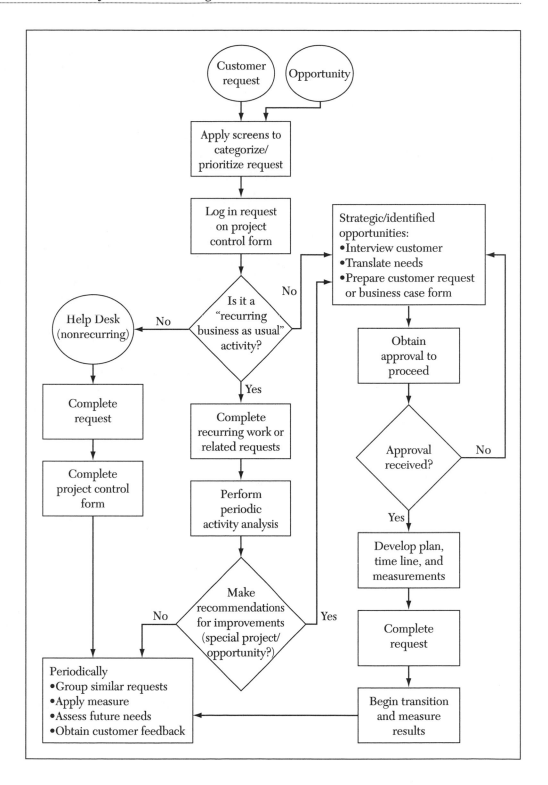

of value to the system. It gave everyone a better understanding of what consulting was about. It even spurred them to learn more about measurement and improve their consulting skills, especially facilitation and negotiation. It also gave everyone a basis for measuring their own efficiency and effectiveness.

THE IMPORTANCE OF A VISION AND MISSION

I am a big believer in vision and mission statements and create them for every assignment and project plan. Whenever I get frustrated with the need to develop one more vision and mission statement for myself or a client, I keep this saying, from an unknown businessperson, in mind: "The purpose of planning is to uncover the things we must do today in order to have a future."

I've learned that I have to create a vision to be effective and that a mission statement helps me stay on track. I may or may not share my vision and mission with my client; nevertheless, they are an integral part of my process for understanding what a client wants and needs, and they provide a basis for evaluating my effectiveness.

A vision statement describes what you see as the possible and desirable future state of your role or function or of the project or the task. A mission statement says what you, the role or function, or the project or task is about. I always start with the vision and then develop the mission. The sequence doesn't really matter; what does matter is having a sense of the future and being clear about your purpose. Figure 1.12 presents my vision and mission for this fieldbook.

Figure 1.12. Vision and Mission for This Fieldbook

Vision: That training and HRD professionals will be recognized and rewarded for their expertise in performance consulting through the use of innovative yet practical tools that engage team members and clients in the process of discovery, diagnosis, problem solving, and measuring results.

Mission: To provide training and HRD professionals with the tools and techniques to:

- Move into performance consulting
- Establish themselves as credible members of the management team
- Use their current activities (delivery, development, facilitation, and others) to build their consulting skills and position themselves as capable, savvy businesspeople
- Give management a more comprehensive picture of the factors that impede and support human performance
- Get the information they need to identify, compare, and recommend appropriate interventions likely to achieve alignment between goals and outcomes
- Join with management to measure the impact or results of the interventions

FIELD NOTES: THE FINANCE TEAM'S VISION AND MISSION

Mike's finance team developed the mission and vision statements presented in Figure 1.13. The group's vision indicates their desire to see systems in place that will enable their clients to make wise business decisions on their own. The group hopes for a day when the system's guidelines and information systems and the client's competence level are sufficient that the finance group can permanently get out of the help desk business.

Figure 1.13. The Finance Team's Vision and Mission Statements

Vision: A financial infrastructure that will enable the product managers and their supply chains to make effective business decisions.

Mission: In our efforts to achieve our vision, the financial team will:

- Provide leadership on strategic initiatives
- Provide leadership in the development of financial guidelines
- Establish a baseline of financial and technical competencies for all product managers
- Provide leadership in the development of a business and financial information structure
- Take and communicate a position and provide recommendations on current business issues

The group's mission indicates the relationship they want with the client (one of leadership) and what they will do to achieve their vision (provide guidance, set standards, offer expert opinions and recommendations).

FIELD TECHNIQUES: SETTING A GOAL FOR YOURSELF

To shift your role from a specific discipline to performance consulting, set a goal for yourself:

1. Look at the consulting continuums in Figures 1.1 and 1.2. Where do you fall on these continuums today? Where do you want to be one year from now? What will you accept as evidence that you have made a change?

2. Review the attributes that distinguish performance consultants from other types of consultants. How closely do those attributes reflect how you are perceived by your clients or how you work with them now? What do you want to change about how you work with your clients and about the type of work you do?

3. Review what the literature says about performance consulting. When can you come up with a definition that works for you?

4. Look at the different consulting processes discussed in this chapter (Figures 1.9, 1.10, and 1.11). Do you have a standardized process for how you consult? What will it take for you to develop a process of your own or adopt a process similar to one of these? How do you want to change the process so that it better fits your situation?

5. Look at the ISPI HPT Standards in Figure 1.6. Download the self-assessment at www.ispi.org, and assess your experience at demonstrating the standards.

6. Use the operational definition worksheet (Figure 1.7) to define performance consulting for yourself. You might want to develop separate definitions for each task. As you work through this fieldbook, return to this worksheet and list what you think it is critical for you to know and to be able to do and what you will take as evidence of success. Figure 1.14 lists some of the competencies I think performance consultants need. Play with it, build on it, and make it work for you.

7. Develop a new vision and mission for your role or function.

SUMMARY

If you want to operate as a performance consultant, you have to define performance consulting for yourself and develop a process for how you will do business. Just calling yourself a performance consultant is not enough. You need a process, coupled with procedures, tools, and techniques, that:

- Integrates the attributes of an expert with those of a facilitator
- Puts you in a position to join with clients as a partner
- Allows you to monitor, measure, and improve your own effectiveness
- Enables you to efficiently and effectively deliver all of your services
- Helps you measure the results of your services

WHERE TO LEARN MORE

The HPT Standards. Silver Spring, MD: International Society for Performance Improvement, 2001. The complete set of standards, self-assessment, and application for the certification can be found at www.ispi.org.

Kaufman, R., Thiagarajan, S., and MacGillis, P. (eds.). *The Guidebook for Performance Improvement.* San Francisco: Jossey-Bass/Pfeiffer, 1997. This basic reference for performance consultants addresses the origins of performance consultancy, direction finding and goal setting, analysis, design and development, implementation, and evaluation.

Self-management

- Make accurate self-assessments (reality testing).
- Have self-confidence (establish a presence).
- Have self-discipline (maintain a sense of priority).
- Maintain an efficiency orientation (always look to do it better).
- Manage your image (maintain external status).

Social/interpersonal

- Maintain social objectivity (detachment).
- Establish rapport (connectedness).
- Engage in group processes (play the task and social roles).
- Cultivate social power (build alliances).
- Be spontaneous (act freely in the here and now).
- Generate cognitive dissonance (purposely provoke reflection).
- Be politically savvy (know whose agenda it is).
- Make use of reciprocity (trade favors without loss of integrity).

Communication

- Describe abstract concepts (models, analogies).
- Describe and explain relationships, goals, and interdependencies (show the link).

Reasoning

- Maintain perceptual objectivity (view events from multiple perspectives simultaneously; engage in heuristic or systemic thinking).
- Engage in conceptualization (identify and recognize patterns in an assortment of information, and develop a concept that describes the patterns or structures; think inductively).
- Use concepts diagnostically (test information by systematically applying it to a concept; think deductively).
- Practice logical thought (place events in a causal sequence).
- Be proactive (provoke activity to some purpose).
- Be concerned with impacts (assess impact on multiple elements).

Performance management

- Interview, observe, and survey (gather data).
- Analyze descriptive, inferential, and financial data (determine significance and correlations).
- Analyze language, symbols, behavior, norms, and rituals (understand social systems).

Figure 1.14. My List of Consulting Competencies

Pershing, J. (ed.). *Handbook of Human Performance Technology.* San Francisco: Jossey-Bass/Pfeiffer, 2006. This updated version of the original handbook, edited by Harold Stolovitch and Erica Keeps in 1992, reflects the latest thinking on performance consulting.

Robinson, D. G., and Robinson, J. *Performance Consulting.* San Francisco: Berrett-Koehler, 1995. One of the early books on performance consulting.

Ukens, L. *What Smart Trainers Know: The Secrets of Success from the World's Foremost Experts.* San Francisco: Jossey-Bass/Pfeiffer, 2001. This book is full of pointed and salient advice on change management, organizational culture, and assessment.

Van Tiem, D., Moseley, J., and Dessinger, J. *Performance Improvement Interventions.* Silver Spring, MD: International Society for Performance Improvement, 2001. This book is full of job aids and examples of how performance technologists do their work.

Chapter 2

The Transition

Some training and HRD departments find the transition to performance consulting difficult. There are a number of reasons that the journey is not a simple one. For example, it requires changing how you operate, learning a different set of skills, and revisiting your own premises about what you can and cannot do.

FIELD NOTES: FALSE STARTS

Doug changed the name of his department from Training and Development to Training and Performance, but he made few other changes. When people asked him what was now different about what his department did, he had difficulty answering. Doug lacked a clear picture of what performance consulting is and a plan for making the transition to it. As a result, nothing in his department really changed.

Doug's situation is common. Training departments often try to move into performance consulting simply by changing their name. Although a name change can help, it is not enough. You have to be able to explain what performance consulting is, why you are moving to it, and how you will operate differently as a result. You have to offer the products and services a performance consultant provides, measure what you do and how you do it, and promote your new services. You need a plan.

EXPERIENCES FROM THE FIELD: PLANNING

When I'm asked about how to make the transition to performance consulting, I talk about the importance of having a plan. The plan should include:

- A *destination*. It is hard to arrive anywhere without a destination in mind. Defining performance consulting and preparing a vision and a mission statement will complete your picture of where you are headed. A vision describes how your world will be once you have completed your mission. A mission statement explains what you are all about, what you do, and the business you are in.

- A *list of available resources.* Every trip requires resources. In this case, resources include your consulting processes and procedures, your current products and services, your skills and knowledge, and your relationships.

- A *strategy.* This is the game plan for getting to your destination. Your game plan might be to leverage your resources or to get out of what you are doing now so that you can redirect your resources toward performance consulting. Another game plan might be to build strategic alliances.

- *Measures.* Measures will help you prove that taking on the new role of performance consultant has been a benefit to your organization and your clients.

The process of developing and carrying out a plan is not particularly linear, but having a destination in mind at the beginning helps. Once you have decided on a destination, you can think about how you will get there, what resources you will need to get there, and how to measure your success once you've arrived. For example, if your strategy is to leverage your resources, those resources have to be well established. If your strategy is to build strategic alliances, you may not have to do anything to your resources. If your strategy is to stop what you are doing now so that you can redirect your resources, then you may have to find someone else to take over what you no longer want to do. If your strategy is to expand your services, you may have to develop your skills so that you can take on new responsibilities. What is important is to look at where you are now and decide on a reasonable course of action. You can't always finish one step before going on to the next. As you learn and gain success, you may have to circle back and pick up some steps you passed by earlier.

FIELD TECHNIQUES: MAKING THE TRANSITION TO PERFORMANCE CONSULTING

Here are some ways you can move from your current role to that of performance consulting (notice that the topics covered in Chapter One, making definitions and mapping out processes, occur early in the plan):

Choosing a Destination

- Define the role of performance consulting.
- Develop a vision and mission statement.

Identifying Your Resources

- Define and describe your process for how you will do business (that is, how you will work with your clients).

- Identify the products and services you now offer, those you want to offer, and to whom you want to offer them (this is covered in this chapter).

- Develop tools and techniques to help you build skill and confidence in your new role (this is covered in Chapters Three and Four).

- Refine your processes for and approaches to discovery, diagnosis, treatment, and measurement (you will find models you can use and modify for this purpose throughout the fieldbook).

- Identify the resources you will require to be effective (additional processes, skills, systems, and so on).

Developing a Strategy

- Continue to learn about the dynamics of organizational and people performance, what organizations can do to improve performance, and how to measure performance and results.

- Build strategic alliances with key staff (such as finance, legal, and marketing managers) and line personnel from the organization's core business.

- Identify a willing customer with a need, and build your confidence by taking on projects that are just at the edge of your comfort zone.

- Manage your relationships and image.

- Market and promote your services and successes.

Defining Measures

- Establish your performance standards.

- Measure the results of what you do and the interventions you recommend.

- Measure your own efficiency and effectiveness.

It is important to start with your destination; however, you will probably move back and forth from resources to strategy to measures and back to resources again. For example, this chapter jumps ahead to measures (setting performance standards) and then goes back to resources (defining your products and services).

FIELD NOTES: MAKING THE TRANSITION

Kelly was head of a centralized training department at a large insurance company. The company had experienced layoffs in the past, and training was one of the first departments to be eliminated. Kelly did not want to go through that again. She believed that by limiting her department's services to training, she and her staff would be at risk for future layoffs. She wanted to expand their services to include consulting on how to improve people performance. She knew the transition would not be easy: her staff were all trainers, her line managers asked only for training, and her students wanted only classroom training. Yet the cost of training was increasingly under attack. Neither she nor her clients could show how training made a difference to the company. She had to change what her department did and how it operated so the value they added to the company could no longer be questioned.

She began by redefining what her department did and how it would do business. She and her staff built a new vision and mission for the department. They changed the name of the department to Learning and Performance Improvement. They expanded their list of products and services to include analysis, coaching, and consultation on evaluating performance. The process of building a plan gave everyone a much deeper understanding of what they did, what they wanted to do differently, who they wanted to serve, and what they had to do to make the change. Their next step was to learn more about assessment and measurement. They defined their processes and added new tools to help them operate more efficiently. They found a friendly and willing client. They tried out their processes and tools. They became known as performance consultants.

ESTABLISHING YOUR OWN PERFORMANCE STANDARDS

About the same time that you are working on your plan, you should begin to think about how you want your work to be evaluated. There will come a time when someone will ask you about the value of performance consulting, and you will be in a better position if you have already set up your measures of success. Your consulting process and plan should help you come up with some performance standards. Otherwise, you cannot compare your performance today with what you did in the past and what you will do in the future. You do not have to know what your assignment is to set your performance standards. Instead, set standards based on your process and the tools and techniques you will use to carry out your assignments. Figure 2.1 lists the standards I use.

With these standards as my guide, I can measure how well my processes, tools, and techniques have enabled me to develop the qualities I need as a performance consultant:

Figure 2.1. My Consulting Process Standards

My *efficiency standards* set targets for

- The time it takes to scope out the job and determine what it will take to deliver on the request
- The time it takes to fulfill the request (cycle time)

My *responsiveness standards* set targets for

- How much time passes before I respond to the request
- How much time passes before I start the assignment

My *accuracy standards* set targets for

- Allowable differences between cost and time estimates and actual expenditures
- Allowable differences between what I expect an assignment to be and what it actually turns out to be

My *effectiveness standards* set targets for

- Acceptable levels of client commitment, cooperation, and confidence
- How well my interventions accomplish what I intend them to accomplish

My *cost standards* set targets for

- The cost-benefit ratio of my services
- The cost-benefit ratio of the interventions I recommend

Efficiency

- How quickly did I scope out a job and determine what it would take, in terms of time and money, for me to deliver the requested product or service?
- How long did a project actually take? (What was the cycle time?) Even if the cycle time for a project is longer than it should be because of events beyond my control, measuring it gives me information that will help me improve how I handle what is under my control on the next job.

Responsiveness

- How long was it before I got around to meeting with the client to find out what the request was?
- How much time passed before I got started on the assignment? Delays may be beyond my control, but they still add to my costs. Tracking this information puts me in a better position to negotiate for faster turnarounds on approvals, reviews, and so forth in the future.

Accuracy

- Did my estimate of how much of my time the assignment would take differ significantly from what it actually took?

- Did I acquire an accurate understanding of the job in the beginning, so that my surprises were few? Every job brings with it the possibility of unanticipated complications. It is only by comparing what I thought at the beginning of a job with what I knew at the end that I can improve my process for qualifying jobs and clients.

Effectiveness

- Did I gain the client's commitment to proceed? Did I secure the client's cooperation throughout the project? Did I build the client's confidence in what I did and how I did it?

- Did the solutions I suggest work? Again, a lot of variables can come into play when it comes to implementing a major program. If I don't measure my results, though, I'll never know how well I managed the variables that were within my control or helped the client manage those within its control.

Cost-Effectiveness

- Did the client feel that the investment in my services was worth it?

- Did the benefit gained from the solution or intervention exceed the cost? When clients get my bill, I want them to think only about the value they received. Even internal consultants should be sensitive to cost-effectiveness. Your services did cost your client: whether you are an external or an internal consultant, you want your clients to feel that their needs were met and that your involvement was worth what it cost them.

You can use the following suggestions to develop standards that will help you measure how effective your processes are and how well your suggestions meet your clients' requirements.

FIELD TECHNIQUES: MEASURING WHAT YOU DO NOW

1. Create a process for meeting with the clients to discuss each assignment or request.

2. Create a mechanism (a time log, calendar, or project plan, for example) for tracking how long it takes you to develop an understanding of the client's

request, put together a proposal or work plan for a client, execute each step of the plan, and measure the results.

3. Track your time over one month or for at least one assignment.

4. Classify the time you spend on each phase or specific step of your process in terms of efficiency, and use this information as a point of comparison for future work (that is, as a baseline).

5. Identify phases or steps for which you think you could develop better procedures or improve your skills to reduce your cycle times or make better use of your time.

6. Set standards for yourself in terms of how efficient or effective you want to be.

7. Continue to track your time, and compare it to your standards or baseline.

8. Continue to identify the phases in which you think you could work more efficiently.

9. Redesign your process or improve your procedures in ways that help you become more efficient.

FIELD NOTES: MEASURING THE CONSULTING PROCESS AND RESULTS

Because each of Mike's subteams (training, finance, IS, logistics, and word processing) now followed a common consulting process, Mike could develop a way to evaluate everyone's performance. To do this, he developed a table of consultant behaviors and results (Figure 2.2). The column heads list the five areas of performance Mike wanted to evaluate. The first column lists different levels of consulting proficiency, starting with least proficient (the bottom row) and progressing to most proficient (the top row). The examples in column 2 illustrate how consultants at various levels of proficiency use processes, from not at all (in the case of the least proficient consultants) to systematically and expertly (in the case of the most proficient ones). Columns 3 and 4 deal with how well a consultant estimates the resources required to fulfill a request and then assesses his or her estimates against what is actually required. The last two columns are about how effective a consultant's subprocesses are at measuring customer satisfaction and determining cost-benefit ratios for the work performed.

The rows list behaviors and outputs that Mike used as baselines to measure performance. The first three rows list behaviors and results that reflect inadequate performance. The fourth row lists behaviors and results that Mike would accept as evidence of meeting expectations. The last row lists behaviors and results that indicate the consultant exceeds expectations. To exceed Mike's expectations, a consultant has to use well-defined, efficient processes that result in services that meet customer needs and add value to the system.

Level of proficiency	Using systematic processes	Estimating efficiency
Optimum. **You exceed expectations as part of your regular way of doing business!**	You are considered an expert at performance consulting.	You can estimate the cost to diagnose a performance problem (not including required outside resources) and recommend appropriate interventions within twenty-four hours.
Capable. **You meet expectations; you've got it!**	You always follow a systematic process for working with clients.	You use a regular process to predict what will be required to fulfill each request in terms of time and expenses.
Stable. **You're close.**	You follow a systematic process on all major projects.	Your process for predicting what is required can be completed within one week.
Visible. **There is room for improvement.**	You may follow a systematic process for one or two major projects.	You may follow a process to predict what is required.
Not visible. **You are not meeting expectations.**	You do not use a systematic process in your work with clients.	You lack a process for predicting the resources required to fill the request.

Figure 2.2. Mike's Expectations for Consulting Proficiency

The operational definition that the team came up with based on Mike's definition of consulting (Figure 1.8), the picture of the consulting process they produced (Figure 1.10), and Mike's list of performance measures (Figure 2.2) gave everyone a better understanding of the behaviors and results Mike was looking for.

ALIGNING YOUR PRODUCTS AND SERVICES WITH YOUR NEW ROLE

Once you have a destination in mind and a plan drawn up, take a hard look at what you do and compare it to what you *want* to do. I find that people who work in training and HRD have usually inherited what they do. They may have initiated and developed some of their programs, but for the most part their department's programs were in place when they were hired. I also find that people often don't know why they do what they do. The reasons, or business drivers behind a program, have long been forgotten.

Estimating accuracy	Assessing customer confidence	Measuring results
You demonstrate continuous improvement in your ability to diagnose problems, recommend interventions, and measure results.	You are asked to do nontraditional work and are perceived as an expert in measurement.	You quantify the benefits of interventions to the organization and have a system to predict future benefits.
You have a process to compare your predictions with reality.	You have a process to assess customer confidence by measuring benefits received and overall customer satisfaction.	You institutionalized your process for doing a cost-benefit analysis.
You track all actual costs.	You follow a process to determine customer satisfaction with emphasis only on the quality of your work.	You follow a process to determine benefits and costs over time (for example, ongoing maintenance costs, administrative costs, and execution costs).
You may follow a process to track actual requirements.	You may follow a process to determine customer satisfaction (such as a survey).	You may follow a process to determine costs and benefits.
You have no process for comparing what you predicted would be required to what was actually required.	You have no way to clearly demonstrate customer satisfaction.	You cannot show your clients a clear cost-benefit relationship.

Figure 2.2. Mike's Expectations for Consulting Proficiency, *cont'd.*

The business driver is the reason that organizations agree to fund the development and delivery of programs and services. Most programs and services are created in response to a business need or because someone in the organization wanted them and got the funding under the guise of meeting a business need.

Programs and services that are created in response to a business need include these examples:

- Job-specific training that is implemented because there is no other cost-effective way for people to learn the job. These programs are offered to new employees and people who are transferred or internally promoted because the job or task is not easily learned through traditional academic or on-the-job programs.

- Mandated programs that are in place because there is no other cost-effective way to satisfy a regulatory requirement. These programs are offered so the organization can comply with a particular law or regulation. Examples are safety programs and other programs used to certify or maintain a certification.

- HR programs initiated because they are an integral part of a process, such as orientation for new employees, performance appraisals, and performance management.

- Programs used to support or deploy an organizational strategy. Examples are new technology efforts, applying quality improvement principles to work processes, shifting work away from individuals and toward cross-functional teams, and working with customers to identify their requirements.

- Skill-building programs offered in response to an identified skill deficiency, such as in financial analysis, coaching, or developing standards. Career development programs are in this category too.

- Product or market support programs created to support the selling of new products or the servicing of new markets.

FIELD TECHNIQUES: IDENTIFYING BUSINESS DRIVERS

Before you can align your products and services to the needs of the organization, you need to examine why the organization maintains the programs and services it now has. Start by asking these questions:

- Why is this program or service offered?

- Has the need been satisfied? If not, is there a better way to satisfy the need? If yes, then why is it still being done?

- Who would be affected if the organization no longer offered the program or service? How would they be affected?

FIELD TOOLS: PRODUCT PORTFOLIO WORKSHEETS

Before you can become something different, it helps to examine what you do now and assess the demands it places on you. There are two worksheets here for doing that. Product Portfolio Worksheet 1 (see Figure 2.3) gives you an overall picture of your current products and services, that is, the business you are in today. Product Portfolio Worksheet 2 (see Figure 2.4) gives you a picture of how well your current and future products and services will perform. Together these worksheets help you better understand:

- Your current and future products and services
- The business reason, or driver, behind each product or service you provide
- The people who depend on your product or services
- The resources required to deliver those products and services
- What, if any, products and services you can eliminate or devote fewer resources to
- What, if any, products or services would bring greater value if they were delivered differently
- Where you can develop a business case for changing what you do or improving how you do it

Both worksheets help you identify opportunities to modify and improve what you do. With them, you examine your current products or services and any new ones you add as a result of moving into performance consulting.

Product Portfolio Worksheet 1

Use Product Portfolio Worksheet 1 to:

- Clarify and gain consensus on what you do now, for whom you do it, why you do it, and the resources required to deliver your current products or services

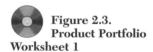

**Figure 2.3.
Product Portfolio
Worksheet 1**

Products and Services	Customer	Business Driver	Methods (how delivered)	Resources Required
1.				
2.				
3.				
4.				
5.				
6.				
7.				
8.				
9.				
10.				

Part 1								
1. Product or Service	2. Customer	3. Driver	4. Dates	5. Percentage of Market	6. Delivery	7. Frequency	8. No-Shows and Cancellations	9. Owner

1. What is the name of the program or service?

2. Who are the customers?

3. What was the initial reason behind the service? What problem was it designed to solve?

4. When was it introduced? When was it last updated?

5. What was the size of the target market? How many have been served to date?

6. How is it delivered (electronically, by contract personnel, by professional staff, self-administered, on-the-job)? Who does the delivery (an instructor, a supervisor, a vendor, a local college)?

7. How frequently is it done (daily, weekly, quarterly, when asked)?

8. What is the average level of participation (class size)? What is the trend in no-shows or cancellations?

9. Who owns the program (your organization or a vendor)?

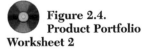

**Figure 2.4.
Product Portfolio
Worksheet 2**

- Reach consensus on what it is you want to do in the future, for whom you want to do it, why you want to do it, and the resources your proposed products or services will require

- Communicate to clients what you do today and what you want to do in the future

The worksheet is a simple matrix that you can modify to meet your needs. The column headings I find most useful are (1) a description of the product and service, (2) a description of the customer or user, (3) a definition of the business driver, (4) a description of how the product or service is currently delivered, and (5) an account of how many resources it requires. You can modify the columns to meet your own needs.

Part 2						Part 3		
10. Rating						11. Measures Used	12. Resources	13. Comments
Q	IC	DC	E	L	O			

10. You and the people who help you administer, schedule, and deliver the program or service should individually and then together rate each program or service on a scale from 1 (worst/least positive) to 5 (best/most positive) for each of these factors:

Q: Quality (Q)
Indirect costs (IC)
Direct costs (DC; together IC and DC tell you what it costs to deliver)
How easy it is to provide (E)
How well it is linked to business drivers (L)
Overall customer response (O)

Note: a rating of 2 or below means attention or action is needed.

11. How do you measure or judge the value of this program or service? For example, is it by the frequency of the request, customer feedback, the revenue it generates, the fact that it is required by a regulatory agency, or something else?

12. What is the overall resource commitment required to deliver this program or service?

13. This is a place for everyone involved to say whatever they want about the program or service.

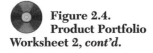

Figure 2.4.
Product Portfolio
Worksheet 2, *cont'd.*

Here is how to use the worksheet:

1. *List the program, product, or service* you currently offer. Be sure to include services like contracting, managing projects, screening and selecting vendors, preparing documents of understanding, training trainers, qualifying trainers, registering students, administering student files, producing and maintaining course materials, scheduling, and managing facilities and equipment.

2. *List the customers* for your products or services.

3. *List the business driver* behind each product or service. For example, is it mandated, connected with turnover, or required for certification?

4. *Briefly describe how you deliver the product or service.* For example, is it delivered one-on-one or in a classroom setting? Is it delivered electronically, or is it self-administered? Is it offered at a local college or outsourced to a vendor?

5. *List the resources required to deliver it.* Be specific about the number of people required and the amount of time they spend. For example, who does the work required to deliver the product or service? How much time do they spend doing it? Which and how many are qualified to do it?

Once you have a picture of what it is you do and why, discuss these points with your colleagues or clients:

- Whether it is appropriate to continue delivering this set of products or services. You might ask, for example, whether there is still a business driver behind each service or what the consequences would be if we stopped providing a certain service or committed less resources to it.

- How you might reduce the amount of resources it takes to deliver your current set of products. For example, you might ask where there are opportunities to outsource or make better use of technology, whether the client could do this instead of doing it ourselves, and what the consequences would be if others did it.

- Which of your current services you would not provide if you were in the business of performance consulting.

- What services you would add if you were in the business of performance consulting. Include the things you wish you could do but do not now because you lack the skills, customer relationships, or resources to be successful.

- How you would have to operate differently if you were performance consultants.

- What internal support systems and processes you would want to add or improve so that you could be effective as a performance consultant. For example, can you track your costs now? Do you have a way to value your time? Do you have a formal process for doing needs assessment?

If you get stuck because you are thinking about *how* you can offer new products and services instead of *what* you want to offer, consider how you might leverage your current set of products to support your transition to performance consulting. For example, you might ask which of your current products or services give you legitimate access to influential people, which ones allow you to develop the skills and confidence required to move more into consulting, or which ones give you access to critical information that a consultant should know.

Create a new worksheet that lists the products and services you want to offer in the future. Include potential clients, the business drivers behind what you would like to offer, the resources that will be required, and whether you have those resources now.

Depending on the number of programs or projects you are responsible for, you may want to fill out different worksheets for each program type (training, facilitation, consulting, services), each client, each different curriculum, or each delivery mechanism.

FIELD NOTES: ALIGNING PRODUCTS AND SERVICES

Deborah was hired to be the new director of training at a national communications company. The company wanted her to change the focus of the training department from technical training to performance improvement. She started by learning more about her staff, what they did, and what their capabilities were. Next she met with key line managers from the field and found out what they expected of her and her people. She asked the staff directors at the home office staff what they wanted from her department. Learning what her field and home office customers wanted gave Deborah a lot of ideas about how her department could better contribute to the company. For example, she saw the need to adopt a more efficient delivery system; work with managers to reduce turnover; propose a more effective, targeted selection program; coach managers on how to support new employees better; and develop expert systems to accommodate regulatory changes more efficiently.

To make these changes, she would have to find out what resources the department had and how it used them. Deborah and her staff decided to take a closer look at exactly what it is they did. Together they created a worksheet and recorded what they did; their customers, stakeholders, and sponsors; the drivers behind their services; how their services were delivered, and the amount of resources their services consumed. Figure 2.5 shows what they came up with.

It was clear from the exercise that Deborah's trainers were consumed with supporting customer service training to new employees (note the resources devoted to the first two services). The few people who were left were dedicated to coaching managers, delivering technical training beyond what was covered in the program for new employees, and participating in corporate projects.

Deborah and her staff then reviewed what their field customers wanted. They had learned that the managers at the call centers wanted more competent

Products and Services	Customers	Stakeholders
1. Deliver product training for new employees	Customer service reps (CSRs)	Supervisors and center managers
2. Deliver sales training for new employees	CSRs and supervisors	Center managers
3. Deliver product training	CSRs Supervisors	Marketing
4. Deliver updates on procedures	CSRs Supervisors	Methods and procedures
5. Deliver management skills training for HR	Supervisors Center managers	HR
6. Facilitate meetings on request	Center managers	Center managers
7. Coach managers on sales on request	CSRs and supervisors	Center managers
8. Maintain the accuracy of technical training content	CSRs	Center managers
9. Participate in corporate projects	Corporate office	Varied; based on criteria for participation

Figure 2.5. Deborah's Portfolio of Current Products and Services

trainers, more sales training, shorter learning curves for new employees (it was taking them from four to five months to get up to speed), and a more efficient way to keep customer service representatives current on product changes, regulatory changes, and competitor information.

Managers from home office functions like finance, IS, and quality assurance wanted reduced turnover (it was as high as 30 percent in some departments); help with message design, to reduce the risk of lost revenues and fines from giving inaccurate billing information to customers; an expert system that would reduce the time to train call center personnel; advice on designing procedures and help screens; and ways to get information to the front line faster, at less cost, and in a form that could be understood and readily accessed.

Deborah and her staff then created a second worksheet. This time they listed the products and services they thought they must offer to get customers to accept them in the new role:

Sponsor	Driver	Methods	Resources
Sales vice president	Turnover and growth	Instructor-led classes and multimedia	Forty instructors, full time
Sales vice president	Turnover and growth	Instructor led	20 percent of five consultants' job
Sales vice president	Steady stream of new products	Instructor led	30 percent of two consultants' job
Internal audit	Constant change in regulations	Memos and announcements	100 percent of one designer's job
HR	Turnover and growth	Training trainers, evaluating trainers, scheduling trainers	Contract trainers
Sales vice president	Shift to a more team-oriented culture	In person	20 percent of two consultants' job
Sales vice president	Shift to a sales culture	In person and phone contact	20 percent of two consultants' job
Sales vice president	Changes in product attributes	Team member or leader	80 percent of two designers' job
Sales vice president	Changes in product attributes	Team member or leader review	80 percent of two designers' job; 20 percent of three to five consultants' job

Figure 2.5. Deborah's Portfolio of Current Products and Services, *cont'd.*

- Developing tools clients could use to improve performance (such as a process for supporting sales, a model for coaching, standards for trainers, and a better hiring process)

- Developing cost models that they and their clients could use to determine current costs and do cost-benefit analyses

- Serving as subject matter experts in learning, performance, message design, electronic delivery systems, and expert systems

- Administering and monitoring (through new technology) training registration, schedules, and learners' course completion

- Serving as team leaders for major corporate initiatives

Figure 2.6 lists their new products and services.

Products and Services	Customer	Driver	Methods	Resources Required
1. Manage the delivery of product and sales training for new employees	Call centers	Lower cost of training	Instructor-led courses; multimedia courses; coaching of trainers	Scheduling software; qualified trainers; trainer coaches
2. Deliver ongoing product and procedures training	Call centers	Changes to products and procedures	Instructor-led courses; self-administered training; online help; job aids	Scheduling software; qualified trainers; trainer coaches
3. Screen and brand vendor training	Call centers and HR	Lower cost of training	Repackage and confirm they meet instructional criteria	Criteria; evaluation process; contracting process
4. Select and qualify contract trainers to deliver HR training	HR and call centers	Improve quality; control costs	Train and certify trainers	Training standards and certification process
5. Facilitate meetings	Managers	Faster results	Use facilitators	Qualified facilitators
6. Coach managers to improve sales and performance	Call centers	Retention; higher sales goals	Use consultants	Qualified performance consultants
7. Do needs assessments and organizational reviews	Vice presidents	Higher sales goals	Partner with HR, IT, Finance, and other departments	Well-defined process; survey technology
8. Develop performance measurement tools	Vice presidents	Align merit with results	Partner with HR, marketing, and other departments	Evaluating and measuring processes and tools
9. Consult on technology, job, and message design	Call centers	Lower costs; speed	Lead teams and consult	Contracting process
10. Update and maintain training	Call centers	Fines	Use instructional designer	Authoring system

Figure 2.6. Deborah's New Products and Services

Product Portfolio Worksheet 2

Product Portfolio Worksheet 2 is well suited for evaluating programs and services from Worksheet 1 that you want to examine in greater detail. Depending on how many different client groups or curricula there are, you may want to fill out different worksheets for each. The worksheet will help you:

- Decide what programs or services still bring value
- Identify what you can do to improve those programs or services or reduce the cost of providing them
- Better manage the life cycle of your programs and services
- Identify which programs or services are worthy of additional time or money for improvement

Product Portfolio Worksheet 2 (Figure 2.4) has three parts. Part 1 lists some variables or factors to consider for each product or service you offer or plan to offer. This includes some of the same information in Worksheet 1. Part 2 has space for you and the other people who support your products or services to rate them based on their quality, cost, and other criteria. Part 3 lists measures used in evaluating the products or services, the resources they require, and comments from anyone involved. You can customize the first two parts to meet your needs.

Part 1: Variables. The first time you use the worksheet, be sure to record the appropriate information for each of the variables or factors listed (see the numbered list of questions at the bottom of the figure).

Part 2: Ratings. Use a Likert scale to rate the program or service according to those criteria. A Likert scale is a five-point scale used to rate something. What distinguishes it from other scales is that it allows people to give neutral or noncommittal ratings (by selecting the midpoint, or 3, on the scale). When you create the scale, be consistent as to which value is positive (the 1 or the 5); do not switch back and forth.

Part 3: Evaluation and Resources. Part 3 is about evaluation and resources. On it you can indicate:

- How you evaluate each program now (for example, using Kirkpatrick's levels 1, 2, 3, and 4, or some other method). Level 1 measures learner's reactions to the program and how it was delivered. Level 2 measures how much people learned by testing them on the content of the program. Level 3 measures the degree people's behavior on the job changed or the frequency with which they applied the information covered in a program. Level 4 measures the impact or results gained from people having attended a program.

- The amount of resources you must commit to it (for example, equipment, space, administration, testing, setup, materials, instructors, and other qualified personnel)

Part 3 also includes a space for general comments.

FIELD TECHNIQUES: EVALUATING THE WORTH OF WHAT YOU DO NOW

Using Product Portfolio Worksheet 2, follow these steps to evaluate the worth of your current products or services:

1. Ask yourself what you want to know about what you do now. (Use your answer to come up with the variables you want to consider.) For example, do you want to know:

   - Which products or services consume the most resources?

   - Which products or services cost more to deliver than the value they generate?

   - Who your customers are for each product or service?

   - Whether you have exhausted the market for a given product or service?

   - If there are other customers for a product or service?

   - If your customers really value a certain product or service?

   - What percentage of your customers use each product or service?

   - What the driver was behind each product or service, whether that need has been met, and whether that product or service is the best way to meet that need? How to find out this information?

2. Based on your answers, create a worksheet and include a column for every variable.

3. Fill out the portfolio as best you can. Solicit input from customers where appropriate. Pay attention to what you do *not* know about a specific program or service, especially if you do not know how much it costs to deliver or support.

4. Ask others who are directly involved in supporting the service to rate it according to the variables you have selected.

5. Ask them to add any comments they want.

6. Once you have gathered the information, question the worth and value of each program and service. Look for indicators that the worth or value is less than it might be. For example, is it costly to deliver? Is the link to the organization unclear or weak? Is the number of cancellations and no-shows high?

7. Identify the products and services that would benefit from changing the delivery system, the number of offerings, when the product or service is offered, how it is offered, and so on.

8. Identify the products and services you can stop offering or outsource.

FIELD TECHNIQUES: FINDING A WILLING CLIENT

You may find that you already offer many of the products or services listed in your new product portfolio. However, if there are some that you have not offered or lack experience with, think of a client who might be willing to give you that experience. This is what Kelly, who worked for the insurance company, did. You probably already have well-established relationships with your clients. If you do:

1. Select a client you think will be responsive to your assuming the new role of performance consultant.

2. Begin by explaining what you want to accomplish.

3. Explain why you think the client would benefit from your doing this or participating in some way.

4. Ask if there is an issue or problem the client would like to have a better understanding of.

5. Ask if there is an initiative, team, or problem where your skills in analysis, measurement, or facilitation would be of value.

6. Negotiate for your involvement.

7. Develop a charter for the assignment, and clarify what the deliverables might be. A charter describes what a group has been commissioned to do and by what date.

8. Identify or develop some measures for your performance and the deliverables.

9. If appropriate, develop a project plan, with a time line and milestones.

10. Fulfill the request.

11. Evaluate the results and how you went about completing the assignment.

12. Share the results with your own colleagues so that you can improve. Share them with other potential clients so that they can see the possible value to them of your products and services.

USING THE PRODUCT PORTFOLIO WORKSHEETS WITH CLIENTS

You can use the techniques described so far not only to help yourself be more effective in your practice but also to help your clients be more effective in what they do. The processes of defining what they are all about and how they do business, measuring their performance and that of their products or services, and so on are the same. For example, I use the operational definition to help my clients and their customers come to a shared understanding of their respective roles, responsibilities, and practices. The definition serves as a reality check for all concerned. It can help both you and your clients tell others who you think you are and what you are all about. Your customers can then judge whether this description is supported by your behavior and the results you produce.

You can modify the product portfolio worksheets for use with your clients as you see fit. To use the worksheet with a client, follow a similar process as you would use for yourself. For example, help the client come up with a list of questions about its products and services, such as these:

- Who are our customers?

- Is this the business we want to be in?

- Do our customers value these products and services?

- What other products and services do our customers want?

- Are we cost-effective and competitive?

- What do we want on this list that would allow us to add even greater value to our organization?

 **FIELD TECHNIQUES: BUILDING YOUR PLAN**

To make the transition from what you do now to performance consulting:

- Look at the elements of the plan. Identify the elements you want to act on, and give yourself a deadline to do so. Add other steps you think will help. How far along do you expect to be one year from now? What will you accept as evidence you are making progress?

- Review the standards and measures in Figures 2.1 and 2.2. If you were to evaluate yourself against any of these criteria, where would you fall today? What do you have to do to begin exceeding your clients' expectations? How might you use these measures to support your plan to move to performance consulting? How would you change these measures to better reflect your situation? How easy would it be to start using measures like these?

- Look at the product portfolio worksheets (Figures 2.3 and 2.4). How might you modify these worksheets to capture the information you want about what you do now? How might you use the insights you gain from these worksheets to build a case for becoming a performance consultant? Are you currently offering services that you should not be or services that should be provided by someone else? What resources would be freed up if you were to change what you do and how you do it?

The act of evaluating your current products and services, assessing their worth against some predefined criteria, and questioning the reason for them are the kinds of things a performance consultant does. If you don't think so, review the list in Chapter One of the four things that distinguish performance consultants from other consultants. Congratulations! You are now on your way to becoming a performance consultant!

SUMMARY

It takes more than a name change to make the transition to performance consulting. You have to mold a plan, define measures of success, and develop the kinds of products and services a performance consultant offers. Most important, you have to start acting like a performance consultant. The easiest place to start is with yourself. In the process, you will increase your skills and better understand your new role.

WHERE TO LEARN MORE

Block, P. *Flawless Consulting.* San Francisco: Jossey-Bass/Pfeiffer, 1981. Block presumes consultants operate from a position of power whether that be based on expertise or position.

Fuller, J. *Managing Performance Improvement Projects.* San Francisco: Jossey-Bass/Pfeiffer, 1997.

Lippitt, G., and Lippitt, R. *The Consulting Process in Action.* (2nd ed.) San Francisco: Jossey-Bass/Pfeiffer, 1986.

Ranshaw, J. *101 Tips for Marketing Your Services.* Chicago, IL: hoosierjanebooks, 2005. This update of the 1995 edition includes tips for marketing on the Internet along with original tips for novice and seasoned consultants, and it has a new section on pricing.

Reddy, W. B. *Intervention Skills: Process Consultation for Small Groups and Teams.* San Francisco: Jossey-Bass/Pfeiffer, 1994. This is a classic.

Ukens, L. (ed.). *What Smart Trainers Know.* San Francisco: Jossey-Bass/Pfeiffer, 2001. This is a collection of tools that successful consultants use.

Chapter 3

Costs

*O*ne of the most overlooked prerequisites of effective consulting is the ability to understand the economics behind poor performance. Unlike trainers, consultants must be able to qualify the costs of a client's processes and practices as well as determine the cost benefits of their own recommendations. Here is what happens when neither the client nor the consultant understands costs and what drives them.

FIELD NOTES: COST OF SALES

The vice president of finance at a large corporation confronted the vice president of sales over the rising costs of sales at their company. Until then, no one had ever talked about the cost of sales. Everyone knew the sales cycle: down in the first two quarters, up in the third quarter, and way up in the fourth quarter. The company didn't launch its sales campaigns until the end of the third quarter, and it based its sales reps' bonuses on their fourth-quarter sales. But sales reps were expected to entertain clients, take them to lunch, and travel to their offices all year long. The subject of cost of sales had never come up before. Sales reps were never even given any information about what it costs the company to make a sale.

The vice president of sales turned to the director of training and demanded that he provide a workshop on territory management at the next regional sales meeting. He specified what the content should be and how the success of the program would be measured. But no one asked why he thought that poor territory management was the reason behind the "high" cost of sales. Because the training wasn't budgeted, the director of training argued that the cost of the session should go in the budget for sales, not the budget for training.

The circumstances described in the story did not emerge overnight. The company's sales costs were driven by business practices that had been considered quite acceptable for years. Unlike Mark in Chapter One, who wondered how he could best improve the financial performance of his Midwest plant, the vice president of sales at this company seems uninterested in finding out which costs are high and by how much, if they are high for all sales staff or just a few, or even what the real problem is. The director of training seems interested only in not having the cost of the workshop show up in his budget.

EXPERIENCES FROM THE FIELD: UNDERSTANDING COSTS

When I speak on the subject of evaluation at national conferences, the questions I'm most frequently asked concern how to prove return on investment (ROI) and how to do Kirkpatrick's level 4 evaluation (that is, how to prove that the training solved the business problem or improved performance). Just like performance consultants, clients often must struggle with how to estimate the value of a product or service or prove its worth. My experience is that trainers, HRD professionals, and consultants and their clients often face similar problems: they don't understand how to value, or quantify, the problem they want to solve in economic terms, and they don't have the systems in place to isolate costs and determine what causes them. These problems are compounded by the fact that people think they are supposed to know these things, as if this information were just hanging around waiting for someone to notice it. It's not that easy. Here are some things I've learned that I've found very valuable when working with clients:

- *Organizations classify their costs depending on their unique needs; they don't all do it in the same way.* Furthermore, organizations vary significantly in their ability to isolate costs and identify what caused them. Find out exactly how your clients identify and classify their costs.

- *Not all costs are valued the same.* Some are looked on less favorably than others (specifically, indirect, fixed costs).

- *Costs don't just happen; they have a cause.* The customers, business practices, processes, or people who cause them aren't necessarily the ones charged with or held accountable for them. Find out what or who caused the cost you're investigating, not just who gets blamed for it or is held responsible for reducing it.

- *Cost management is about managing the causes of costs.* You have to manage the cause, or cost driver, to reduce, avoid, or eliminate the cost.

- *Most efforts to reduce costs don't; they just shift the cost to someone else.* Find out what the implications are on others before you claim your program reduces costs.

- *The cost to develop and launch a solution is not the same as the total cost of ownership or sustaining a change.* Encourage discussions about the effort required to sustain an initiative over time. A simple example is the cost to keep training content current or administer multiple offerings in multiple formats in future years. The discussion should be about who will bear these costs and whether the organization is committed to funding the solution over the long term.

- *The cost of the infrastructure (facilities, systems, and equipment) required to actualize a solution is frequently assumed or undervalued, yet the long-term effectiveness depends on it.* You should encourage discussions about what exists or will exist if it is necessary for the solution identified.

How Organizations Classify Costs

There are different types of costs, yet we often talk as if all costs are the same. There are some universal rules and guidelines for classifying costs, yet how an organization classifies specific costs depends on its unique needs. You need to understand how your organization or client classifies costs so that you can isolate which costs your services are expected to reduce and compare the cost of doing something with the cost of doing nothing. This information is key to being able to quantify a problem and justify recommendations for change.

Figure 3.1. Major Cost Classifications

Organizations classify costs depending on the type of business they are in and what they want to do with the information. For example, they typically start by distinguishing product or service costs from the cost of selling the product or service, the cost of support services, and management costs (that is, the costs of running the business; see Figure 3.1).

Organizations further classify their costs within each of these major categories. The headings or labels under which a company or business unit classifies costs usually represent its larger cost components. For example, service organizations almost always distinguish salaries from overhead. Capital-intensive businesses almost always separate out depreciation costs. Manufacturers separate the cost of making their products from the costs of selling, servicing, warehousing, and shipping them and the costs of managing the business (see Figure 3.2).

Organizations pay attention to the costs that affect profits, pricing, and bonuses. For example, manufacturers pay attention to the cost of these components:

- The *raw materials* used to make their products, because raw materials are frequently the largest part of a product's cost. Manufacturers want to know when the cost of raw materials changes and what causes the change, as this

**Figure 3.2.
Manufacturers' Major
Cost Components**

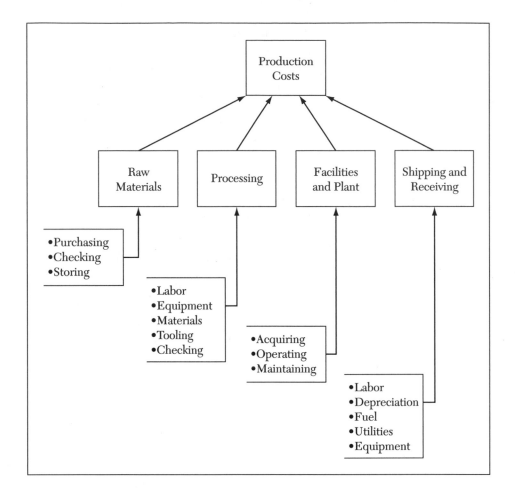

cost directly affects their ability to price products competitively and make a profit. They also pay attention to whether the raw materials add hidden costs because they require extra handling.

- *Processing or assembling* the raw materials (specifically, the costs of labor, equipment, materials, tooling, and testing). Labor can be a significant part of a product's cost; therefore, companies pay attention to how much they are paying employees. Poorly scheduled or untrained people can add unnecessary costs.

- Their *plants and facilities* (specifically, the cost to acquire, operate, and maintain them, including depreciation, utilities, insurance, and taxes). Because facility costs are significant, companies pay close attention to what percentage of their facilities is dedicated to producing products. Underused space can increase the overall cost of a company's products and services, forcing an increase in its prices or a lower profit margin.

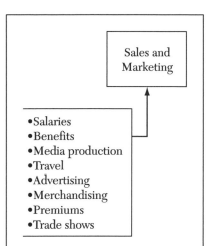

Figure 3.3. Cost of Sales

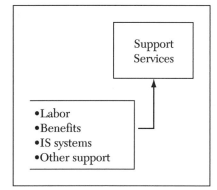

Figure 3.4. Cost of Services

• *Warehousing and shipping* the product (specifically, labor, depreciation, fuel, utilities, insurance, taxes, pallets, and refrigeration). These costs, too, get added to the price or reduce the profit margin.

All companies are particularly concerned with the cost of sales and the cost of service. Figure 3.3 shows what is typically thought of as the cost of sales, and Figure 3.4 shows the items that usually make up the cost of service. Your clients may include other or different costs, however.

Determining the cost of running the business (see Figure 3.5) is more complex, because what is included depends on the type of organization and its reason for tracking some costs and not others.

How Organizations Value Costs

Businesses do not treat all costs the same. They look on some costs more favorably than others. The kinds of costs most look on more favorably are those that are easier to isolate, control, or pass on to customers; these are generally incurred in direct proportion to the amount of business being done. The kinds of costs that businesses look on less favorably are those that are harder to isolate, control, and pass on; these are usually incurred independently of the amount of sales.

Rule No.1: Find out how your clients classify their costs and how they distinguish direct costs from indirect costs.

Organizations pay attention to:

• *Direct and indirect costs.* Direct costs are easier to isolate and can be linked (and charged) to a specific customer, product, or service. For example, the cost of raw materials, fuel for delivery trucks,

**Figure 3.5.
Cost of Running
the Business**

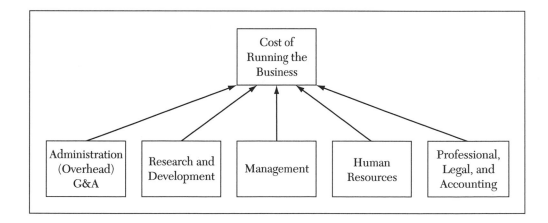

and technicians who make service calls are all direct costs. Indirect costs, frequently referred to as *overhead,* are harder to isolate and link to a specific customer or product; therefore, they are spread across products and customers. Indirect costs include sales, marketing, management, human resources, and administration.

- *Variable and fixed costs.* Variable costs fluctuate based on the volume of work being done (raw materials costs are variable, for example); therefore, they are somewhat controllable. Fixed costs, such as depreciation, do not fluctuate and are thus less controllable. Some costs are partially fixed and partially variable. The cost of electricity is an example: companies use electric power all of the time (the fixed portion), but they use more power when production lines are up and running (the variable portion).

The Relationship Between Direct, Indirect, Variable, and Fixed Costs

Most direct costs are variable costs—for example, the cost of raw materials and the cost of production labor (regular and overtime wages and benefits). You can attribute these costs to a specific product or service, and you most likely incur them when you have business (you don't buy raw materials without customer orders, and you can lay workers off when business is down).

There are a few direct costs that are fixed. Consider depreciation on the equipment used to manufacture products. You can attribute the cost of the equipment to the product it produces (making it a direct cost), but you still have the cost (depreciation) whether the equipment is running or not (making it a fixed cost).

Most indirect costs are also fixed costs, because companies continue to incur them regardless of the amount of sales or production. Changes in the volume of work have minimal effect on them. When organizations want to cut costs, they usually start by looking at their fixed indirect costs, which include management salaries and benefits and perhaps facility costs for management offices, and overhead, or general and administrative (G&A) costs. G&A costs include administrative costs; insurance costs; real estate taxes; the cost of licenses; interest expense; rent and leasing costs; the cost of heat and other utilities; depreciation and amortization of assets not easily linked to specific products, services, or customers; marketing and advertising costs; research and development (R&D) costs; training and HR costs; and accounting and legal costs. (Administration, marketing and advertising, R&D, training and HR, and accounting and legal costs include costs for salaries and benefits, facility use by the specific function, and depreciation on equipment used by the specific function.) Figure 3.6 briefly defines and provides examples of variable direct costs, fixed direct costs, and fixed indirect costs.

Figure 3.6. Examples of Costs

Type of Cost	Examples
Variable direct costs: allocated to specific products, services, or customers; fluctuate with the volume of business.	• Raw materials • Labor used to build products or provide service • Consultants contracted to develop or facilitate programs • Vendor courses • CSRs' overtime
Fixed direct costs: allocated to specific products, services, or customers; do not fluctuate in proportion with changes in the volume of work performed	• Depreciation of capital equipment used to make specific products or dedicated to servicing specific customers • CSRs (salary, benefits, and percentage of facility use) who are dedicated to a specific product line or customer group and whose hours do not fluctuate in proportion to volume • Supervisors whose departments are dedicated to one business line, product, or customer • Professional staff dedicated to one business line, service, or customer • Corporate university facilities or dedicated space
Fixed indirect costs: not dedicated but spread across products, services, and customers; do not fluctuate with changes in business volume	• Management salaries and benefits • Staff salaries and benefits • Corporate office expenses

Depreciation is a reduction in the value of producing a fixed asset because of wear and tear from normal use. Examples of assets that are depreciated are facilities (buildings) and capital goods (equipment and vehicles). Companies with high depreciation costs (like manufacturers) are more capital intensive. *Amortization* is the gradual reduction in the book value of a nonproducing asset that has a limited life. The original cost is spread over the life of the asset. Examples of assets that are amortized are patents, copyrights, and franchises.

What Businesses Include in the Price of a Product or Service

The price of a product or service includes its direct costs, plus some portion of the business's indirect costs, plus some margin for profit (see Figure 3.7). Organizations strive to reduce their costs so that they can maintain or lower their prices (to become more competitive) without reducing their profit margin.

Rule No. 2: Find out how your organization, department, or client classifies its costs. Find out what costs, if any, are considered direct and what costs are considered indirect. Whether you as a performance consultant are a direct or indirect cost, find out how your time, space, and equipment are valued and thus allocated, or spread.

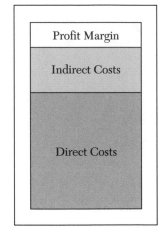

Figure 3.7. **Components of Price**

FIELD TECHNIQUES: LEARNING HOW YOUR ORGANIZATION CLASSIFIES COSTS

I've presented a simple explanation of costs, but it's enough for you to begin to have a conversation with your client's or organization's finance department. You have to find out how your client or organization classifies costs, why it uses that method, and how well it can isolate its costs. Here is a technique for doing so:

1. Meet with someone in the accounting or finance department and ask how the organization classifies costs.

2. If your client or organization uses broad categories like overhead, management, G&A, and so on, ask what costs go into each category and who makes those decisions.

3. Ask which costs are considered direct and which are considered indirect.

4. Ask which costs are fixed (less controllable) and which are variable (controllable).

5. Ask which costs are the larger cost components.

6. Ask how changes in business volume affect costs and which costs are most affected.

7. Ask how the organization recovers its fixed costs when volume or business is down.

8. If the organization is capital intensive, ask how it allocates and recovers depreciation when volume or business is down.

9. Ask which costs the company attributes to you or your department (salaries, facilities, equipment, and so on) and how it classifies them. If some of your costs are direct, ask which products, services, or customers they are linked to. If some or all of your costs are considered indirect, ask on what basis they are spread across customers, lines of business, or products (that is, equally in proportion to usage).

FIELD TOOLS: VALUING TIME

Sometimes consultants and clients do not know how to value their time. Thus, even if they are able to eliminate activities or become more efficient, they don't know how to assign a value to the time they have saved. Figure 3.8 provides a worksheet for figuring out how much your time and your client's time is worth.

Figure 3.8. A Formula for Valuing Time

1. Identify an appropriate pay grade, and select the annual salary at the midpoint of that grade.

   Enter that figure here. _____

2. Divide that figure by the number of available hours in the year (see below). ÷ 1,800

   Enter the result here. _____

3. Add a percentage for overhead (an indirect, fixed cost). A commonly used number is 35 percent. × 1.35

   This is your hourly rate. = _____

This formula gives you an hourly rate you can use to value your time and your client's time. Once you know the formula, you can change its assumptions based on the situation.

The figure of 1,800 work hours per year is derived from this formula:

52 weeks a year × 40 hour work week	= 2,080 hours
Less minimum vacation time (2 weeks)	– 80 hours
Less an average 11 personal days and holidays	– 88 hours
Less typical number of training hours	– 50 hours
Less typical time spent in meetings	– 40 hours
Less typical miscellaneous and sick time	– 22 hours
Available hours per year	= 1,800 hours

Add a percentage for overhead (an indirect, fixed cost) to your hourly rate. A commonly used number is 35 percent. This gives you an hourly rate you can use to value your own and your client's time.

FIELD NOTES: SPREADING FIXED COSTS

Jennifer headed the word processing group in her company's shared services department. Her group's costs (salaries, benefits, depreciation of equipment, materials, travel, and space) were treated as fixed indirect costs, classified as overhead, and spread evenly across the seven departments she served. Jennifer decided to find out how much time her group spent working for each department and the nature of the work they performed for each customer. She compiled work records for eight months. She discovered that 33 percent of her work was done for the company's U.S. product managers, 33 percent for the remaining five departments, and 34 percent for her own department. She also looked at the average number of pages word-processed for each customer group and the extent of the revisions they required. She recommended that the company no longer spread her group's costs evenly but instead spread them in proportion to each department's use of their services. Spreading the costs evenly had given the U.S. product managers and the other departments a distorted picture of their true costs.

COST MANAGEMENT

Cost management is about taking direct action to reduce, avoid, or eliminate costs. The term *cost management* is actually somewhat misleading. What you manage is not costs but what causes those costs (this is similar to time management, where you manage what you do with your time, not the time itself).

Rule No. 3: Find out what drives, or causes, your costs.

Here is what causes costs:

- Companies engage in activities to create products and deliver services.
- Those activities consume resources (time, materials, space, and equipment), and resources cost money.

Activities are directed by a product or service's requirements, the processes used to create the product or provide the service, customers' requirements, and business practices. By linking resources to an activity, then to the product or service, and eventually to the requirement, process, customer, or practice, you can trace the true source of the product's or service's costs. By identifying what drives unnecessary activity (such as an unnecessary requirement of the product or the customer, a poorly designed or executed work process, or poor employee performance), you can find ways to eliminate or reduce the amount of activity and reduce costs. Thus, you can reduce costs by eliminating activities or reducing the amount of resources they consume.

Rule No. 4: Look for hidden costs.

Hidden costs is the term I use for costs an organization either does not or cannot isolate because they fall outside the system for isolating and tracking costs. Such costs frequently get shifted between groups: the group that gets charged with a cost may not be the group that created it. For example, when sales reps fail to get complete or accurate information about new accounts, the cost of getting that information is shifted to someone else, like accounting or customer service. The failure to get complete or accurate information in the first place increases the cost of sales, but that portion of the cost is hidden or buried in overhead because it shifted to accounting or customer service. This is why Jennifer wanted to track her department's activities to specific customers. She wanted to know which customers drove her activities and thus her costs. She discovered that five of her customers were paying more than their fair share and two were getting off easy.

UNNECESSARY COST DRIVERS

You and your clients have unnecessary costs when:

- Product or service requirements are excessive.

- Processes are not well designed.

- The customer's requirements are not fully understood, and this results in doing more work than required (rework) or doing work the customer doesn't value.

- The information, equipment, space, and tools to do the job are insufficient or inappropriate.

- Employees lack the necessary skills.

- People's behaviors force others to incur costs (that is, they shift costs to others).

- Jobs or tasks could be done with less costly resources, such as through automation or outsourcing.

- Management does not provide adequate direction, resulting in unnecessary activity.

Rule No. 5: To manage costs, you must identify and isolate them, find out what they are made up of, and determine what causes them.

Once you know what causes a cost, you can change the requirements (product, service, or customer), improve your processes, or eliminate practices that shift it around.

FIELD TOOLS: ISOLATING AND MANAGING COSTS

Organizations use a number of tools to isolate costs and find out what drives them:

- *Activity-based costing systems.* Not all accounting systems are designed to help manage costs. In fact, most accounting systems are designed only to report costs. Activity-based costing is an accounting system specifically designed to identify costs and support cost management.

- *Statistical process control* (SPC). SPC identifies variance within products, pinpoints what causes it, and suggests ways to improve processes to eliminate all predictable causes of variance. (*Variance* is the degree to which individual products deviate from a standard. It results in rework, which adds unnecessary costs.) SPC identifies causes of variance: poor employee performance; bad process design; deficient equipment, tools, or materials; inaccurate or incomplete information; and others. SPC helps you focus on how you can reduce variance and not just shift costs to other parts of the company.

- *Process mapping and analysis.* Clients do this to identify and describe all the elements that go into a process (that is, to make the process visible) so that they can identify which elements are unnecessary or contribute to excess costs.

FIELD TECHNIQUES: FINDING COST DRIVERS AND HIDDEN COSTS

When you meet with your client's or organization's finance or other managers, ask them:

- How they track costs
- Which cost management techniques they use, why they use them, and how effective they are
- Which costs they want to manage (direct, indirect, fixed, or variable)

When your clients talk about wanting to reduce costs, ask them:

- Which costs they want to reduce and what systems they have in place to determine what those costs are now
- If they can effectively isolate costs (product requirements, customer requirements, inefficient processes, poor people performance, and so on)
- What departments, work groups, or individuals are doing now that increases indirect or fixed costs

FIELD NOTES: REDUCING THE COST OF NONCOMPLIANCE

Deborah's boss sent her a memo that said her department had to reduce the cost of noncompliance by 35 percent by the end of the year. The first thing Deborah did was meet with her boss and the head of finance to get clarification. She wanted to know:

- Whose costs she was expected to reduce. (It turned out to be customer service and field sales.)

- What this would mean in dollar terms. (She had to cut out $5 million.)

- How the cost of noncompliance was currently calculated. (It was an arbitrary process. The vice president of finance and her boss had added the direct costs [salary] and indirect costs [percentage of overhead] of the customer service reps and field sales reps together and guessed that there was 35 percent waste in the system.)

- What the causes of noncompliance were. (They weren't sure, but assumed it was because people didn't know how to do certain aspects of their job.)

One of Deborah's first tasks was to get management to better define *noncompliance,* identify whose noncompliance they were concerned about, specify who would bear the cost of reducing it (the perpetrator or someone else), and what they would take as evidence of improvement. She was told to focus on noncompliance in the call centers and among the customer service reps (CSRs) in particular. The cost of the CSRs was classified as overhead and considered a fixed indirect cost. The customer service centers' costs were spread across all the products and markets. However, a small portion of their cost was considered part of the cost of sales (for example, when the CSRs took customer orders). This part was direct (it could be attributed to a specific product or service) and variable (it was driven by the number of customers who called wanting to buy). However, no one had tracked what portion of the CSRs' time was spent taking sales orders and what percentage was spent answering service calls. Deborah began by finding out what percentage of the CSRs' time was spent resolving customer complaints, correcting billing errors, checking the status of shipments, and other mistakes caused by breakdowns in other departments. The source of this type of noncompliance was not the CSRs. She also wanted to know the percentage of time that CSRs spent on callbacks because a problem had not been resolved the first time; this represented noncompliance by the CSRs. Once she knew the scope of the problem, she could place a value on it and find out the root cause.

IMPROVING PROCESSES AND PRACTICES TO REDUCE COSTS

Poorly designed (or poorly executed) processes add unnecessary costs. Processes include all the activities, decisions, and resources (equipment, information, time, money, and people) used to take an input (for example, a customer request, a course evaluation, a new training requirement), add value to that input by changing it in some way (engage activities that transform the request into a new product or more useful information), and produce an output a customer wants (a training course, a report with recommendations, or modified materials, for example).

Processes vary in size and scope. There are processes within and across departments and functions. Some are considered primary because they are linked to the core business. Examples are receiving, producing, marketing, selling, servicing, and distributing products and services. Other processes are considered secondary because they are performed by departments that are considered part of overhead. Examples are purchasing, HR management and development, and information systems management.

Rule No. 6: Understand business processes and practices.

Business practices are a business's regular way of operating. One could argue they are simply part of the business's processes; however, I consider them separately as practices because they consume excess resources. Poorly designed practices shift costs to other parts of the organization or result in hidden costs.

MANAGING COSTS IN PERFORMANCE CONSULTING

Before you can help clients manage their costs, you have to understand your own costs and manage them. One way to do this is by describing, evaluating, and improving your processes and practices.

When you describe a process, you identify all the activities, decisions, and resources that make up the process. You also find out what drives the process, that is, whether it is performed in response to a customer requirement, a program requirement, or a business requirement. The description communicates what is done and in what order, which resources each activity consumes, and how time is spent.

There are different ways to describe a process, but all should capture the following information:

- The activities that occur
- The resources consumed by each activity
- The activities' relationships to one another (that is, which are done sequentially and which are done concurrently)

Once you have described a process you will be in a better position to question:

- What the process does, how it does it, and why it does it
- What information the process uses and where that information comes from
- What information the product produces and who uses it
- What technology the process uses, what resources that technology requires, and the cost of those resources

A process or practice adds unnecessary costs if it uses too many resources, uses resources that cost too much, or produces products or services that do not meet customer expectations.

To improve a process, you must first make it visible; this means you should describe or map it. Then you will be in a position to identify the resources consumed and their cost. You will also be in a better position to identify where and how activities or tasks shift costs to other processes, departments, or suppliers.

FIELD TOOLS: PROCESS OR TASK PERFORMANCE WORKSHEET

Use Figure 3.9 to help you evaluate your own processes or tasks. Like the product portfolio worksheets in Chapter Two, this worksheet is meant for you to customize so that it will capture the information you currently do and do not have about what you do and how you do it.

The worksheet will help you determine which processes or tasks you need to formalize so that you can determine if and how they add unnecessary costs. The worksheet drives discussions about:

- How well defined your processes or tasks are
- How well you measure the costs of your processes or tasks
- How many resources your processes or tasks consume
- Which resources or costs add unnecessary costs
- The value added (or not added) by doing what you do in the way that you do it
- How you will measure any improvements you make

FIELD TECHNIQUES: IMPROVING YOUR PROCESSES AND TASKS

Create a process or task worksheet of your own, or modify the one in Figure 3.9 to fit your own business. Then follow these steps to complete it:

1. *List your processes or tasks.* Meet with the people you work with. Together list the processes and tasks you would like to better understand in terms

1. Process	2. Purpose or Reason	3. Resources Required	4. Cost	5. Criteria					6. Comments
				D	E	N	V	U	

1. What is the process or task you are evaluating?

2. Why is it done? Whose need does it meet?

3. How many resources does it take? How many people or what percentage of their time is dedicated to or involved in this process or task?

4. What does it cost to perform this process or task in terms of dollars, time, or resource commitment?

5. Ask each of your colleagues or key customers to independently rate the process or task according to these criteria (add criteria to meet your needs). Use a Likert scale or some other scale (1 = very positive, 3 = noncommittal or indifferent, and 5 = very negative).

   • How well is the process or task described or documented? (D)

   • How efficient is this process or task is? (E)

   • How well does it meet customer or department needs? (N)

   • How much value does the customer or department gain from this process or task? (V)

   • How easy is this process or task to use or do? (U)

6. Add any other comments. Based on everyone's understanding of the process or task, which ones are worthy of your improving?

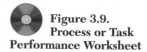

Figure 3.9.
Process or Task
Performance Worksheet

of time, resource costs, output, and value. Look at the product portfolio worksheets from Chapter Two to get ideas about what you do and for whom you do it. For example, some services are processes themselves, and other services require intake procedures to identify the customer's requirements. All of your services should have a process for evaluating customer satisfaction and your effectiveness. To help you get started, think about how you:

- Identify customer needs

- Scope out customer requests

- Select contractors and vendors

- Develop and maintain training courses

- Register and administer people who attend your programs

- Manage and maintain facilities (meeting rooms, classrooms, computer systems, and so on)

- Train and develop your own staff

- Evaluate your products and services

2. *Identify their drivers or customers.* Why are these processes or tasks required? Whose needs are they meeting? You may want to revisit Product Portfolio Worksheet 1, where you listed what you do and for whom you do it.

3. *Identify the resources they require.* Again, look at what you wrote in Product Portfolio Worksheet 1. Ask how many people (employees or contractors) are engaged in each process. Ask what percentage of their time they dedicate to these activities.

4. *Determine their costs.* Put a value on the resources you identified in step 3. What are your direct costs for each process or task?

5. *Rate them.* Set some standards or expectations for your processes or task management—for example: how well you describe or document the tasks or processes, how well you understand what and how many resources they consume, how well people use them, or how easy they are to use.

6. *Identify opportunities for improvement.* Focus your attention on those processes and tasks for which you can identify ways to reduce costs, once you understand them better.

FIELD NOTES: REDUCING FIXED AND HIDDEN COSTS

Linda, the director of training and performance improvement at her company, was concerned that so much of her staff's time was spent marketing training programs instead of consulting on performance improvement initiatives. One day she decided to examine what drove her department to stay in training (selling instructor-led workshops) instead of moving more into performance improvement. She looked at her budget with this question in mind.

The company evaluated Linda's performance based on her ability to recover her costs. Most of her costs were in facilities. Her department owned six buildings, all of which had classrooms set up especially for instructor-led courses. Linda suddenly realized that she was in the real estate business, not the performance improvement business. She was selling classrooms to cover a fixed cost. With this realization, she put all six buildings on the market, sold them, and leased classroom space as needed. She changed her fixed cost for classroom space to a variable one. She also got out of the real estate business, which allowed her to direct her staff's efforts toward performance improvement.

Kelly hired contractors to deliver training to field offices. One day she was looking at her instructor costs (variable direct costs charged to specific programs) and noticed that all of her instructors charged essentially the same fee. All had also received similar evaluations from students. On the surface, it looked as if each instructor added the same amount of cost to deliver a course. When she discussed the instructors with her administrative assistant, however, she discovered that one instructor was difficult to support. This instructor always lost materials, requiring second shipments. She wouldn't set up the classroom, which meant a local administrative person had to come in early to do this work. She wouldn't check out the computers, overhead projects, or any other equipment, so a technician had to be on call during her classes. She didn't have her classes break or go to lunch on schedule, which caused traffic jams in the cafeteria and made students in other courses late in getting back to class. Kelly realized that her direct costs per instructor may have been the same, but her indirect costs were not. This instructor was actually much more expensive than the others, and her higher cost was being borne by others in the company. Kelly decided to rethink her evaluation of this instructor.

When Russ's manager asked him to reduce his operating budget for the coming year, Russ turned to his two largest fixed costs: salaries for full-time staff and depreciation on medical equipment purchased for use during training. He asked that all staff track their time for a month and note what they were doing and who they were doing it for. He discovered that three administrative staff members spent approximately 60 percent of their time rescheduling people for classes, including no-shows (people who didn't show up for training and later called to get in another class). Russ thought their time could be better spent on activities that added value. He documented the cost of rescheduling students and went to his supervisor with a recommendation on how to reduce this cost. The departments of the no-shows suffered no financial consequences for their behavior, but it increased Russ's costs significantly. Russ wanted this cost to be borne by the offending students' departments, not his.

Next, Russ looked at depreciation. The company's business policy stated that when a department used a product the company made, that department had to purchase the product. Therefore, Russ's technical training group had to buy the equipment it used to train field technicians to install and repair equipment. Some of this training equipment cost over $1 million. Russ couldn't resell the training equipment because he had to be able to train technicians on all models of equipment. The cost of delivering technical training was charged to the field service department; however, this did not include any costs associated with the training equipment. Russ went to his finance department to discuss the implications of leasing the equipment instead of buying it.

FIELD TECHNIQUES: HELPING CLIENTS IMPROVE THEIR PROCESSES

If you participate on a process improvement team as part of your performance consulting services, here are some ways you can add value to the team's activities:

- Facilitate the mapping or describing of processes. Be sure to help the client identify all the activities involved and assign a value to them. Then clarify how costs are classified and assigned (to a department, product, service, customer, or spread among these).

- Facilitate discussions about which activities add value and which ones do not. Identify which activities should be eliminated because they are redundant or unnecessary, consume too many resources or unnecessary ones, or cause other processes to engage in activities that do not add value.

- Help the client identify where it can use fewer or less-costly resources and still achieve the same or better outcomes.

- Work with the client to identify where any false economies might exist because current processes or business practices shift costs to other processes or departments.

- Ask if there are any policies, standards, or requirements that result in activities or the use of resources that do not add value, add unnecessary costs, or shift costs.

- Ask about the technology used by each process and whether it results in non-value-added activities or the use of unnecessary or too-costly resources.

Once you and your client have identified what drives the cost of the client's processes, you can decide whether to redesign them or better manage their cost drivers.

SUMMARY

Performance consultants must understand costs, what drives them, and how they become hidden or shift around. Unnecessary costs are the result of poor people performance, poorly designed processes, misunderstood customer requirements, and non-value-adding business requirements. Besides helping your clients, understanding costs will also put you in a better position to define your own costs and prove that your activities add value. If the training director in the story at the beginning of this chapter had better understood costs, he could have helped the vice president of sales isolate the company's sales costs, identify their causes, and develop a plan to eliminate or reduce them. If the vice president of sales had better understood how to make managing the cost of sales an integral part of his job (and thus a criterion for judging his performance), he could have avoided his confrontation with the vice president of finance.

WHERE TO LEARN MORE

Since the first edition of this book came out, a fair amount has been written about how to evaluate the impact of specific interventions, training in particular. Here are two books with practical tools:

Hale, J. *Performance-Based Evaluation: How to Measure the Impact of Training.* San Francisco: Jossey-Bass/Pfeiffer, 2002. This book contains over forty-four tools on a CD-ROM that include how to measure the transfer and impact of soft and hard skills, how to determine appropriate sample size, and how to analyze and interpret qualitative and quantitative data.

Seagrave, T. *Quick Show Me Your Value: A Trainer's Guide to Communicating Value: Connecting Training and Performance to the Bottom Line.* Alexandria, Va.: ASTD Press, 2001. The book comes with a CD with ready-to-use templates.

The following books explore how organizations think of costs and business economics. Although some of them were published more than a decade ago, they remain relevant, and all are very readable.

Cokins, G., Stratton, A., and Helbling, J. *An ABC Manager's Primer Straight Talk on Activity-Based Costing.* Montvale, N.J.: Institute of Management Accountants, 1992. Highly recommended as readable and useful.

Cooke, R. *36-Hour Course in Finance for Nonfinancial Managers.* New York: McGraw-Hill, 1993. Highly recommended by my clients, who find the ideas informative and useful.

Gill, J. *Understanding Financial Statements,* and *Financial Analysis: The Next Step.* Menlo Park, Calif.: Crisp Publications, 1990. A practical book about the fundamentals of understanding financial reports.

Hawkins, P. *The Ecology of Commerce.* New York: HarperCollins, 1993. Chapter Nine, on the opportunity of insignificance, brings to life how, in our efforts to reduce costs, we only shift costs and burden others.

Levitt, S. D., and Dubner, S. J. *Freakeconomics: A Rogue Economist Explores the Hidden Side of Everything.* New York: Morrow, 2005. A counterculture look at economics.

O'Guin, M. *The Complete Guide to Activity Based Costing.* Upper Saddle River, N.J.: Prentice Hall, 1991. One of the better books on cost management and very readable. It is particularly useful to help clients understand when they are shifting costs rather than reducing them.

Stack, J. *The Great Game of Business: Unlocking the Power and Profitability of Open-Book Management.* New York: Doubleday, 1992. An insightful book about business economics and how an educated workforce can avoid, reduce, or eliminate costs.

Stalk, G., and Hout, T. *Competing Against Time.* New York: Free Press, 1990. Provides excellent examples of reengineering and process redesign. Be sure to check the rules on pages 76 and 77.

Chapter 4

Credibility and Influence

*P*erformance consulting requires more than knowing how to design needs assessments and participate on cross-functional teams. It takes a special mindset combined with political and image management skills.

FIELD NOTES: THE NEED FOR CREDIBILITY

Doug, the director of training for his company, complained he couldn't get management to change career development policies because they would not listen to him. He believed they wouldn't listen because his position was too far down on the organization charter. Doug believed he would have greater influence if only the company would promote him.

Marilyn, who headed the training unit at one of the field offices, complained that managers from corporate headquarters would tell her and the other field training managers what to do. Although she saw opportunities to add value to the company beyond training, she hesitated to offer her ideas because she was not from corporate.

Having position power and being part of the corporate team can make it easier to be an effective performance consultant. These things are not required, however, and they don't guarantee that your voice will be heard or your ideas considered. The ability to influence other people's decisions and actions requires a combination of position, expertise, courage, and skill.

Whenever others ask me how to get people of higher status to accept them as a professional, I use the analogy of a recipe. The essential ingredients are:

- *Relevant information.* Know your stuff and know the client.
- *The courage to speak up.* Believe that what you have to offer is worthy of consideration.
- *Interpersonal skills.* Make people comfortable with you.
- *Integrity.* This is the essential ingredient; without it, nothing else matters. It means being true to your word, honoring your commitments, and keeping the best interests of the client and society in mind at all times.

The spices are:

- *Trust (with verification).* Assume people's good intentions, but challenge their information and seek corroborating evidence. Remember that opinions and myth are not facts, and hope by itself never makes things happen.
- *Political savvy.* Never forget whose agenda it is, and make sure that person comes off looking good.
- *Dissonance.* Make people uncomfortable enough that they will pause and consider new information.
- *Status.* Make sure your clients know that people outside their group or organization think well of you.

The cooking instructions are:

- *Establish a presence.* Manage your image.
- *Remain impartial and objective.* This doesn't mean you shouldn't form an opinion; just don't take sides. Remember that everyone can be right at the same time.
- *Stay focused.* Never lose sight of where you want the client to go and why. Don't confuse being liked or accepted with the goal of improving performance.

It is difficult to separate the key ingredients from the spices and the preparation. It takes all of them to produce a tasty dish.

THE ESSENTIAL INGREDIENTS: INFORMATION, COURAGE, INTERPERSONAL SKILLS, AND INTEGRITY

Information

In an article in *Performance Improvement* (September 1996), Byron Stock states that the two top obstacles to optimum human performance are lack of information and lack of measures. Training and HRD departments may be particularly vulnerable. They are way down the information chain in many organizations. They are the last to know and the last to be involved and are generally called on after others have already decided on a solution. Unfortunately, the solution may not be based on a thorough understanding of the factors that influence performance. Training and HRD professionals have to move up the information chain if they are going to operate as performance consultants.

For some people, asking to be included in the decision making feels pushy or even illegitimate. The problem then seems to be how to gain involvement in a way that feels legitimate. One strategy is to contribute useful information at every opportunity. Another is to establish relationships and set up systems that will give you timely access to information. These strategies work together because getting information depends on having information to share, and having information allows you to get more.

When I'm asked how I stay current so that I have something useful to contribute, I tell people what I learned from studying David McClelland's research on what made people in the foreign service effective (McClelland, D. C., and Dailey, C. *Evaluating New Methods of Measuring the Qualities Needed in Superior Foreign Service Officers.* Boston: McBer, 1973]). The discriminating factor was not having graduated from a specific school but the ability to engineer opportunities to get useful information.

Relevant information—information that helps people make more informed decisions—is a valuable commodity. Sometimes the information people find most useful is the old or proven principles, which is why it helps to be grounded in the fundamentals of performance improvement. Other times, however, people want information about what is going on now because they like to feel they are in the know. A question I'm asked frequently is, "What are other companies doing?" Rather than answer the question directly, I find that talking about what other companies have learned proves I know my stuff better than talking about what they are doing does. This was reinforced by an article I once read in an internal company management magazine about an innovative safety program. The program, which touted the use of peer pressure to support safety goals, certainly made sense. Later, I asked a manager from the company how the program was working. The program, he said ruefully, was a bust because it pitted coworkers against one another, and rather than turn on one another, the company's workers simply chose to ignore the program. In the end, the program was unenforceable and a waste of money. Obviously it would have been misleading to simply share with a client what this company did without also pointing out what it learned from the experience.

Courage

When I'm asked about the courage to speak up, I often refer people to a test I found in Richard Byrd's *Guide to Personal Risk Taking* (New York: AMACOM, 1974). The test listed sources of personal power such as seniority, desirable personal traits, interpersonal skills, professional friendships, confidence, expertise, and access to information. Byrd's premise is that the more personal power you have, the less you need to rely on position power to take risks; the less personal power you have, the more you need to toe the party line. I was interested to find from taking the test that some of the factors that determine personal power were outside my control, such as seniority and the desirability of my personal traits. However, most of the factors were within my control, such as improving my interpersonal skills, increasing my information, and building relationships.

In fact, most of the factors are interdependent. If you are willing to take responsibility for one of them, such as relationships, the success you have there will affect the others. For example, improving your interpersonal skills leads to friendships, which lead to information; better information leads to expertise, which leads to confidence; greater confidence leads to the courage to create opportunities.

I've also learned not to be afraid of criticism. Lyle E. Schaller, in his book *Getting Things Done* (Nashville, Tenn.: Abingdon Press, 1986), includes the willingness to stand up to criticism as one of the thirteen essential characteristics for leading and influencing. Peter Senge, in the *Fifth Discipline* (New York: Doubleday, 1990), also comments on the willingness to be criticized. When you speak up, it is less important to be right than to bring about reflection and examination. The irony is that staying silent also has consequences: it reduces your chances of being included in decision-making processes. Think about what it takes to be a professional athlete. They know everyone is watching and their every move will be criticized. When an athlete executes a successful play or maneuver, everyone cheers; when he or she fails, everyone's a critic. Yet without the athletes, there would be no game. Only by being in the game are you in a position to influence the outcome.

If you want to influence someone, you have to stick your neck out. I once saw an inspirational poster advertised in an airline magazine. The poster had a picture of a golf ball, with a fairway in the background. Under the picture was the caption, "You'll miss every shot you never take." Speaking up when it matters is a risk. So when I'm considering the need to speak up, I reflect on Byrd's list about personal risk taking and recall the importance of doing the things that can raise my score. If I create opportunities to stay informed, I can take more risks because my comments will be grounded in facts. If I strengthen my relationships, others will be open at least to considering my comments. And when I find I'm wavering, I recall Peter Drucker's words:

> Courage rather than analysis dictates the truly important rules for identifying priorities:
>
> - Pick the future as against the past;
> - Focus on opportunity rather than on problem;
> - Choose your own direction—rather than climb on the bandwagon; and
> - Aim high, aim for something that will make a difference, rather than for something that is "safe" and easy to do [*The Effective Executive.* (New York, HarperCollins, 1967)].

Interpersonal Skills

Interpersonal skills are a combination of nonverbal and verbal communication skills and social and cultural sensitivity. It is often apparent from other people's reactions whether someone has interpersonal skills. Some people are able to establish a rapport with people of one social group but not with those from another. The key variable is the ability to pick up on social cues concerning which behaviors are acceptable and then to adapt your behavior to that of the group. I don't know of any shortcuts to obtaining interpersonal skills. They are developed in interacting with people of different backgrounds and different levels of interpersonal skills. At a minimum, you have to be aware of your own behavior, observe how people interact, and be willing to take responsibility for establishing relationships with others.

Integrity

Integrity is about unwavering adherence to a code of conduct or set of values. People with integrity are consistent, can be counted on, and have altruistic motives. Integrity is sometimes thought of as the person's character—the distinctive qualities that set him or her apart from others. Qualities like trustworthiness, reliability, and honorable motives add up to integrity. Integrity is earned by being consistent in actions and motives. Once it is lost, it is difficult, but not impossible, to recover.

When I speak on the subject of performance consulting, I reference some work done many years ago by Stephanie Jackson and her partner, Don Tosti, on earning others' trust. Stephanie and Don have been presidents of the International Society for Performance Improvement and have won awards for their work with organizations. They listed the specific behaviors they believe are core to earning, deserving, and sustaining trust: keeping your word, maintaining confidences, and not misrepresenting your capabilities. They also addressed what to consider when you are deciding whether to trust someone else:

- Is the information this person is giving me timely, accurate, and in my best interest?

- Does the person send mixed messages, for example, make light of what he or she says is important?

These questions are about motives and whether the other person has a hidden agenda. I have found it helpful to be explicit when my agenda changes. I let people know when my motive or purpose has shifted to another agenda and why.

Sometimes I am asked to do things that I do not believe are in the best interest of the organization but may meet the needs of the immediate client. In these situations, I remind the client that I'm being paid by the organization and therefore see him or her only as an agent of the company. I also hear vendors disguised as consultants whose motives are to sell a predetermined solution, thus meeting their needs rather than those of clients. I encourage clients to question motives.

FIELD TECHNIQUES: EVALUATING YOUR PERSONAL POWER BASE

Figure 4.1 has questions to direct your thinking about how you might increase your personal power. Answer the questions about each variable for yourself. Later, you might want to discuss your answers and ratings with someone you think knows your situation very well. Use your insights to develop a plan to increase your personal power.

After you give yourself a score for each area, determine which areas you want to work on in the next six months, identify some resources you might use to help you, and periodically check to see if you have improved in the areas you think will be most valuable to you.

There is no substitute for the right ingredients. Good information, the courage to speak up, effective interpersonal skills, and integrity are essential to gaining other people's trust. These are elements you can acquire and develop with education and experience. However, it is hard to compensate for their absence even with skills in needs assessment and measurement.

Company friendships. The more people you know in your organization—both within and outside your own department or unit—the better.

How many company friendships do you have?

1	2	3	4	5
Few		Some		A lot

Where do they work in the company?

1	2	3	4	5
Same work group	Mostly people in staff positions	Mixed	Mostly people in line positions	People from all departments

Desirable organizational traits. What is desirable depends on the environment you work in. In some organizations, being an engineer is desirable; in others, it might be having military, sales, or international experience.
List the traits most admired by your organization.
Rate the degree to which you collectively possess the traits.

1	2	3	4	5
Few		About half		A lot

Information. Stay current on issues the organization is wrestling with and decisions that have been made in relation to them. You may know someone who has this information even if you don't personally have it.
Rate the degree to which you are in the know.

1	2	3	4	5
Very low		In the middle		Very high

Perceived expertise. This is *not* what you know or can do, but what people think you know and can do.
Rate your perceived expertise.

1	2	3	4	5
Very low		In the middle		Very high

Opportunity. This is about being able to participate in existing situations or create new ones that provide you a chance to meet new people, hear what is going on, and contribute.
Rate the opportunities you have.

1	2	3	4	5
Few and far between		Somewhere in the middle		A lot

Personal confidence. This is about how capable you feel and the degree you believe you have something worthwhile to contribute.
Rate your self-confidence.

1	2	3	4	5
Low		Somewhere in the middle		High

Interpersonal skills. You need communication and cultural skills to work effectively with people from all areas in the organization.
Rate your interpersonal skills.

1	2	3	4	5
Limited		Somewhere in the middle		Very high

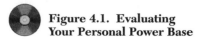

**Figure 4.1. Evaluating
Your Personal Power Base**

FIELD TECHNIQUES: GETTING INFORMATION

Here are some ways to acquire relevant information in a timely manner:

- Listen carefully to find out what the business is doing and the politics behind its choices.

- Learn your customer's business—what it does and how it does it. Identify its products, customers, and competitors. Find out where it stands financially and how financial decisions are made. Look at its Web page and its Dun and Bradstreet rating. Check the Web sites of its industry trade associations to begin to identify industry trends.

- Get to know the librarian at your company, your local public library, or a local college or university. Indicate your interest in and need for quick access to timely information. Talk about how he or she might support your need for information.

- Scan the business section of your newspaper daily. Pay particular attention to news about technological developments and your client's or organization's competitors, suppliers, and key customers.

- The *Wall Street Journal* contains the latest information on the legal front. Take note of emerging legal precedents.

- If you don't have a stock broker, introduce yourself to one. Periodically ask this person for financial information about your client and its major competitors, suppliers, and customers. Learn how to read a prospectus, annual reports, and financial statements.

- Subscribe to research journals or find another way to review them, such as at your local public library, your local college or university library, or online. When you get them, scan the table of contents. Look for research studies about technology, change, productivity, and improving performance. A journal I find useful is the *Performance and Instruction Quarterly*.

- Pay attention to the best-seller list in the *New York Times,* particularly books about new management theories, corporate success stories, and solutions to cutting costs (taking over the market and increasing productivity, for example). Check the book section in your local Sunday paper as well for reviews of new books. Your customers may not have read them, but may know about them. You do not have to read the whole book, but do try to scan the salient chapters.

- Develop professional relationships with colleagues from other organizations. Join professional organizations such as the ISPI, Society for Human Resource Management, and the American Quality and Productivity Council. Use those relationships to set up user groups and special task forces to share information and commission studies.

- Create opportunities to learn and build skill at information sharing. For example, submit proposals to present at local and national conferences, join committees, volunteer to be a greeter at local meetings, and submit articles to the local chapter's newsletter.

- Make a habit of doing searches on the Internet for timely information.

FIELD NOTES: DEVELOPING THE ESSENTIAL INGREDIENTS

Deborah now had specified her department's vision and mission, described its products and services, defined its processes, and established measures to evaluate those processes. The next step was to meet with her staff to develop a plan for getting information more quickly about what was going on in the company. The team decided they needed a better way to get information from within the company about their markets and new developments in performance improvement. The plan they came up with called for them to create strategic relationships, establish carefully selected professional affiliations, subscribe to targeted journals and newsletters, and become more skilled at using the Internet.

They also wanted to establish strategic relationships with the company's finance and marketing departments. Those relationships would be key to finding out early what programs the company was funding, which managers were seeking the funding, and what new products and marketing campaigns were under development. Early access to this information would allow the team to recommend simultaneous creation of help screens, funding for training, and funding for just-in-time documentation. All that was needed was to create an opportunity to build the right relationships.

To learn more about new developments in performance improvement, two members of her team decided to contact noncompeting organizations in their area to see if they would be interested in getting together to share what each was doing. They contacted the major employers in the area, and ten companies decided to participate. The companies created a purpose statement for the group and some guidelines about when and how often to meet, who to invite, and how they would share information. Deborah's group believed that finding out what other companies were doing would not only help them personally, it would make it easier to build a relationship with members from their own finance and marketing departments.

THE SPICES: TRUST, POLITICAL SAVVY, DISSONANCE, AND STATUS

Trust

One of the things I've learned is that people tell the truth. However, their truth is based on what they know, what they've heard, and what they've surmised. During the time I was a commercial arbitrator, I learned a lot about facts and hearsay. I also came to understand that most people do not distinguish between the two. There are many ways to get an accurate and complete picture of a situation. However, they all require some political savvy. It helps to remember that:

- People base their conclusions and opinions on what they have experienced and what they have heard others talking about.

- Perceptions are real, but they are not the same as facts.

- People, especially senior managers, do not want to be embarrassed because of something they could have known but didn't.

Here are some ways to verify what others have told you:

- Find out if their conclusions are based on one incident or if they have corroborating evidence.

- Ask questions to help people distinguish direct evidence from hearsay. For example, ask, "How exactly did you find that out? Did you come across that information yourself, or did someone tell you about it? Is this a one-time event, or has this happened before?"

- Point out whether what you are hearing is hearsay, folklore, or based on direct observation. For example, say, "Oh, so you're basing your conclusion on what Joe told you. Boy, I sure would like to see that for myself. I get nervous when I'm relying on someone else's interpretation of what happened without some additional or corroborating evidence." Or ask, "So, you saw the numbers yourself?"

Political Savvy

A key play in chess is the gambit: one player makes a move to get the other player to expose his or her queen. An analogous move exists in social settings. For example, you might tell a story or make a comment that exposes some weakness or frailty about yourself, for example, your discomfort, despair, or fatigue about a situation. The other person has three choices for responding: match with a similar exposure, ignore what you said, or discount what you shared. If the person responds with a mutual admission (for example, "I know. I get pretty exasperated myself and wonder if it's all worth it"), there is evidence of some regard for your position. If the person ignores your disclosure, you need additional information before concluding he or she will give your ideas serious consideration. If the person discounts your disclosure, you have initial evidence he or she will discount your ideas.

I use the concept of the gambit in business settings to test how well my ideas are being accepted, how open the client is to critical discussion, and how people in the group work together. For example, if someone mentions mistakes made during the development or launch of a program, I listen to how the conversation unfolds. Others in the room might point out what was learned and how that can be used in this situation, or they might ignore, contradict, or discount the remark. How they respond provides valuable cues to how I should proceed.

In other situations, I share stories of common mistakes and false starts and then note how the stories are received. Again, those listening might match with a story of their own false starts, ignore them altogether, or discount them as lacking foresight. If my or other people's ideas are discounted, I know I have to work harder at influencing decisions.

Dissonance

Dissonance is another technique for getting people to pause, reflect, and reconsider. Most people are familiar with dissonance in art; for example, an artist will show water falling the wrong way or stairs going in circles. Some well-known comic strips use dissonance as the basis of their humor, among them, *Doonesbury, The Far Side,* and *Non Sequitur.* Teenagers try to create dissonance by challenging social customs (a friend calls the teenage years the age of costume, hair, and body jewelry). People who fit in and behave as expected or talk the party line do not cause dissonance. Dissonance occurs whenever our sense of the expected is disrupted. In business settings, you can create dissonance with new and unexpected information, for instance, by introducing an unexpected thought, a new interpretation, or a different perspective. You can create dissonance by telling a story or using an analogy that gets people to think about the situation in a new way. Your goal is not antagonism, unpleasantness, or, like the teenager, to be noticed. It is to get people to be open to new perspectives and possibilities while not losing face.

The importance of being willing to tolerate criticism or opposing views is illustrated by a story my father once told me. He believed you can judge the health of an organization by the degree to which leaders allow at least one person in their ranks who is different. My father called it "looking for the guy in the brown suit." In the 1940s and 1950s, all corporate leaders were male. They all wore navy or black suits, white shirts, plain ties, and black oxford shoes, and their socks matched their pants. Dad always looked for the guy with gravy on his tie, whose jacket didn't match his pants, who wore loafers instead of oxfords, or whose shirt was blue or pink. His premise was that if the leaders could not tolerate deviation from the dress code, they probably wouldn't entertain constructive arguments. Today, the "brown suiters" are the conscience of the organization. Much of the work of the performance consultant is to act as a conscience. We are the ones who raise the issues of proof, facts, and fallout. I am a brown suiter and proud of it.

Status

Status inside the organization depends on the person, the organization, and the norms of the group. The common sources of status are academic degrees and other credentials, specific experiences, and ties to leadership. For example, if the organization is a chemical engineering firm, a degree in chemical engineering carries a fair amount of status. If the leaders of the organization have a military background, having served in the armed forces will bring you some credibility, at least initially. Leaders with experience in social service will probably look favorably on previous Peace Corps service.

Status outside the organization is similar to internal status. Although having the same academic and life experiences helps, external status comes more from associations with people, agencies, and ideals the organization looks on favorably—for example:

- A formal relationship with a professional, industry, or community organization
- Being cited positively by the business or industry press
- Having had a professional relationship with other groups your organization wants to be like or learn from
- Having access to influential people in the press, industry, or community

Verifying information, being politically astute, creating dissonance, and using status are the instruments to leverage your information. They are what help you get an audience. Moreover, they are what you use to find out what is really going on.

FIELD TECHNIQUES: DEVELOPING POLITICAL SAVVY, DISSONANCE, AND STATUS

Here are some suggestions for learning to be appropriately skeptical and more politically astute, instill dissonance, and acquire external status:

- Always look for corroborating evidence.
- When you hear second-hand information, point out that it is hearsay. Ask for direct evidence and where to find it. For instance, ask, "Who has read the report [or seen the numbers or heard the comments] and would be willing to give us his or her interpretation of what happened? Could we see the report ourselves?" Engage the client in conversations about who benefits (and how) from the perpetuation of hearsay and who is affected when you operate from facts instead.

- When there is a dispute over the accuracy or interpretation of some information, try to get each party to assume the other person's role or position and then interpret the information from that standpoint.

- Identify the sponsors of ideas and programs. Find out what they have to gain if their ideas are accepted or lose if they are not.

- Exemplify as many of the client's characteristics, norms, language, and values as you can. But don't be exactly like the client; a little deviation helps, as long as it does not conflict with the client's values.

- Observe what happens when one person in the group challenges or tries to promote critical dialogue about an issue. You will learn who has the most influence in the group, how open the group is to opposing ideas, and to what degree the group is in real consensus versus silent compliance.

- If there is something that everyone thinks is obvious but really isn't, raise the question under the guise of being new to the group, needing to explain it to someone else later, or wanting to get a richer picture of the situation. If no one supports your request, negotiate to talk about it after the meeting with one or two people.

- Establish some source of external status. It won't carry you over the long haul, but it will help you in the beginning.

FIELD NOTES: LEARNING TO COOK WITH SPICES

Deborah was in a meeting with two of her peers. During the conversation, her peers began to argue over who was responsible for certain items in the budget. As the argument grew more heated, they began to accuse each other of deliberately trying to duck their responsibilities. Deborah interrupted with the statement, "I think you two are operating from different data sets." She got them to pause long enough for her to continue. "You are both referring to what sounds like the same financial report, but you understand the company's finances too well to be this far apart. Is it possible you are actually referring to different reports that happen to go by the same name? Why don't the two of you get a copy of the report you are talking about so we can all look at it together." They reluctantly agreed. When they returned, they had indeed been talking about different financial reports.

Chris, one of the consultants in finance who reported to Mike, was meeting with the head of accounting, Frank, and the head of production, Brian. The goal of the meeting was to come up with recommendations for improving communications between the two departments to reduce administrative costs. They decided to map how information flowed between accounting and production starting from ordering raw materials to billing customers for receipt of finished goods. Frank and Brian began to argue over what information existed, where information went, how it got there, how often, and in what form. The two men were becoming more polarized in their positions. When they looked to Chris to take sides, he said to them, "You're both right, and you're both wrong. You're right based on what you know. You're wrong because you have only part of the picture." She suggested that they spend one day at each other's site. While there, each one was to observe only, with no criticism allowed. The assignment was to find out exactly what information the other one worked with. The three of them agreed to meet again in two weeks after Frank and Brian had completed their assignments. Frank and Brian learned that each worked from different—and incomplete—information. They returned with a stronger conviction that the new information system had to provide both of them with a better picture of administrative costs.

THE COOKING INSTRUCTIONS: ESTABLISHING A PRESENCE, REMAINING IMPARTIAL AND OBJECTIVE, AND STAYING FOCUSED

Establishing a Presence

I remember a TV interview with Marilyn Monroe. She was asked why she didn't wear hose or jewelry. Her answer was something about wanting people to focus on her overall sensuality, not her hair or jewelry. She considered comments about her hair (or dress, or any other discrete item) as evidence that she had not managed her image well.

I've often used Monroe's philosophy as a model for myself. Although I'm not interested in selling sensuality, I am interested in selling useful information and myself as an expert. I want clients to experience our collaboration as an instrument to help them make sense out of what is happening in their work environment. I want them to know that I have their best interest in mind. Therefore, I'm careful not to send distracting or conflicting messages. Distracting messages happen when something we say causes people to question our motives, our materials are unclear about who we are and what we do, or our materials contain conflicting messages.

I've also learned that getting to the point quickly is part of managing my image. My brother once told me about wanting material for his "elevator conversations," since he frequently had only the brief time in the elevator to communicate the value of his department. He had to quickly establish a presence, negotiate for resources, and get permission to proceed. Therefore, he used only a few phrases, facts, visuals, or stories that could convey in a nutshell his successes, breakthroughs, results, and dilemmas.

I've thought of that conversation often. At times we all want and need an audience with the right people. So many times, however, we ask for a ninety-minute or two-hour meeting, even while knowing that time is the most valuable resource we all have. Asking clients to give us their time is a costly, sometimes even painful request. When we take *their* time to tell *our* whole story, we're meeting our needs, not theirs. It takes skill to get to the point quickly, say what you mean, and ask for what you want. Clients are appreciative when you respect their time.

Remaining Impartial and Objective

Another thing I've learned is to be impartial and objective. When you take sides, someone loses, and people don't let go of their losses. They go into hiding and wait for another opportunity to bring up the issue again or get even. Therefore, try to make everyone a winner.

I begin where the client currently sees the situation, not with how I want that person to see it. This means I have to accept the client's assessment of the situation and solution to the problem. I always acknowledge to them that they have taken the time to think through the problem and arrived at a logical conclusion. Once I'm sure they know I accept their ideas, I can move on in these ways:

- Present new information they may not have been privileged to receive but should know.

- Talk through another interpretation of the situation under the guise of making sure I fully understand their perception of the situation.

- Talk about how much better they would look if they were to let their solution evolve into one that incorporated the opposing view (in the case there is an opposing view). I tag on something to the effect that they and their adversary are smart enough to come up with an innovative solution that will make them both look good.

- Solicit the help of their peers in coming up with a way for the client to change his or her position and save face.

Staying Focused

Although it is important not to take sides, it is just as important to express an opinion if that opinion is based on a solid understanding of the situation. As an expert, you are expected to have an opinion. I've also learned, however, that it is important for people to save face.

Once I was asked to bid on a multimillion dollar job. I was told the client had made up his mind and not to present any suggestions. The client had attended a trade show and had seen an example of how a company changed its culture and saved money through the use of new technology. The client had asked the vendor, "Can you do this for us?" A more appropriate question would have been, "What has to be in place for us to experience the same results?" Very few people will admit they can't do something (especially a salesperson).

I believed this idea wouldn't work in the client's organization and got facts together about hidden costs and what it would take to implement the suggestion. I called one of the client's best friends and quickly related my understanding of the situation, presented the problem, and said, "Your friend could be making a decision with negative career consequences. I need your help to get him to at least consider these other factors and do it in a way that helps him save face. He bought into this idea with insufficient information. Let him know it's okay to change his mind when the change is based on more complete and accurate information."

I've also learned that some of the strangest things can get people off task. Instead of focusing on the problem, how to solve it, and what the implications might be, they often direct their energy to nonrelated subjects. Introducing new language that is not part of the client's vocabulary is an example of something that can throw people off track. Clients talk about costs, problems, missed opportunities, and solutions. They talk about reorganizing, implementing programs, and changing selection criteria. They do not talk about *interventions;* that's our word, and *performance technology* is our label. If you want your ideas to be heard, use your clients' language; don't ask them to learn yours. Language can be a barrier if people feel left out because they aren't familiar with the lexicon. This is true whether the language is chemistry, finance, marketing, manufacturing, electronics, or performance technology. When you introduce unfamiliar language, the focus of the conversation shifts away from healthy debate to something else. It may in fact shift to questioning your credibility. Staying focused on the task, not on you, helps assure clients that your motives are in their best interest.

FIELD TECHNIQUES: ESTABLISHING A PRESENCE, REMAINING IMPARTIAL AND OBJECTIVE, AND STAYING FOCUSED

Here are some ways you can create a presence and thus enhance your credibility and enlarge your sphere of influence:

- Create a logo—a visual image for your department.

- Create a slogan or a few phrases that quickly capture what you do or your work group does and how you work with clients.

- Volunteer to be on your client's team or committee as a scribe or coordinator. Once there, be sure to contribute; don't just sit on the periphery. Fill the task and social roles as needed.

- Produce solutions, recommendations, and programs the client sees as adding value. Talk through implementation, downstream costs, and the implications of your suggestions for other systems.

- Document your results in terms of revenue or cost reduction. Be willing to share the glory.

- Develop and practice your elevator conversations. Be clear in what you want to accomplish, and always think about your audience. Ask yourself what they want to know and why. Give them only what they need. If they ask for more, give it to them, but let the client drive the agenda.

FIELD NOTES: FOLLOWING THE COOKING INSTRUCTIONS

Deborah wanted to establish a strategic alliance with the vice president of finance and asked if they could meet for ten minutes. She went prepared with a ten-minute overview covering who she is, her department's mission, and what she wanted from the meeting. She included two brief examples illustrating how the lack of her early involvement had added costs. One of her goals for the meeting was for the vice president to understand her department's capabilities and establish an ongoing, mutually beneficial relationship. The two of them communicate regularly now, mostly during ten- to fifteen-minute meetings.

Kelly, the head of training at a large insurance company, continued to meet with her staff to discuss some of the problems they were having gaining acceptance as performance consultants. Kelly was particularly troubled by their spotty access to senior management. The group wondered why it was so hard to be accepted in their new role despite their expertise in needs assessment and facilitation. They wondered why external consultants could come in and immediately be accepted as credible. After studying ISPI's standards, they asked themselves: "What are the skills and knowledge behind these standards? What do we have to do differently?" And most important, they asked, "What do we have to change about ourselves to be effective in this new role?" It became clear to Kelly that they all needed to develop their political savvy and learn more about influencing decisions and marketing their services.

Kelly called Dave, a colleague from another company whom she had met at a professional meeting. Dave had put together a full-scale marketing plan for his training department with these components:

- Changing the name of the department from Training to Performance Development.

- Creating a slogan, "A Small Investment for Big Returns," and putting it on all department materials.

- Putting together a seven-minute briefing his staff could deliver about what they have done and are doing, their plans for the future, and the driving factors behind their services.

- Reorganizing the department so they were more closely aligned with the core business.

- Arranging for department staff to work in the field for three to six months (although his company greatly valued field experience, Dave's staff did not come from the field).

Kelly knew she could implement parts of Dave's plan. She also realized her staff had no marketing strategy and little presence outside her department. She and her staff met to come up with image-enhancing ideas. They assembled a portfolio of the materials their department produced. When they looked at it, they realized there was no one look, no logo, nothing that identified these materials as being from their department. Instead, the materials simply described the department's processes, with no information about results or benefits to the client. Kelly quickly arranged a meeting with marketing to learn how to communicate the department's message better.

FIELD TOOLS: QUALIFYING THE CLIENT

So far the focus of this chapter has been on building your credibility and influence. The irony is that clients sometimes will need to do the same for themselves. Clients can be unsophisticated in getting good information and knowing when to speak up. They may lack interpersonal skills and political savvy. They may have trouble staying focused on what is important. As a professional, you can develop your own skills, but as a consultant, you must learn how to work effectively with your clients no matter how skilled they are.

I was once asked about my process for qualifying my clients. The question led me to document the factors I intuitively look for when I first meet the client—the information that helps me decide if I want to do the job and what it will take to work effectively with this client. Based on my reflections, I compiled a survey, provided here as Figure 4.2, which you can use to assess your client's sophistication and to distinguish your issues from the client's issues. Using this tool will help alert you to the factors you will have to manage in order to be effective with the client.

Read over the questions before you meet with your client to identify which issues you want to confirm in your early interviews when you are still scoping out the job and deciding what resources (time and people) it will take to fulfill the request. You and your colleagues can answer the questions separately, share your answers, and then use your answers to develop a strategy for working with the client. Figure 4.3 lists some suggestions for how to proceed.

Client Capabilities and Commitment

1. To what degree has the client defined the problem?

Unclear	Can't tell	Very clearly
1	3	5

Comments: _____

2. To what degree are the different groups within the client's organization in consensus about the problem?

Polarized	Wide variance	In consensus
1	3	5

Comments: _____

3. To what degree has the client defined the solution or how to handle the problem?

Unclear	Can't tell	Very clearly
1	3	5

Comments: _____

4. To what degree are the different groups within the client's organization in consensus about the solution or how to handle the problem?

Polarized	Wide variance	In consensus
1	3	5

Comments: _____

5. How well does the client understand what is meant by *competent performance?*

Naive	All over the map	Sophisticated
1	3	5

Comments: _____

6. How well does the client understand how skills, knowledge, and values relate to competence?

Naive	All over the map	Sophisticated
1	3	5

Comments: _____

7. How well does the client understand what research is already available about competence and performance?

Naive	All over the map	Sophisticated
1	3	5

Comments: _____

8. How well does the client understand the organizational factors that influence competent performance?

Naive	All over the map	Sophisticated
1	3	5

Comments: _____

9. How do people feel about the project?

Resistant	Not sure	Supportive
1	3	5

Comments: _____

10. How willing is the client to consider new possibilities and take risks?

Mind made up	All over the map	Skeptical
1	3	5

Comments: _____

11. How skilled are the client's people at working as a team?

Unskilled	Wide variance	Very skilled
1	3	5

Comments: _____

12. How skilled are the client's people at representing customer groups?

Unskilled	Wide variance	Very skilled
1	3	5

Comments: _____

13. How skilled are the client's people at managing projects?

Unskilled	Wide variance	Very skilled
1	3	5

Comments: _____

14. How skilled are the client's people at processing written information?

Unskilled	Wide variance	Very skilled
1	3	5

Comments: _____

15. How skilled are the client's people at processing statistical information?

Unskilled	Wide variance	Very skilled
1	3	5

Comments: _____

Figure 4.2. Qualifying Survey for Clients' Readiness and Maturity

continued

16. How skilled are the client's people at processing oral information?

Unskilled	Wide variance	Very skilled
1	3	5

Comments: _____

17. How skilled are the client's people at building communications plans?

Unskilled	Wide variance	Very skilled
1	3	5

Comments: _____

18. To what degree has the client already determined who will do the work?

Entrenched	Unclear	Open
1	3	5

Comments: _____

19. To what degree has the client already determined how the work will be done?

Entrenched	Unclear	Open
1	3	5

Comments: _____

20. To what degree has the client already determined how much the work is worth?

Entrenched	Unclear	Open
1	3	5

Comments: _____

21. How well developed are the client's systems for gathering customer intelligence?

Not well	Wide variance	Sophisticated
1	3	5

Comments: _____

22. How well developed are the client's systems for analyzing data?

Not well	Wide variance	Sophisticated
1	3	5

Comments: _____

23. How well developed are the client's systems for disseminating information?

Not well	Wide variance	Sophisticated
1	3	5

Comments: _____

24. How well developed are the client's systems for identifying trends and drivers?

Not well	Wide variance	Sophisticated
1	3	5

Comments: _____

Demographics

25. What business is the customer in?

26. What are the business drivers?

27. Who is the customer's competition?

28. Where does the customer's organization stand in the market?

29. How is the business organized? What is its organizational structure?

30. How many employees are there?

31. Who is involved in this project?

32. Who will be most affected by the project?

33. Does the project have a sponsor? Who is it? Where is he or she in the organization?

34. Is the team in place?

35. Has the client developed a scorecard or defined the criteria to measure the results of this project? If so, what are the criteria and standards? How does the client plan to get the information needed to determine if the objective was achieved?

36. Is the project budgeted?

37. Is there a timetable for the project?

38. What software does the customer use now that might be appropriate for this project?

39. How geographically spread are the team, the customers of the project, and the organizational decision makers?

40. Is this project part of a larger goal?

Figure 4.2. Qualifying Survey for Clients' Readiness and Maturity, *cont'd.*

If the client organization	*Then*
Is very clear or has defined the problem	• Confirm how the client came to that conclusion. • Look for evidence the client was thorough in the process.
Is not clear or has not defined the problem	• Work with the client to develop a process or suggest a process for defining the problem.
Is not in agreement	• Plan to meet with representatives of the varying views to confirm what they disagree over. • Use that information to bring them to consensus or come up with a new view they can all support.
Is naive or all over the map	• Plan to bring all the players to a similar level of understanding about what supports competent performance and what undermines it.
Is resistant to the project	• Add to your strategy a process for overcoming resistance and getting buy-in.
Is skeptical	• Find out the source of the skepticism.
Has its mind made up	• Find out about what, and the reason behind this position. • Acknowledge the legitimacy of the position and, if you believe it is unproductive, create enough dissonance to introduce doubt while at the same time complimenting the client for being conscientious. • Provide the information the client needs to come to a more informed conclusion. You may want to ask a neutral party to participate or be the one to introduce new information.
Is unskilled	• Add coaching or training, teaming, project management, data analysis, or something else that you think will be useful to the client.
Is open to who will perform the work and how the work will be done	• Add to your process facilitating discussions about who might do the work and how the work will be done.
Is entrenched, and you or others disagree	• Find out their reasoning. • Acknowledge their rationale. • If the entrenchment is based on old hurts or wounds, make public the reasoning. • Identify who gains and who loses from the decision. • Create enough dissonance to get them to reconsider. • Recommend a solution that still satisfies their need. • Negotiate for them to join with the others to come up with a process they can all support.
Does not have systems suited for the project	• Explain the implications of this deficiency on cost and time. • Work with a design that accommodates the systems in place or help the client negotiate for additional resources.

Figure 4.3. If-Then Table: Developing a Strategy from the Survey Results

FIELD TECHNIQUES: STRENGTHENING YOUR CREDIBILITY AND INFLUENCE

If you want to be credible and influence your client's actions and decisions, you must develop your own plan:

1. Begin by coming up with ways to build on the essential ingredients, that is:

   • Come up with ways to get the *relevant information,* Find out what is going on and who is behind what initiative; then stay in the know.

   • Have the *courage to speak up,* ask for an audience, and present information you believe is worthy of being considered while managing the risk. Answer the questions on the power test (Figure 4.1) to assess how much influence you have now and what you can do to get a higher score.

   • Continue to develop your *interpersonal skills.* Cultivate your skill at building relationships and your ability to gain others' trust.

2. Work on the spices:

   • *Trust people, but always verify* the information they give.

   • Develop your *political savvy.* Find out what people's hidden agendas are, and try always to make others look good.

   • Strategically *create dissonance* when people are entrenched or polarized to get them to pause long enough to incorporate new information or rethink their position.

   • Increase your *external status.* Take steps to build your professional reputation.

3. Perfect your cooking:

   • Learn to *establish your presence* and manage your image.

   • Practice *remaining impartial,* but do not hesitate to offer a well-founded opinion.

   • Periodically ask where the discussion and the action are going to *stay focused* on what matters.

4. Learn to consciously assess where your clients are, how sophisticated they are, what their attitudes are, and what their commitment is to the project at hand. Use that information to come up with a strategy for working with them effectively. In the process, you will strengthen you credibility and influence.

SUMMARY

Doug and Marilyn, in the stories at the beginning of the chapter, were looking to their organizations to legitimize their roles and gain a voice in decision making. Having position power and being close to the action can help, but they do not replace accepting responsibility for managing your image and establishing a reputation as a credible professional. These are things only you can do. The ideas in this and the previous chapters offer you a template for building a presence in your organization.

WHERE TO LEARN MORE

American Society for Training and Development. *Models for HRD Practice.* Alexandria, Va.: American Society for Training and Development, 1996.

Byrd, R. *Guide to Personal Risk Taking.* New York: AMACOM, 1974. This book is out of print but can still be found.

Cialdini, R. B. *Influence: Science and Practice.* Needham Heights, Mass.: Allyn & Bacon, 2001. This book describes a detailed process for gaining and using influence to shape others' ideas and actions.

International Society for Performance Improvement. *Human Performance Technology Standards.* Silver Spring, Md.: International Society for Performance Improvement, 2001. These are the standards for the certified performance technologist certification. They are available at www.ispi.org, along with a self-assessment.

Iverson, K. *Plain Talk.* San Francisco: Jossey-Bass, 1997.

Langdon, D. *The New Language of Work.* Amherst, Mass.: HRD Press, 1997. This book addresses the need for consultants to understand and be able to use the language of their business customers.

Pershing, J. (ed.). *Performance Technology Handbook.* San Francisco: Jossey-Bass, 2006. This handbook, sponsored by the International Society for Performance Improvement, is a solid reference for both aspiring performance consultants and veterans.

Ranshaw, J. *Consultant's Quick Guide to Grammar and Style.* Chicago: Hoosierjanebooks, 2005. This guide provides practical tips for writing clearly, an essential skill for consultants.

Schaller, L. *Getting Things Done.* Nashville, Tenn.: Abingdon Press, 1986. The ideas and techniques presented will help you get people over whom you have no position authority to make and carry out commitments.

Watzlawick, P., with Weakland, J., and Fisch, R. *Change: Principles of Problem Formation and Problem Resolution.* This provides an excellent explanation of how our mental models of the world and ourselves prevent success and is especially constructive on learning how to look at situations from a different perspective (which lead to breakthroughs) and stay focused on solving the real problems.

Chapter 5

Sustaining Change

*O*rganizational performance is improved when we are able to institutional-ize new behaviors that lead to long-term results in ways that are effective, ef-ficient, and ethical. Unfortunately a lot of our work is event driven. We and our clients stay engaged until a program is launched; then everyone's involve-ment and attention fall away as we go on to new challenges.

FIELD NOTES: STOPPING RUTHLESS BEHAVIORS

Carol and her team had developed and delivered a half-day workshop to all one hundred senior managers on the four continents that her company had offices in. The objective of the program was to get senior managers to stop one set of behaviors and adopt another. The focus was not on skill building; they already knew how to do the new behaviors. But they had determined it was more impor-tant for them to be efficient than engage in those behaviors. In fact, the managers had not become more efficient; rather, they had become ruthless, and the result was increasing health costs and waste. Premature retirements and increased disability claims due to stress-related health issues had increased by 20 percent, absenteeism was up 30 percent, and key staff members were leaving the orga-nization because of the stressful working conditions.

During the workshop, the managers reviewed and publicly committed to fol-lowing a series of protocols that they had developed: setting agendas with spe-cific outcomes for meetings; including in meetings only those who needed to be there; developing and trusting backups and not relying on the same people to do everything; using the appropriate communication vehicles instead of copy-ing everyone on e-mail and voice mail on the guise that everyone has to know everything; planning work instead of insisting everyone be available 24 hours a day, 7 days a week, 365 days a year in case someone had a question (employees were required to be available by cell phone 24/7); and scheduling international conference calls while taking the different time zones into consideration. The premise was that the leadership set the norms because their behaviors communicated what was expected of others.

Getting everyone to participate in the workshop was a challenge in and of itself; Carol knew the bigger challenge was sustaining the new behaviors.

In a perfect world, program sponsors would think through how to sustain new behaviors beyond the workshop; typically, however, they too are distracted by new demands or move on to new assignments. I believe it is the performance consultant's job to raise the question about how to sustain change and suggest ways to make it happen. Four techniques that I outline here will help clients better appreciate what it takes to reap the benefits of a new program or initiative: tracking adoption, dramatizing causality, sustaining ownership, and ongoing measurement and reporting of results.

TRACKING ADOPTION

In the past five or so years, a lot of attention has been directed to measuring impact, or in the language of Kirkpatrick, measuring results. However, the most meaningful results may appear only after a substantial period of time. I believe we instead should focus on the degree to which the ideas, concepts, and behaviors espoused in training and communication programs are adopted or implemented. To track adoption cost-effectively, we must trust the participants and their supervisors to report their success at incorporating the new behaviors in their day-to-day work. The tracking and reporting of adoption is an intervention in itself, as it reinforces the new behavior and subjects the participants to some public scrutiny. There is no need to track everyone all of the time. According to Mary Gelinas and Roger James—in their book titled *Collaborative Change* (San Francisco: Jossey-Bass, 1998)—a change can be sustained if a critical mass in the organization (51 percent) adopt the new behavior. However, to get to that 51 percent, you must have early and middle adopters. The distribution of who is adopting in an organization depends at least partly on the culture. Once the middle adopters are on board, the late adopters usually fall in line.

DRAMATIZING CAUSALITY

Dramatizing causality using examples, stories, and visuals to show the relationship of the need, the proposed solutions, and the eventual results helps to sustain change. The goal is to create for program sponsors and developers a mental model of a solution's place in the larger scheme of improving performance. Ideally, this is done near the beginning of a project, but it is effective even after a program is launched. The technique should document the group's logic: the evidence they used to justify the dedication of resources to a solution and what they will accept as success.

As organizations move people around on the premise of developing talent, institutional memory is lost. The rationale for why things were done or done in specific ways is forgotten. The intended beneficiaries of a program and the new leaders of the department that originally sponsored it lack the depth of understanding to support it over time. Perhaps this is why training departments and HR in particular have difficulty showing their value and get the reputation of purveyors of "flavor of the month" solutions. Performance consultants are in unique position to be keepers of history and serve as the conscience of the organization because they should know the rationale behind solutions and are in a position to make the logic explicit and codify it.

FIELD TECHNIQUES: DRAMATIZING CAUSALITY

One way to capture, communicate, and document why a program was funded and the results it was intended to achieve is through illustrations. My preferred technique is to create a picture of client's logic (see Figure 5.1). The goal is to capture in a single illustration the need, the solution, and the measures of success at the organizational and participant level.

**Figure 5.1.
Logic Chain:
From Need to
Measured Results**

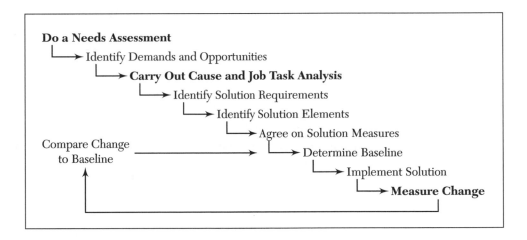

The following information should be captured in the illustration:

• Results of the needs assessment (the problem to be solved)

• Results of the cause or job analysis (the factors and behaviors that are contributing to the need because they are absent or inappropriate)

- Elements of the solution (training topics, job to be redesigned, and so forth)

- Measures of effectiveness at the organizational level (key performance indicators such as improved efficiency, less waste, or faster market penetration, for example)

- Measures of effectiveness at the participant level (improved learning or rate of adoption)

- The baseline or current state (what will be used for comparison to show improvement)

Documenting the measures of success at the organizational and participant levels can show the correlation between the change in participant behavior and the impact on the organization.

Other techniques are to capture war stories that highlight the problem and evoke the solution and use quality tools like a fish bone diagram to document the problem and its root causes.

FIELD NOTES: REINFORCING NEW BEHAVIORS

Carol knew that she had to get about 50 percent of the senior managers in manufacturing, operations, quality control, marketing, and sales to make a concerted effort to change their ways. This group used a goal-setting form to document their personal goals and track progress, so she decided to modify the form to accommodate the behaviors covered in the workshop. Her logic was that using a well-established planning tool would increase the chances the managers would use it. The form assessed the managers' maturity at using the new behaviors. It had a place for the baseline, action steps for getting started, action steps for staying focused, and action steps for making the new behaviors a priority for how they worked. On the form were suggested observable behaviors in three of the areas of emphasis (adhering to the communication protocol, enforcing time away from work, and recognizing good performance), which embedded the concepts of delegating to a backup, not requiring people to be on call all of time, planning work, and using people's time respectfully and purposefully.

Next, Carol created a picture that documented the story behind the workshop (see Figure 5.2). It captured the need, the solution, and the measures of success. She gave the illustration to the company president, who agreed to use it as a reference during the quarterly meetings with all senior managers.

Figure 5.2. A Logic Chain for Reducing Stress: Need, Solution, Measures of Success

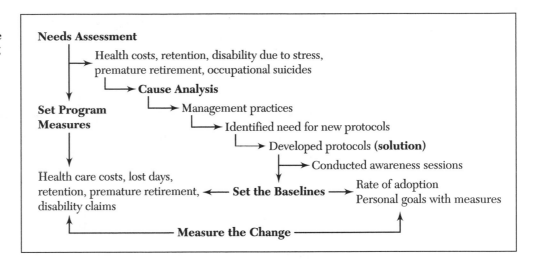

FIELD TECHNIQUES: BUILDING PROFICIENCY IN COMMUNICATING LOGIC

To increase your understanding of and proficiency in the use of illustrations to capture, communicate, and document the rationale behind a program, use your interest in making your transition to performance consulting for practice:

1. In conjunction with a client and colleagues, identify the need for performance consulting.

2. List the barriers to adopting performance consulting as an integral part of your current function.

3. List what must be in place for performance consulting to be adopted.

4. List what you, your clients, and your colleagues will use as evidence of adoption of performance consulting (for example, number or types of assignments requested that require you to use new behaviors or skills).

5. List what you will use to measure the impact of adopting performance consulting (for example, the ability to show improved performance of people, processes, and systems).

6. Describe the current state (remember that absence can be a baseline measure).

7. Identify ways to track your adoption of the behaviors and skills you want to make use of.

Now answer questions 1 to 7 for a program that you were responsible for or participated in its creation and delivery. When you have finished, use these questions for reflection:

- What insights did you gain from this exercise?

- Were some questions more difficult to answer than others? Which ones?

- How might you use this technique to point out logic errors or weaknesses when asked to assist with future programs?

- Use or modify the template in Figure 5.3 to document your story.

Figure 5.3. Logic Chain Template

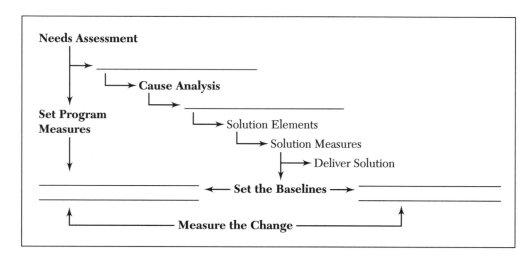

SUSTAINING OWNERSHIP

Another barrier to sustaining a change or the incorporation of a program's principles into everyday practice is the loss of the original sponsor. Sponsors come and go for a variety of reasons, ranging from leaving the organization to getting promoted or reassigned. The problem is that accountability for a program does not travel with the original sponsor and is not passed on to his or her replacement. The problem is compounded because sponsors are usually evaluated and rewarded for getting initiatives launched, and sometimes short-term results, but not for the long-term success of the program.

Organizations in general are terrible at succession planning for key personnel and rarely think of it in connection with programs. Therefore, having a conversation about the need for sustained sponsorship and accountability legitimizes the need for it. The conversation may start out asking, "What do you want us to do about the program when you retire [or get promoted or want to focus on other initiatives]?" "Who is the best person to take over the program when you leave [or want to do other things]?" "How might we orient this person to the program and its importance?" "What incentives might we suggest that would make adopting the program attractive to this person?" The goal is to start the conversation and make succession planning a legitimate activity.

FIELD NOTES: SUSTAINING OWNERSHIP

The program on behavioral change came about because the company's president saw the need and personally owned the program. But Carol knew that his tenure with the company would not last forever. He was still a young man who would be attractive to other companies and no doubt eventually would move on. She believed that without his ongoing commitment to the program, there would be few incentives for the managers to sustain the behaviors specified in the protocols, and the program would gradually fade away.

Shortly after the program was launched, she asked the executive vice president of HR to initiate a conversation with the president about planning how to transfer sponsorship should he want to direct his attention elsewhere. The president recommended the vice president of operations as sponsor because his division had the highest incidence of premature retirement and disability claims due to stress in the workplace. The president and the executive vice president of HR began a plan to transfer sponsorship. Then the executive vice president and Carol practiced the strategy for succession planning because they knew they could apply it to other major programs underway in the company.

FIELD TECHNIQUES: SUSTAINING OWNERSHIP

Addressing the following questions will help you become more proficient at initiating conversations about ongoing sponsorship:

- Who is the current sponsor of a program that would be put at risk if sponsorship stopped?
- How long do people stay on average in this position?
- When do you anticipate losing the sponsor?
- Who might be a likely replacement?
- What would make taking over sponsorship attractive to someone else?
- When might you create or take advantage of an opportunity to initiate a conversation with this person about succession planning for the program?
- What might you say to start the conversation?

ONGOING MEASUREMENT AND REPORTING OF RESULTS

The final barrier to sustaining an initiative is the lack of ongoing measurement and reporting of results. It is not unusual for organizations to measure at the beginning of a new project, but even that is rare. Instead, most organizations believe that once something is funded, the benefits are automatic.

There are a number of reasons for a lack of measurement; among them are the loss of sponsorship, a lack of systems to track meaningful measures, and the failure to leverage measurement activities already in place. The act of dramatizing causality and illustrating the link between the need, the solution, and the results should have identified those factors the solution was expected to have an impact on and ways of measuring that impact. Ideally, you should have identified what the organization was already measuring, reducing the need to set up new measures or new ways of tracking results. Organizations track a lot of information that training and HR professionals fail to leverage when evaluating the impact of their work. For example, manufacturing organizations track safety incidents and costs, and productivity and waste. Service organizations track the number of transactions, the cost of service, and the number of unrecoverable or unbillable hours. Most organizations track customer satisfaction and employee satisfaction. If the goal of a solution is important, it can usually be tied to something the organization is already tracking.

FIELD NOTES: REPORTING RESULTS

In addition to ensuring ongoing sponsorship, Carol knew it was important for the managers to report on their success at adopting the behaviors on a regular and long-term basis. Getting the president to agree to make reporting the rate of adoption of the new behaviors a standing agenda item for the next eight quarterly meetings was a step in the right direction. Carol wanted it to be a standing item on each department's internal meeting agendas as well, so she met with the company's health director, who normally tracked health care costs, including disability claims, health insurance costs, and premature retirement actions, and the HR executive vice president, who tracked turnover and its causes. She asked the health director if he would be willing to prepare a brief quarterly report on this information to share with all managers and the executive vice president if he would write a short paragraph each quarter reinforcing the importance of following the protocols, which would be sent to the heads of all of the divisions worldwide.

FIELD TECHNIQUES: MEASURING AND REPORTING

To encourage you to think more about the importance of measuring and reporting results as a way to sustain commitment to an initiative and reap the long-term benefits, here are some things you can do with your team and client:

1. Identify a program in which you have or will have a role in the implementation.

2. Identify information that the organization is already tracking or capturing that you might use to monitor whether the new behaviors are being adopted and implemented.

3. Identify who is responsible for tracking that information, and put together a plan to develop a relationship with that person.

4. Identify opportunities to report on the adoption of the new behaviors. Consider regular meetings, the schedule for updating a Web site, the production schedule of project reports or internal newsletters.

5. Identify who you need to work with to obtain the information and provide it to the people who need to know.

6. Determine how you will position the need to measure and report progress on a continuing basis.

7. Create a measurement and reporting plan that lists the people who will be responsible for getting and reporting the data, who must approve the communication, and who else needs to be involved and why.

8. Put together a timetable for reporting progress and how this will be accomplished.

SUMMARY

If we as performance consultants want to show the impact of our work on the organization, we need to stop being event driven and look for ways to sustain behaviors and results. At a minimum, we must initiate conversations about how to sustain the behaviors that will lead to success, including finding ways to track the adoption of the desired behaviors, ensuring ongoing sponsorship, reminding clients of the rationale behind their decision to support a program, and communicating progress well after a program's launch.

WHERE TO LEARN MORE

To learn more about the impact of job-induced stress and the rising incidents of suicides, go to www.afsp.org.

Three books on the subject of sustaining change are of interest:

Gelinas, M., and James, R. *Collaborative Change: Improving Organizational Performance.* San Francisco: Jossey-Bass/Pfeiffer, 1998. This is a comprehensive description of how to institutionalize new behaviors.

Mourier, P., and Smith, M. *Conquering Organizational Change.* Atlanta, Ga.: CEP Press, 2001. This well-researched book is full of useful ideas.

Hale, J. *Performance-Based Management: Things Managers Should Do to Get Results.* San Francisco: Jossey-Bass/Pfeiffer, 2004. The examples, stories, and tools presented in this book can help consultants and managers understand what is required of them for people to perform to standard.

Part Two

Performance Consulting

Chapter 6

Environment and Norms

*N*ot only do performance consultants need a special set of skills, they also need specialized knowledge. For example, they should understand how work environments and social systems in organizations shape performance. Here is what happens when these things are not understood.

FIELD NOTES: ENVIRONMENTAL PITFALLS

The bank was considered the model of sound banking practices. The main branch was an architectural wonder, with soaring marble columns and a grand portico. The people who worked at the bank, known for being polite and loyal to the bank, were shocked when the local TV newscaster announced the bank was on the brink of financial failure. The bank's senior management, it turned out, had been speculating in risky investments.

Day after day, the feature story in the local newspaper focused on the bank: it reported possible fraud and malfeasance and editorialized on the need for stronger government controls in the banking industry. Every day brought disturbing new developments, like the firing of an experienced auditor over a dispute about investment practices. The bank's employees found themselves facing embarrassing questions from neighbors and colleagues. The questions about why it had happened seemed unending. Why hadn't someone spoken up, challenged what was happening, and reported it to the government?

When new management took over, they decided a culture change was needed. They sent out a memo to all employees telling them to lighten up and that telling jokes was appropriate behavior and placed advertisements in the local newspaper depicted the bank as a buffoon. In response, morale among employees dropped to an all-time low, and the incidence of serious illness by mid-level managers had increased. The new management did not understand how deeply the betrayal of trust at the bank had undermined employees' self-esteem.

EXPERIENCES FROM THE FIELD: ORGANIZATIONAL DYNAMICS

Rather than starting Part Two of the fieldbook with a set of guidelines on how to do performance consulting, it's important to set out some of the underlying principles of organizational dynamics. I have found that clients and peers do not always have the same understanding of how the work environment affects performance. One reason is that we come from such different backgrounds. My standing joke is that at least accountants studied debits and credits and doctors studied anatomy. The performance consulting industry isn't so lucky; performance consultants' professional and academic backgrounds vary widely. And even those of us who have degrees in human resources, education, or business cannot assume we studied the same concepts, since academic programs are shaped more by the philosophies and strong personalities of professors than by a codified body of knowledge.

Therefore, before getting into the processes of needs assessments and selecting interventions, I'll start by explaining two concepts on which these processes are based. Think of this section as a primer. My intent is to give you an understanding of my thinking behind the tools used in the later chapters.

I taught graduate courses in management for the Insurance School of Chicago for fourteen years. The courses were part of the insurance industry's Chartered Property and Casualty Underwriting (CPCU) and Management (IIA) programs. In addition to finance, the courses stressed management theory, analytical decision-making models, and organizational behavior. In the early 1980s, I had the opportunity to hear Richard Boyatzis and David McClelland speak on their methodologies for defining competence. They presented a powerful case that competence depends on context, that is, the work environment. This helped me understand what was going on in the insurance industry. Insurance companies hired one another's employees. The assumption was that if an underwriter who held the CPCU designation and was a good performer at one company would perform equally as well at another company. This proved not to be the case. Companies forgot to consider that each one had its own policies, products, procedures, and culture. Earning the CPCU designation and having experience in underwriting was not enough to ensure that a person could perform well in different environments. With this observation in mind, I created two models for understanding how environment affects performance. The first model concerns the work environment, and the second is about group norms.

THE WORK ENVIRONMENT

Three variables have to come together, or be in harmony, for an individual to achieve optimum performance in a particular job:

1. The resources of the larger organization, including its mandate, technology and systems, and financial strength

2. What the job is expected to produce—the output

3. What the individual knows, believes, can do, and is willing to do

The more the three variables overlap, the greater the chance is that optimal performance will result (see Figure 6.1). The further apart they are or if one of the three is not in sync with the other two, the greater the likelihood of marginal or poor performance. I visualize the area of overlap as the zone of competence.

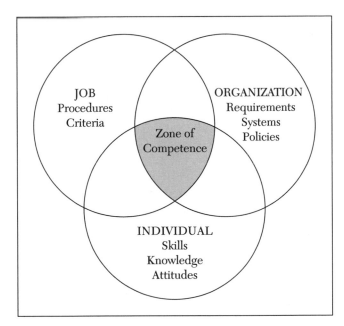

Figure 6.1. The Zone of Competence

The Organization

People performance depends on what the organization can offer. The term *organization* can describe a whole company, a division within it, a department, a function, and even a work group or team. For example, companies have reputations, and so do departments and teams. Companies have financial and other resources, and so do departments and teams. Companies are more or less attuned to developments in the marketplace; departments and teams too can be more or less attuned to developments in the larger organization. Companies may or may not make the latest technology available to their workforce; departments and teams too may or may not have available the latest technology or systems. Whether you are dealing with the organization as a whole or just a work group, its customer profiles may not be clearly defined and its customers may not have similar needs. No matter what the size, the organization shapes what people do and how they do it. The organization shapes performance through its culture and values, leadership and guidance, information systems, core processes and technologies, product mix and customer profile, economic strength, and reputation in the marketplace.

These elements make up the characteristics of an organization. When people are hired or assigned to a position, they are either attracted to or accept these characteristics. People who accommodate and adapt to those characteristics will usually be successful there. When these characteristics change, whether by choice or in response to outside forces, the balance between the organization, the job, and the individual is disrupted. Balance can be restored only when the elements of the job and the capabilities of the individual also change.

The Job or Task

The activities and duties that make up the job or task also shape performance. People's performance is affected by:

- How well the organization has defined its roles, responsibilities, and relationships

- How well it has designed the rules, procedures, and processes used to perform the tasks

- How efficient and appropriate the technology is that is used in the job

- How mature and functional the business relationships they must deal with are

- How clear, accurate, and timely the information is that they must work with

- How similar and reasonable their customers' expectations and needs are

These elements make up the characteristics of the job. Some jobs and tasks have well-developed, thoroughly documented procedures; others do not. Some jobs put people in long-established, mature relationships; others do not. Roles and relationships are well defined for some jobs and less so for others. A change in procedures, relationships, or any of the other elements disrupts the balance. Whether the change is looked on positively or negatively, the organization and the individual have to accommodate and adapt to restore the balance. If they do not adapt, performance suffers.

The People

Different people bring different skills, knowledge, emotional and physical capacity, and motives to the job. Their performance can be enhanced or threatened when there are changes in their capacity (intellectual, physical, emotional) or personal motives. For example, people who leave work to return to school may find their old job less fulfilling than they originally did. People who find themselves with increasing personal or family responsibilities may be less enamored with a job that requires a lot of travel. People who are faced with increasing complications from chronic health conditions may find it harder to execute certain procedures or use more sophisticated technologies. Again, when people's capacity and capabilities change, the balance is disrupted. To restore the balance, the organization might dedicate more resources or redesign the job.

What is important is to separate changes in the work environment from those in the job and those in the people. Because the organization, the job, and individuals are always adapting, this can be very difficult to do.

FIELD NOTES: CECIL AND THE COMPUTER

Cecil worked in petroleum logistics. He was responsible for calculating the fuel requirements for the U.S. Air Force during World War II, the Korean War, and Vietnam. To do his job, Cecil had to solve complex mathematical problems. Remember math problems from algebra that started with a story of a train and a car? *A train leaves Los Angeles traveling 80 miles per hour. You leave Washington, D.C., driving 50 miles per hour. Who will get to the Mississippi River first? You or the train?* Cecil had to solve problems like this, but they were much more complex. He had to consider things like:

- Where the storage fuel tanks were located all over the world, their capacity, and how much fuel they contained at any given time

- How many planes there were of every type, how much fuel they consumed, where they were stationed around the world, and where they had to be

- How many fuel tankers there were, where they were located, how much fuel they had on board, how fast they could travel, and how far they had to go

- How many storage tanks were destroyed or could possibly be cut off

- Where ground forces were, how many there were, and how many miles they were from surface and air support

He was then given a "what-if" situation like, *What if we lose this many tankers?* or *What if it takes the tankers this long to get somewhere?* or *What if the landing strips are too damaged for planes to land?* He had to consider all of these factors and figure out how many planes could be kept in the air and for how long in a variety of situations.

The demand for accurate calculations was critical. The military depended on its intelligence sources and its suppliers for information. The computing power we take for granted today did not yet exist. Whenever there was a threat of an international incident, Cecil was not allowed to come home. He was taken to a heavily secured area, where he remained for days at a time. Cecil was given the information he had to work with orally or through written intelligence reports.

The job required highly developed skills at solving complex math problems without the benefit of today's technologies. Cecil had to be a quick and good thinker. Because he had not gone beyond his sophomore year of high school, he had never been formally trained in the language of math and could not read algebraic formulas. As a consequence, he could not communicate how he calculated an answer. He could only tell you what the answer was, and that was all he was asked to do.

Twenty-five years after Cecil started in the job, the air force put in a "big" computer and hired ten people with Ph.D.s in mathematics. The Ph.D.s and Cecil were given the same problems. The Ph.D.s converted their information into formulas and gave the formulas to computer programmers, who then built programs for the computer. Cecil and his two helpers worked as they always had. Cecil would meet periodically with the Ph.D.s and compare answers. But although Cecil knew the answer, he could not talk to the Ph.D.s in their language. He didn't know how to translate his thinking into formulas that computer programmers could use. He only knew the answer. The introduction of the computer changed his job and the skills required to be effective in it.

FIELD TECHNIQUES: ISOLATING ENVIRONMENTAL CHANGES

Assume that people's performance has deteriorated in your client's organization. To understand whether changes in the job environment have affected their performance, start by watching people do their work. To find out if anything has changed, pay attention to:

- *Where they get the information they use, what form it comes in (electronic, oral, written), and the language or symbols it comes in (words, icons, tones, colors).* You want to know if a new technology or reporting relationship has changed some aspect of the information people use to do their jobs.

- *The equipment and tools they use.* You want to know if the equipment that people use requires a certain level of strength, manual dexterity, fine motor skills, or visual and auditory discrimination. If people's performance has changed, find out if their tools or equipment changed and if those changes require new skills.

- *The workplace layout, air quality, noise level, and lighting quality in the workplace.* A change in layout can disrupt relationships and work habits. Poor air quality and ambient noise can contribute to fatigue. Shadows and glare can contribute to mistakes.

You would then use this information to support your recommendations about what has to change in either the work environment or a specific job to restore balance and productivity.

FIELD NOTES: ADDING A NEW PRODUCTION LINE

Russ, who works in HRD at the medical manufacturer, was assigned to a team to find out why production errors at one of the production centers were up and to make recommendations for improving performance. The center made plastic tubes for lotions, ointments, and salves. Russ asked to spend a day at the plant to see how it operated and talk to the production line crew. Two people worked the lines each shift. The lines had to be cleared, cleaned and sterilized, and recalibrated for each type of tube at the end of each shift. The same workers had been with the center since the plant had opened five years ago. Another person worked the swing shift and covered for the others when they were ill or on vacation.

Russ saw that there were six production lines in the plant. The newest line was added two months ago. He also noticed that the equipment used in four of the lines came from different manufacturers. He learned that the procedures for setting up, calibrating, and line clearance were significantly different depending on the manufacturer. The crew pointed out there were a lot of differences in the equipment. For example, the dials were in different places, some instruments had digital readings and others were analog dials, some had two-way valves and others had three-way valves, the color red meant off on one line but signaled a problem on another, and so on. The number of variables the crew had to deal with had more than doubled over the past five years.

Russ used this information to support his recommendation that an industrial engineer be hired to see if some of the variables could be removed. He also wanted the engineer's opinion on whether more people should be hired. He recommended that visual symbols and job aids be added to each machine to cue the crew in the proper sequence of steps for clearance, cleaning, and calibration. Removing or reducing the number of variables and adding resources (people and job aids) would help restore the balance.

VARIABILITY IN JOBS

Jobs with the same output requirements may not really be the same. Varying circumstances or situations can make the same job very different for different employees. For example, an employee at a field location may face very different conditions from an employee doing the same work at corporate headquarters. Different geographical locations can change a job significantly. Salespeople assigned to different territories may face different markets. Their customers may not have the same level of sophistication, buying power, or needs. Their sales managers may be more or less skilled at coaching. Some may service concentrated markets, reducing their need to travel. Others may service dispersed markets, requiring greater travel or skill at using electronic communication systems. Yet because the salespeople represent the same products for the same company, people will be inclined to think their jobs are the same. It may well be that the job is the same, but the conditions under which the work is done are quite different.

Building engineers who service heating and air conditioning systems for small retail businesses face very different circumstances from engineers who service hospitals or laboratories that require uninterrupted service and consistent humidity and temperature. Although these differences may be understood, they are sometimes overlooked when companies reassign (or even promote) a high performer. The ability to perform the job well under one set of circumstances does not always translate to a different set of circumstances.

If nothing has changed in the work environment yet performance among group members is not the same, look for variability in the job. Pay particular attention to the conditions the different group members work under (ask about them, or go see for yourself). You want to investigate:

- *The working conditions.* Are they the same for everyone in the same or similar jobs? Look at number or frequency of disruptions, sophistication of processes, and so on.

- *The relationships the job requires.* Are similar relationships required for everyone in the same or similar jobs? Consider, for example, protocols, culture, business norms, and language.

- *The job inputs.* Are they the same for everyone in the same or similar jobs? Look at information, customer requirements, and expectations.

- *The geographical location.* Is it the same for everyone in the same or similar jobs? Consider the effects of distance from headquarters and working in different time zones.

If you discover that people in similar jobs actually work under very different conditions, describe the differences and somehow make them public or go on the record concerning the differences. Then recommend that the organization either eliminate or reduce these differences by adding resources or equipping people to deal with the differences better.

FIELD TOOLS: CONTEXTUAL JOB DESCRIPTIONS

Traditional job descriptions usually list responsibilities and the preferred education and experience. They are used to support hiring, selection, and salary decisions. My experience is that the traditional job description is silent about work conditions or minimally describes them. I developed a tool for creating job descriptions that considers the conditions of the job (see Figure 6.2). The model serves as both a job aid and worksheet for describing the job and the work environment in particular.

The job description can be combined with the operational definition (Figures 1.3 and 1.7) to give a fuller picture of what it takes to be successful in the job. Just as with many of the tools already described in this book, the job description is best done in collaboration with the client and someone in the job. As a performance consultant, your role is to facilitate the process of discovery and of gaining consensus. The benefits of the tool come from the process. The tool encourages people to question their assumptions about the job and what influences job performance.

**Figure 6.2.
Contextual
Job Description**

1. What is the job's mission and purpose?
   - What business need was it created to satisfy?
   - How would the organization be affected if the job were eliminated?
   - Who within the organization would be affected?
   - Would the effect be positive or negative?
2. Who are the job's customers? Who depends on it and needs it to be done well?
3. What are the underlying and sometimes unspoken assumptions that determine how performance will be evaluated? What demands of the job's work environment require extra skills and knowledge?
4. Who are the people, teams, or groups that a person doing the job has to get along with?
   - What relationships must an employee establish or maintain to be successful in the job?
   - With whom must they be established, and how accessible are the necessary people in terms of time and distance?
   - How different are the people doing the job from one another and from those with whom they must have relationships (in terms of their values, norms, language, knowledge, skills, status, culture, and so on)?
5. What do the people in the job have to produce or deliver to be considered effective? On what basis is their performance evaluated: efficiency? quality of the relationships gained or sustained? quality of the work? cost of the work? cost benefit derived from the outputs of the job? customer satisfaction? revenue generated (indirectly or directly)?
6. What are the typical tasks that make up the job?
7. What do people have to know to do the job?
8. What skills do people have to have to be effective in the job?

**FIELD
TECHNIQUES:
ISOLATING
DIFFERENCES IN
JOB CONDITIONS**

To identify a job's conditions and determine if the conditions differ for different employees, start by asking questions that will reveal some of the unspoken assumptions various people have about the circumstances under which people doing that job must work:

1. Ask employees in the job and their bosses to describe the people, teams, or groups the employees have to work with in terms of:
   - Their values, norms, language, knowledge, skills, social status, and business sophistication
   - How much they differ from each other
   - How much they differ from the employees in the job
   - Which of these differences require additional skills or knowledge on the part of the employees

2. Ask the employees and boss to explain the business reason for the job. Why is the job done? What need was it created to satisfy? How would the organization be affected if the job were eliminated? Who would be affected, and how?

3. Ask the employees what they have to produce or deliver to be considered effective. On what basis is their performance evaluated: efficiency? quality of the relationships gained or sustained? quality of work? cost of work? cost benefit derived from the outputs of the job? customer satisfaction? revenue generated (indirectly or directly)?

From this information, you can gain an understanding of the job and the circumstances under which the people who do it work.

FIELD NOTES: MOVING TO THE INTERNATIONAL DIVISION

Mike was asked to find out why the performance of his company's U.S. product managers dropped significantly when they were transferred to the international division. The product managers are responsible for product safety and brand integrity for specific products. As U.S. managers, they had been assigned U.S. suppliers and supply chains. A supply chain consisted of all the companies involved in getting a product to the store. The companies at the start of the chain produce raw materials. Companies in the middle of the chain convert the raw materials into finished products. And the companies at the end of the chain package and distribute the finished products.

Mike found that a traditional job description already existed for the international product managers and that the job responsibilities, education requirements, and performance expectations were the same as for the company's domestic managers. Product managers had to have a degree in science. Most of the managers' degrees were in agronomy, animal husbandry, or microbiology. The performance criteria for both jobs measured how well their suppliers reduced product costs, ensured uninterrupted supply, protected brand integrity, and maintained product safety. Mike decided to focus on the underlying assumptions and the environmental conditions of the job.

He met with some of the U.S. product managers and their key suppliers. Many of the suppliers had been with the company for over twenty years. The relationship between the suppliers in each supply chain was also well established. The U.S. product managers spent most of their time encouraging their suppliers to embrace the quality principles of process improvement and improve business transactions among themselves to eliminate unnecessary cost.

Next, he met with some international product managers. He learned that in many international markets, local suppliers did not exist. The supply chains there were a combination of local, regional, and international firms. The managers were expected to identify local manufacturers and teach them how to make the product. Because the company had rigorous product standards, the managers frequently had to help local suppliers secure lending to upgrade their production lines. As a result of these factors, the international product managers had to know local lending practices, the import regulations and protocols of a variety of nations, the transportation options within and across various international borders, several languages, and the nuances and protocols of different business cultures.

They had to be able to deal in multiple currencies, negotiate agreements to accommodate varying rates of inflation, decide which currency to do business in (some worked in highly inflationary countries), persuade nationals from different countries with a history of hostility for generations to cooperate, and assess the ability and willingness of suppliers to comply with the company's business ethics.

Mike decided to develop new job descriptions for both groups that focused on the work environment, not just its tasks. Figure 6.3 is the job description he produced for international product managers. Mike recommended that the company better prepare managers for international assignments through training and increasing corporate backup support.

Figure 6.3. Job Description for International Product Managers

---

Job Title: International Product Manager

Purpose

- To provide leadership, stewardship, training, direction, information, and feedback to zone staff, management, and suppliers
- To provide expertise in the areas of standards, raw materials selection, processing, packaging, distribution, manufacturing, and regulatory compliance
- To lead a coordinated effort to link the independent segments of the supply chain (suppliers, distributors, stores) in ways that result in the best value to the system, while providing ongoing tactical distribution support to all markets

Givens

- There is wide variance in supplier and in-country personnel abilities and technologies, technical expertise, and resources.
- Effective relationships are required with people of different countries, values, languages, ethics, business practices, and norms.
- International product managers are expected to operate independent of backup resources, while preserving quality, product, safety, integrity, and supply.
- The ability to demonstrate and perform any step in the process, from raw product to finished product, is required.
- The job requires the ability to operate within a wide range of political and economic environments.

- International product managers must exemplify the principles of Total Quality Management in their own practices, such as by evaluating and continuously improving company processes, being customer oriented, exhibiting leadership, and making fact-based decisions.

Required Activities

- Direct the quality assurance needs within the zone.
- Develop trained professionals in the local countries.
- Locate and develop suppliers who understand the company's standards as evidenced by quality and price.
- Set direction and priorities in conjunction with local country management.
- Perform product and supplier evaluations.
- Maintain knowledge and skills in the technical areas of product technology, sensory evaluation, safety programs, and good manufacturing practices.
- Develop, oversee, and revise specifications and policies related to suppliers.
- Maintain awareness of legislative issues regarding world trade to help local markets understand the potential or real impact on their operations.
- Commit to and exemplify the department's philosophy and values.
- Support the achievement of department objectives.
- Strive for continuous improvement in all activities.
- Maintain competitive awareness.
- Perform all administrative functions required.

When people performance is down but job conditions are relatively equal and nothing has changed in the workplace, it's time to focus on the people. You want to know if they have experienced a change in their physical capacity or personal motives. This is best done in collaboration with someone from HR. You will also need to ask supervisors to cite specific fact-based instances in their examples of the change in performance.

Performance consultants rarely get involved with performance problems related to specific individuals; however, you may want to offer your skills in facilitation and negotiation to help clients experiencing trouble with specific employees. You can facilitate discussions with supervisors about whether performance expectations and the change in performance have been communicated to the employee in question. You can help in the negotiations with the employee to seek medical or other professional help. You may want to join with HR in helping managers understand how to address performance problems due to changes in employees' physical or emotional health. Whatever role you play, you will have to be very astute about discriminating between people's conclusions (what they think has happened) and what has actually been observed firsthand. Here are some guidelines:

1. Meet with the supervisor to find out exactly what has changed. If the supervisor lacks direct evidence, then try to meet with someone who has witnessed the change in behavior or work results firsthand.

2. Ask about the onset and frequency of the undesirable behavior or results.

3. Confirm that the person has been told what was observed, what the observer's conclusions were, and what the consequences will be if the behavior does not change or the results do not improve.

4. Find out if other efforts have been made to coach, train, or counsel the employee.

5. If the employee's performance has met expectations in the past, facilitate a discussion with the supervisor and other appropriate parties about what the organization is willing and is not willing to do.

6. If there is a concern over a health problem, work with HR to understand the policies about requiring medical examinations.

FIELD NOTES: THE EFFECTS OF DIABETES

Kelly, who worked at an insurance company, was asked to find out what was wrong with Mary, an employee in one of the corporate offices. One manager thought Mary should be fired. Kelly found out that Mary had been a consistent performer for years; nothing had changed about her job, and she had had the same boss and coworkers for over five years. What had changed was that Mary would disappear over the course of the workday. One day a coworker found her asleep in the ladies' rest room. She was even found leaning against a filing cabinet asleep. When she was asked if anything was wrong, Mary just complained of being tired. Kelly met with Mary and a representative from HR. They told Mary that a record of sleeping on the job would be put in her file and that if she didn't get a physical, HR would start the process of terminating her. She was given thirty days to bring in a doctor's statement attesting she was able to work. Mary finally agreed to get a physical. She learned she had diabetes. Once it was under control, her performance returned to what had been in the past.

ORGANIZATIONS AS SOCIAL SYSTEMS: MANAGING GROUP NORMS

The second model I draw on is that of organizations as social systems. This model helps me better understand what influences group norms. I use this model when a group's behavior and attitude is not what the organization wants. The term *behavior* encompasses people's interactions (the exchange of ideas and information) and their activities (everything else they do). A group's behaviors and attitudes are often called its *norms*. Just as with the first model, the elements are interdependent: a change in any one element causes some corresponding change in the others. Figure 6.4 illustrates the elements.

In the center of the figure is the nucleus. It is a combination of (1) what the organization requires or expects in terms of behavior and results and (2) the actual behaviors and attitudes that emerge (called the *group's norms*) and results that occur. When both components of the nucleus are in harmony, everyone is happy. When they separate and are at odds with each other, problems occur. The nucleus is surrounded by those elements the larger organization can more immediately control:

- The technology and equipment the people use to do the job
- The physical space where the job is performed (how that space is arranged and designed)

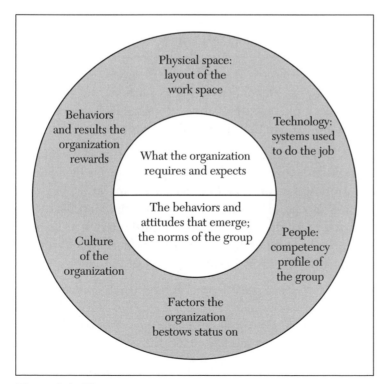

Figure 6.4. Elements of a Social System

- The factors that lead to higher status in the organization

- The behaviors and results the organization chooses to reward

- The culture of the larger organization

- The competency profile of the group

This visual model helps me see the relationships of the elements and reminds me of what the organization can more readily control. Here are some principles I try to remember:

- *People adopt behaviors and attitudes for a number of reasons.* For example, they develop new behaviors to compensate for deficiencies in their organization or in how their job is designed.

- *What is dysfunctional in one context may be functional in another.* People have beliefs or ideas about the world and how it operates, and they tend to act in ways that confirm their beliefs. Sometimes these beliefs lead to behaviors that their organization considers dysfunctional.

- *Norms are what a group's members decide are appropriate behaviors.* Some norms continue to be reinforced even when they are no longer useful. Because norms are usually unwritten, the best way to find out what they are is to observe the behaviors of people who are considered outcasts or non–team members by the group. People who consistently violate norms will be ignored or considered outcasts. People are more likely to conform if the group's norms are close to their own beliefs about the world.

- *People's competencies affect their ability to deal with the world, and competencies influence the number and types of goals people set for themselves.* Richard Gardner proposed in *Multiple Intelligences: The Theory in Practice* (New York: Basic Books, 1993) that there are multiple intelligences, including cultural and social intelligence. His premise is that people possess different degrees of these intelligences, which affects their ability to solve problems and work effectively in varying roles and situations.

- *People choose behaviors that are consistent with their goals, competencies, beliefs, and values even if those choices appear illogical to others.* The behaviors most likely to occur in a given situation are those that best reflect a person's self-concept and worldview.

- *The higher a person's status is outside the group, the higher his or her initial position or rank will be within it.*

FIELD NOTES: CHANGING NORMS

Joe was the director of learning and performance at a major corporation. In the more than twenty years he had been with the organization, he had purposefully moved his team from training to performance by insisting on doing needs assessments and measuring his group's contributions in dollars. He and his managers were highly regarded by senior management and the profession.

But over the years, Joe had failed to recognize the subtle but steady changes in the corporate culture. Senior managers were retiring and being replaced by new people who did not tolerate trainers' asking questions about processes or offering advice; trainers, they believed, coordinated events. Joe's remaining political base was older and was being displaced by younger managers from the outside. When a new HR vice president was hired, Joe reported to her instead of the executive council. She made it clear that trainers took orders and never challenged a line manager's request. In the past, Joe and his team were regularly given accolades because they questioned, offered alternatives, and insisted on solving problems worthy of a solution. Within a year, he went from getting outstanding performance reviews to reviews that said he needed a performance plan. He and his team went from being leaders to being outcasts. Joe retired, two of his managers took jobs in other departments, and three left for positions outside the company.

FIELD TECHNIQUES: IDENTIFYING HOW NORMS AFFECT PERFORMANCE

Here are some guidelines you can use when you want to find out why a group's norms do not support what the organization wants and what to do about it. If there is a performance problem, find out if the problem is unique to an individual or a group. If the problem is unique to a group and you think norms play a role, try to find out what happened that caused the group's norms to get out of sync with what the organization wants. For example:

1. If the technology changed, ask:

   • How the change in technology affected people's activities and interactions.

   • How the change affected the number of people needed, when they must be in certain places, how much latitude they have, the amount of variation in their work methods, and the level of personal judgment that is required or accepted.

   • How the group feels about the change.

   • What kinds of interactions the change has made easier or more difficult.

- What kind of expertise the new technology requires and whether it has affected who can be a member of the group, how often they see each other, and to what degree they are supervised.

2. If there has been a change in how status is bestowed on people, find out how that has affected internal relationships within the group. Find out if valuable members of the group are being ignored because they lack external status or if some people have more influence than their actual work contribution merits.

3. If the level of competency required to do the job has changed, find out if different levels of competence among group members can be tolerated or if the work requires everyone to have the same level of expertise.

What to Do

To influence a group's norms because they do not support what the organization wants, recommend changing those elements over which the larger organization has most control:

- *The job itself.* It could be that group norms are accommodating a poorly designed job or inappropriate expectations, nonperformance of other groups, inadequate technology, or something else.

- *The physical layout of the work area.* Inadequate space and poorly laid out work areas encourage people to take shortcuts and be inefficient.

- *What gets rewarded.* A reward is more than what an organization does to recognize people performance; sometimes it's what it *doesn't* do. For example, there may be no consequences for inappropriate behavior.

- *The technology used to do the work.* It could be that the procedures or work processes are inefficient or can no longer support the work volume.

- *The culture of the larger organization.* If the larger organization celebrates people who bend the rules or focus only on short-term results, the norms of the group may be similar.

If those strategies do not work or if still more change is desired, then recommend:

- Changing the competency profile of the group by changing its membership
- Increasing or decreasing the amount of external status afforded certain members by recognizing only those people whose behavior and accom-

plishments support the organization's goals and withholding recognition from those whose behavior and accomplishments do not

- Replacing group members with people whose beliefs are more like those of the organization (or at least are not in conflict with them)

The last thing you want to do is attack the norms of the group directly because this is usually the least effective course of action.

FIELD NOTES: NEW TECHNOLOGY
AND LOWER PERFORMANCE

Deborah's company asked her to find out why the average call handling time at one of the customer call centers was up. She started out by asking what had changed and found that the call center had put new terminals in about a fourth of its workstations. The terminals ran on a new software and required different keystrokes. The new software gave the customer service rep (CSR) more information about callers, such as credit history and what equipment they owned. This extra information enabled the CSR to extend credit, arrange payment plans that were more or less favorable to the customer, and decide if the customer could receive a different level of service. In the past, only the most senior CSRs were allowed to do these things.

Deborah learned the new terminals were assigned on a lottery basis and were placed in the larger, more attractive workstations. In the past, CSRs had been assigned stations based on seniority. Deborah also learned that the more senior CSRs used to take their breaks together. Now the CSRs' breaks were scheduled by a shift coordinator, who tended to give the high performers the preferred break times. As a result, the senior CSRs, whether they were assigned to the new terminals or not, increased their average call handling times so they could take their breaks together.

Deborah concluded that the new terminals and how they were assigned had disrupted the norms of the group. The lottery violated how the group historically afforded status to its members (seniority). The terminals had also introduced a new technology that allowed people who previously were of lower status greater autonomy in their work. Deborah met with the center managers to confirm what they wanted to change about the group's behavior. She recommended that breaks be assigned on seniority, as in the past. She also suggested a plan that would allow everyone to work on the new terminals over the next six months. After that, the new terminals would be assigned based on a combination of seniority and performance.

Mike was asked to coach Tim on how to get his U.S. product managers to reduce their travel and entertainment expenses. Tim had sent out a memo and made an announcement at a staff meeting about six months ago that some expenses were getting out of hand. No names were mentioned, and no one knew how his or her expenses compared to everyone else. No one had ever been held accountable for expenses. The only person who knew what each person's expenses were was Tim. Mike suggested that Tim publish everyone's expense record, with the names included, every month on a single spreadsheet ranked from the highest to the lowest so people could see where they stood. He suggested the spreadsheet break out everyone's expenses so it became public how the money was being used. He also instructed Tim to not mention the subject of expenses for the next six months. Within six months, the people whose expenses were way above the group's average dropped. The overall average of the group went down, and the variance was narrower.

EXPERIENCES FROM THE FIELD: ABOUT BEING DIFFERENT

Whether you are an independent, external consultant or an internal consultant, your success will be influenced by the resources your clients are willing to contribute to supporting your development and processes. Both external and internal consultants are limited by clients' ability and willingness to dedicate time, people, technology, and space to identifying barriers to performance and developing solutions. External and internal consultants are also influenced by the attitudes of their peers and colleagues. Sometimes when you want to step out of the crowd, take on a new responsibility, or try innovative approaches to your work, you don't get the support you are looking for.

One of the more difficult lessons I learned was that my friends all supported my becoming an independent consultant until I did it. It was as if having the courage to actualize a dream was wrong. The same thing can happen with people who want to be internal consultants. Being a trainer or a facilitator is safe. You work hard, and people know what you do. Being a performance consultant is not safe. You will question business practices, will work to get the facts, and recommend actions that will produce results. I've learned that I have to be my own conscience and my own steward.

FIELD TECHNIQUES: LOOKING AT YOUR OWN ENVIRONMENT AND SOCIAL SYSTEMS

Whether you are an internal or an external consultant, step back and begin to study your work environment:

- What is the larger organization (your employer, your department, or your clients) willing to invest in your development? Will it acknowledge that part of the package in hiring a consultant is to learn about consultants and how they operate?

- What resources are available to you?

- Identify the group you are more closely affiliated with. Who is in it? What are its norms? How will it see your roles of developing processes, setting standards for yourself, AND measuring your own performance?

- Go back to the recipe for building credibility and influence. Will the group support your efforts to develop those skills?

FIELD NOTES: DESCRIBING THE JOB OF A PERFORMANCE CONSULTANT

When Deborah and her team changed their mission, expanded their services to include performance consulting, and learned how to market these new services, work seemed exciting. It wasn't until a few months passed that some of Deborah's staff realized that the job had changed. Some still tried to hold on to old behaviors and activities. The result was seventy-hour work weeks. Others tried to let go of the old behaviors and activities so they could do the new things. But they too found the change difficult. Deborah's staff had been long-term employees who had grown up in the business and had been promoted because they were conscientious and hard working. They gravitated to training because they liked people and knew the content. In the past, they operated very independently, interacting with the instructors only at the call centers. Now they were being asked to interact with the call center managers. They were put on cross-functional teams to design new technology, being asked to track their time, and required to document their processes. It all felt very uncomfortable and even a little off-putting. They had liked operating independently, delivering training and coaching instructors. Now they were in meetings, managing budgets, and tracking expenses.

Deborah decided to develop a new job description for the position. She wanted her staff to apply for their own jobs. Her goal was to help them decide for themselves if this was the job they wanted. If they didn't, she was prepared to help them find other positions in the company. Figure 6.5 is the job description she came up with. You will notice it combines some of the attributes of the operational definition with the contextual job description.

Figure 6.5. Deborah's Job Description

Title: Performance Consultant

Primary customers: Call center managers, instructors, instructional designers and independent contractors, electronic support systems team, methods department, human resources, finance

Purpose: Consultants are responsible for assessing the training and performance needs of their centers, ensuring that qualified resources are available to meet those needs, coaching center management, and providing data so the division's products, people, and initiatives can be measured. They may deliver soft skill training courses. They may supervise clerical staff and coordinate instructor schedules companywide.

continued

Figure 6.5. Deborah's Job Description, *cont'd.*

Why: So centers get the training and services they need and the division's products and services support improved performance and achieve a positive return on investment.

How: Consultants consult with call center managers, staff in the methods department, human resources, finance, information systems, and the team assigned to develop an electronic support system. They participate on major teams, serve as experts in performance improvement, provide data to financial analysts, and negotiate for resources. They may hire contract services.

Structure: They report to the director of performance improvement. They may supervise instructional designers, media developers, and contract personnel. They are members of cross-functional teams.

Givens:

- Performance consultants must acknowledge inherited relationships with call center management.
- Real differences exist between call center managers and their vice presidents in terms of goals, values, and business practices.
- Call center managers get mixed and contradictory messages from senior management.
- Consultants report to people at remote locations, so there is little opportunity for direct interaction with other consultants.
- Procedures for handling exceptional circumstances are missing or unclear.
- Goals of other home office departments are mixed and contradictory.
- No process exists to keep up-to-date.
- Procedures for deploying new initiatives are missing or unclear.
- Multiple initiatives are always underway, and those initiatives compete for resources.

Knowledge: Performance consultants need to know and understand:

- The goals of the division
- The goals and operating style of the other home office departments
- The goals of the centers, the local geography, business protocols, market, and so on
- Instructional design principles and what learning outcomes are
- How people learn; principles of knowledge transfer
- What contributes to or interferes with optimum performance
- Each customer's business drivers and current initiatives
- How to use or apply standardization appropriately
- How to get required resources
- How to manage resources within budget
- How to measure performance and return on investment

Skills: Consultants must be skilled in:

- Managing staff and other resources
- Establishing credible relationships with other home office personnel

**Figure 6.5. Deborah's
Job Description,** *cont'd.*

- Facilitating and coaching
- Confronting and negotiating
- Controlling group dynamics
- Conducting feasibility studies
- Assessing and evaluating individuals, processes, and programs
- Measuring results
- Estimating costs
- Communicating vision with clarity and conviction
- Transferring knowledge
- Working within budget

Typical tasks:

- Assessing developmental needs and performance requirements of centers
- Establishing working relationships with other home office personnel
- Assessing the performance of the division's initiatives
- Coordinating the design, development, and delivery of training
- Assessing home office needs
- Maintaining communication with contract services
- Preparing personal development plans
- Maintaining skills and knowledge
- Participating on cross-functional teams and working on special initiatives

Outputs or deliverables: Productivity measures include:

- Number of services delivered
- Number of new courses developed
- Number of modifications to current courses
- Number of cross-functional teams supported
- Number of technical innovations adopted

Outcomes: Performance and return on investment measures include:

- The time it takes for call center staff and instructors to achieve proficiency
- Positive return on investment on the division's initiatives
- Higher retention and compliance by field personnel
- The division's ability to deliver quality products and services
- The confidence level of call center managers and other home office directors

For the first time, Deborah's staff would be held accountable for and measured against outputs and outcomes. The job description also made it clear that some of them would have to return to school to learn more about technology, the transfer of learning, and organizational behavior. They would also have to learn more about business economics and project management. Some of her staff elected to seek other positions in the company.

SUMMARY

Training focuses its efforts on helping individuals develop the skills and knowledge they need to do the job. But it is important to remember that the work environment significantly shapes performance. If the bank described at the beginning of this chapter had better understood how its culture and norms suppressed critical dialogue, it might have avoided public embarrassment and questionable financial practices.

Organizations are complex systems. They require us to work in partnership and draw on one another's expertise and support. We also have to be willing to challenge our own beliefs about the world and recognize that they can limit our ability to see new possibilities and approaches.

**WHERE TO
LEARN MORE**

Boyatzis, R. *The Competent Manager: A Model for Effective Performance.* Hoboken, N.J.: Wiley, 1982. Chapters One and Two explain the variables that contribute to competent performance.

To learn more about social systems, consult the writings of Alfred Adler, Edward Lawler, Leonard Nadler, and Chris Argyris. Pay attention to the seminal research they reference for a better understanding of how the study of social systems came about and the ideas it has contributed to performance consulting.

Chapter 7

Needs Assessment and Cause Analysis

Many organizations that experience poor results either resort to blaming people or investing in a single, sometimes simplistic, solution. They do not always take the time to find out what, if anything, has changed in the work environment, the job, or the people in question. It's almost as if they think that blaming people and spending money will solve of their problems.

FIELD NOTES: SOLVING THE WRONG PROBLEM

Lisa, an independent consultant, was hired by a large community bank to develop a training program for its managers. The bank president told her he was disappointed that some of his top performers were no longer meeting his expectations. During Lisa's first meeting with the management team and the president, one of the managers challenged the bank's lending policies. The manager commented that the bank was founded on the idea of developmental banking (lending money to revitalize inner cities) but that its current loans were no different from those made by traditional banks. Another manager wanted to know why the bank was expanding internationally. The bank's mission was about helping community business expand, he said, not expanding itself.

Later, Lisa attended a meeting with twenty-five managers and their direct reports, which included professional and clerical staff. She wanted to use this opportunity to get a better understanding of the role of managers in the bank. Lisa asked the professional staff to whom they reported—that is, the person they went to for assignments, to get approval for a day off, and for guidance on how to handle exceptions (for example, in loans and check cashing). She asked a similar question of the clerical staff. Much to Lisa's surprise, everyone gave her the same answer: they all went directly to the executive vice president of the bank. No one mentioned his or her supervisor. It seemed as though everyone in the bank reported to the same person for everything. Lisa began to wonder how the training would help improve the performance of the managers as they apparently didn't do any managing, at least of people.

This situation illustrates why consultants, both internal and external, need a way to discover and verify the performance expectations and determine what is preventing employees from meeting them. Without the facts, you are faced with accepting any solution. It is easier to improve or sustain high performance when you have a clear picture of what is expected and what the barriers to performance are.

A PROCESS FOR IDENTIFYING NEEDS

A needs assessment is the first phase of the front-end analysis process. The needs assessment identifies the need to improve performance and discovers opportunities for improvement. The results are used to guide decisions about what to focus on. The second phase, usually the cause analysis, identifies what is preventing performance. The results are suggested interventions—for example, testing or assessing performance, developing training, or redesigning jobs. The next phase is the job task analysis that identifies the activities people should engage in, the resources they should have and use, and the knowledge and skills they should have to perform a task or job effectively (see Chapter 10). The results are used to design jobs, training, and assessments.

At a minimum, the overall process should distinguish environmental factors from people factors. Most assessments are done because of a performance problem, and in these situations, the client typically starts with a premise—for example:

- People in the job lack the required skills or knowledge.
- Processes are poorly designed.
- Expectations are unclear or conflicting.
- The wrong behaviors are being rewarded.

The goal is to validate if the premise is true.

Sometimes needs assessments are done in anticipation of a change, such as rolling out a newly designed work process, replacing technology, or adding a product line. In these situations, the client starts with the premise that people lack the ability to support the change. In both of these situations, the premises might be right, partially right, or wrong. What I've learned is that when you limit the focus of your investigation to a preconceived premise, you reduce the chances of uncovering critical variables that are causing the problem.

What you need is a process that will help you determine which performance problems are worthy of attention and what is really obstructing performance. The process should remind you to consider the organization's goals, the work environment, the way the job is designed, and people's ability to do the job. It should help you find out what is needed to support a major change. At the same time, it is not always feasible to consider every variable. Therefore, the ideal process is one you can expand or contract, depending on the evidence you have and the severity of the consequences if you are wrong. I use two tools for this process:

- *The scorecard.* This tool helps me determine what is worthy of examination and what will be used to measure success or improvement.
- *The hierarchy.* This tool helps me discover what is currently obstructing performance and what might obstruct it in the future.

FIELD TOOLS: THE SCORECARD

The scorecard is a powerful tool. I use it to facilitate discussions with my clients about what is important to them, what gets their attention, and what they use as evidence that things are bad, good, or improving. The scorecard I'm referring to is not the same as the balanced scorecard, which refers to the importance of focusing on more than one initiative. Organizations usually combine initiatives like customer satisfaction, financial return, market share, process improvement, people development, and product excellence. They have learned that by focusing on only one initiative, they limit their ability to compete in the future. When I introduce the scorecard, I explain that I use it to help me in these ways:

- Identify the costs of poor performance
- Quickly identify performance gaps that need further investigation
- Identify the criteria and metrics for measuring the gap and future improvement
- Link programs like training to the needs of the organization

Two forms of the scorecard are presented here: the job aid, which has examples (see Figure 7.1), and the worksheet, which is a blank and is for you and your client to fill in (see Figure 7.2). Which one you use depends on your situation.

The job aid version of the scorecard helps me break the ice with clients. I also use it when a client wants to implement a major program that requires a big investment, such as a certification program or a blended learning curriculum. It helps clients begin to understand why they need to build a business case for their program and how to do so. The job aid has examples of common organizational initiatives, how companies measure the performance of such initiatives, different performance gap sizes, how to identify the cause of the

Objective: To model how initiatives can be linked to business measures. This job aid will help you communicate what information does or does not exist, what the organization does or does not track, and where a deeper analysis might add value. You can also use it to facilitate discussions about evidence—what it is and how to get it.

1. Key initiatives, strategies, or objectives: What the client pays attention to and values	2. Measures: What the client tracks to measure performance	3. Standards or goals versus actual performance: What the client wants versus what is real; the gap	4. Assessment: How to get the data to identify the cause of the gap in performance	5. Measured results: What has to change for the intervention to be a success and worth it
Customer satisfaction, employee satisfaction	Ratings (five-point scale), number of complaints and grievances	Goal: 4.2; actual: 3.7	Survey data, focus groups, interviews	Higher ratings, fewer complaints
Market share	Percentage compared to potential	Gap over competition	Market research	Increased share
People performance: time, quantity, frequency, rework and waste	Process time, cycle time, number of calls or visits per time period	Non-value-added less than *x* percent, ratio of *x* percent, number per time period, waste of less than *x* percent or *x* dollars	Time sheets, interviews, industry indexes, worksheets, observations	Improved performance of products, people, and processes; less waste
Financial performance: Cost, cost benefit, sales revenue, cash flow	Fixed to variable costs, return on investment, return on assets, return on capital employed, contribution margin, percentage of growth	Cents or dollars per unit, sales call, or proposal; cost of sales less than *x* dollars or *x* percent; incremental sales of *x* percent; growth at *x* percent	Daily reports, actual dollars versus budgeted dollars, sales analysis	Improved ratios, lower costs, higher margins, higher revenues, increased cash flow
Product performance: accuracy, consistency, compliance	Variance, percentage yield, unscheduled service, formal filings	Zero defects, less than *x* percent variance, ratio of unscheduled to scheduled service	Statistical process control data, quality control reports, complaint calls and citations	Less variance, higher yields, better ratios, fewer reportables

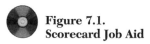

Figure 7.1.
Scorecard Job Aid

performance gaps, and the evidence of improvement organizations accept. In using the job aid with clients, I ask which examples are or are not relevant to them and how they would change the scorecard to make it work for them; their answers give me a much better understanding of what is important to them. The worksheet version is the same, but you fill in the information relevant to your situation. Here is an explanation of what goes in each column:

- *Column 1: Key initiatives.* These are frequently stated as objectives or strategies, like "increase market share," "reduce turnover," "reduce costs," and

Objective: To serve as a worksheet to capture what is important to your client's organization. The worksheet can be used to facilitate discussions about what you and your client expect of each other.

1. Key initiatives, strategies, or objectives: What the client pays attention to or values	2. Measures: What the client tracks to measure performance	3. Standards or goals versus actual performance: What the client wants versus what is real; the gap	4. Assessment: How to get data that will identify the cause of the performance gap	5. Measured results: What has to change for the intervention to be a success and be worth it

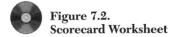

Figure 7.2.
Scorecard Worksheet

"increase sales." They are what the organization (whether it is a major business unit, a department, a small work unit, or a task force) pays attention to.

- *Column 2: Measures.* These are the data the organization tracks and takes as evidence that what it is doing to support the initiative is achieving the goal or purpose. Sometimes these measures are well documented and understood; other times they are chosen intuitively by management. However they've been selected, you need to find out what they are.

- *Column 3: Standards or goals versus actual performance.* This refers to the performance gap: the difference between where the organization is today and where it wants to be. Some organizations have sophisticated systems for tracking their performance against goals. Others do not. You need to know if your client has the capability to measure performance and, if it does, how its performance stacks up to its goal. If the organization does not have systems in place to measure performance, then it is making decisions based on incomplete data—and you need to know this too.

- *Column 4: Assessment.* This is how the organization plans to get data that will identify the cause of the gap and measure its extent. Use this column to identify what information is already being captured, where and by whom it is being captured, what other information would be helpful, and how to get it. What you learn as a result of analyzing the data will help you identify the appropriate interventions.

- *Column 5: Measured results.* This column is used both before and after an intervention is implemented. Use it to specify what has to change for the client to consider the intervention a success and worth the cost. This is where you begin the discussion about how much benefit the client must gain to offset the cost of taking corrective action. After an intervention has been implemented, you can go back and put in what actually changed, how much it changed, and how much it cost.

Sometimes the information you need for the scorecard job aid will not be available. The scorecard brings to light what the organization really knows and where it has to do a better job of defining its expectations, its current performance, and its deficiencies.

FIELD TECHNIQUES: FOCUSING YOUR INVESTIGATION

Depending on your relationship with your client and what you already know about the client, you may or may not want to use the job aid version of the scorecard. I always keep a copy of the job aid in my briefcase, however, should a client need help coming up with ideas about what to focus on or how to measure performance. Throughout the process, you will be working in partnership with your client. At one moment, you might participate by contributing ideas and suggestions; at other moments, you might facilitate discussion among members of your client's group. Whatever role you play, keep your clients' attention focused on identifying where performance problems exist, which ones they need to address, where to get better data, and how to measure success. Here are some guidelines on how to proceed:

1. Meet with your client. If appropriate, show the scorecard job aid to your client and discuss a few of the examples.

2. Explain that the scorecard can be used to identify opportunities for improvement or to target areas with the bigger performance gaps for a needs assessment.

3. If you are unsure what is important to your client, ask about the client's major initiatives, objectives, or strategies. Record the answers on the worksheet version of the scorecard.

4. Ask how the client measures those objectives now. Ask what kinds of data the client uses to measure performance.

5. To identify which performance gaps to work on, explain that you want to confirm:

   • Where there are gaps in performance

   • What costs are associated with those gaps

   • Which gaps are worth examining to find out the cause

   • How much an intervention would have to reduce the gap to be considered a success or worth the cost

6. Help the client identify those gaps for which a more thorough analysis would be beneficial.

7. If the client cannot provide all of the information or is unsure about what gets measured, why it gets measured, or how big a particular performance gap is, help the client decide how and where to get the missing information.

8. Once you have the missing information, return to the scorecard and decide with your client which interventions are more likely to reduce or eliminate the performance deficiency.

9. Work with the client to pinpoint which aspects of performance the interventions will have a positive impact on and what data the client will use to measure improvement.

10. With your client, estimate how much change the intervention will produce and if it will be enough to outweigh what you estimate its costs will be.

FIELD NOTES: USING THE SCORECARD
TO IDENTIFY MEASURES OF PERFORMANCE

Deborah's company asked her to help the vice president of sales improve sales performance at the company's call centers. The president of the company had recently announced that all call centers would soon be evaluated on sales performance, a significant shift from the past, when call centers were evaluated only on average call-handling time.

Deborah began her meeting with the vice president of sales by asking how sales were currently measured, what types of sales were going to be tracked, and to what degree the centers were already meeting their sales goals. During their meeting, she used the scorecard job aid to illustrate the types of things other organizations focus on when they want to improve sales performance. She believed that stressing sales volume alone would not lead to optimum sales performance and wanted the vice president to consider how to reduce the cost of sales.

As a result of their conversation, Deborah identified what her department could do to support overall sales performance, which was to rapidly improve the CSRs' product knowledge and selling skills, develop systems to improve order accuracy, and provide guidelines to qualify customers' creditworthiness. Errors in orders increased costs because someone had to spend time correcting the order. Selling unnecessary products to customers with poor credit also potentially increased costs because such customers were more likely to require special payment plans.

Russ, the HRD manager at a medical supply manufacturer, was asked to lead a team charged with making a new product line successful. One of the company's divisions had announced that its goal was to be the world leader in diagnostic equipment. The company currently had 40 percent of the market worldwide. One strategy for increasing market share was to promote a new line of equipment the company had acquired from another manufacturer. Russ suggested that the team develop a scorecard to make sure they didn't overlook any factors that could significantly jeopardize the product's success. He handed out the scorecard job aid to illustrate what theirs might look like once they had completed it. He talked about the types of initiatives other companies focus on. The team was able agree on the following initiatives:

- *Improving product performance.* The number of service calls due to product failures was higher than the team had originally expected. They decided that they could track service calls, determine the costs of these calls, and measure improvement in equipment performance by the number of service calls received in the future.

- *Improving customer satisfaction.* Survey data indicated that customers had doubts about the capability of the company's field technicians. The team decided to continue to use surveys to measure if customer satisfaction improved.

- *Improving field technician performance.* The company's field technicians reported they felt unprepared to support this new product line. In particular, they felt they were inadequately trained in diagnosing equipment failures. The team decided to survey the technicians periodically to see if the training and performance aids had increased the technicians' confidence.

Now the team could focus on finding out what caused equipment failures and what the technicians needed in terms of skills, knowledge, and performance aids to increase their ability to service the new line of equipment.

PERFORMANCE CRITERIA FOR THE NEEDS ASSESSMENT PROCESS

Once you know what to focus on, you can begin the process of finding out why performance is not at the level the organization wants. At national conferences, I hear a lot about how training was the most expensive, and sometimes the least effective, solution to performance problems. With this in mind, I went about developing a process for discovering and validating what supports performance in an organization and what interferes with it. I began by setting some criteria for my process:

1. It must be based on the idea that the work environment, the design of the job, and the capability of the people involved all contribute to performance. Therefore, it must help me and my clients distinguish among these elements.

2. It must not be biased in favor of a particular solution. If the problem is a lack of skills and knowledge, I want to know that, but if it is something else, I want to know that too.

3. It must be designed to help me get facts and corroborating evidence. Hearsay and folklore are stories people tell to rationalize their behavior. They are not facts. One source of information is not enough.

4. It must help me position myself as an expert in assessment and measurement. It should help me contribute expertise as appropriate, yet facilitate the client's retaining ownership of the problem and the solution.

5. It must work for organizational units of all sizes. I wanted a process I could apply to:
    - Work groups assigned to specific jobs (such as the CSRs Deborah has to support)
    - Teams working on key initiatives, projects, and programs (such as Russ's team assigned to improve equipment performance)
    - Departments (such as Mike's, Kelly's, and Deborah's departments, which all wanted to move toward performance consulting)
    - Functions or larger divisions in the organization (such as the call centers where Deborah had to improve sales performance)

6. It must provide me with a way to organize my approach to identifying the major causes of performance problems.

FIELD TOOLS: THE HIERARCHY

The result was the hierarchy (see Figure 7.3). I call it that because problems at one level cannot be fixed by interventions aimed at a lower level. For example, investing in training and facilities will reap fewer benefits if management is not in agreement on where the organization is going or if processes are

Congruency and Clarity:

1. Vision and mission

2. Goals and objectives

3. Rewards and consequences

Efficiency:

4. Organizational and job structures

5. Work processes, procedures, and practices

6. Documentation and standards

7. Job aids, signage, and labels

Resiliency and Capability:

8. Physical facilities and space

9. Training and development

10. Resource capacity and sufficiency

Figure 7.3.
The Hierarchy

inefficient. I use the hierarchy to identify what is causing poor performance (lack of congruency, inefficiencies, or lack of investment in environmental, job, or people resources) and confirm that people are prepared to support a change.

The Need for Skepticism

To use the hierarchy successfully, you have to be skeptical. You cannot believe just a single source of information; you must look for corroborating evidence. Wherever possible, try to obtain direct evidence—that is, see it, read it, or hear it firsthand. Don't accept hearsay or folklore as proof. Hearsay and folklore do not provide credible evidence of what customers expect, how work gets done, or what adds unnecessary costs. Look for ways to get other evidence that supports or refutes your original source.

The hierarchy is in three sections. The elements in the first section are the most important because there must be congruency and clarity before you can fully benefit from addressing the other issues. Note that depending on what you know about the situation you are addressing, your investigation may be limited to one or more of the three areas (that is congruency, efficiency, or resiliency).

Congruency and Clarity

Considering the first three elements in the hierarchy will help you identify inconsistencies between how the organization has defined itself and its actions. Sometimes what organizations say they are about (their vision and mission), what they focus on (their goals and objectives), and what they do (the behaviors they reward) are not in alignment. They may even be at odds with each other. Investigating these issues will help you determine whether people are clear and in agreement on what they are doing and why. When people are unclear about their roles or what is expected of them or when the company's leaders send mixed signals, resources are wasted and performance suffers.

Efficiency

Investigating the next four elements will help you identify operating inefficiencies, waste, and unnecessary cost. How an organization is structured can result in redundant work and waste. For example, processes that appear efficient in isolation may actually consume unnecessary or overly costly resources because the information required to do the work is incomplete or difficult to access.

Resiliency and Capability

Considering the last three elements will help you determine whether the organization is making appropriate investments in its physical and human resources.

FIELD TOOLS: THE HIERARCHY JOB AID

The hierarchy, like the scorecard, is both a job aid and a worksheet (Figure 7.4 is the job aid and Figure 7.5 the worksheet). As a job aid, it helps me remember all the variables I want to look at. I use the hierarchy in the same way as I use the scorecard: to work with my clients in designing needs assessment studies, drive conversations about what is really known and what is hearsay or folklore, and determine how to get the information we need. Column 1 has sample questions for each of the ten elements in the hierarchy. Column 2 has examples of operating hypotheses. Column 3 lists the types of data you might want to get, and Column 4 suggests ways to get the data.

FIELD TECHNIQUES: GETTING EVIDENCE OF CONGRUENCY

The first three elements in the hierarchy are about congruency and clarity. Your goal should be to find corroborating evidence that confirms that where people say they are going, what they are focusing their energy on, and what they get rewarded for are aligned and not in conflict.

Vision and Mission

Examine vision and mission first because you want to verify there is agreement on what each program, team, or initiative is supposed to accomplish. The vision reveals where people want to go; the mission says what people are about or what business they are in. *Fulfilling the mission should bring people closer to their vision.* The organization's guiding principles should also move the organization closer to its vision. Without a vision, an organization cannot move forward; it will have no basis for building a long-range plan or road map to the future. Confirm that the organization's guiding principles are in alignment with the stated purpose and vision of the program, team, or initiative. Again, be skeptical; your hypothesis or operating assumption should be that the vision and mission (or the people) are *not* in agreement. Then look for evidence that people in the organization have a vision, know what the mission is, and share the same understanding of the vision and mission as their leadership. Seek to prove your hypothesis is incorrect. It is not enough to ask people if they have a vision statement or team charter; instead, ask each person in a group separately to tell you what it is and what they think it means. You can then compare their answers with what the organization says about itself. Find out if the organization has devoted adequate resources to programs that directly support the mission.

1. Hierarchy Model and Questions	2. Hypotheses: What to Confirm	3. Data to Collect	4. How to Get Data
Congruency and Clarity:			
1. *Vision and mission* A. Are there vision and mission statements? B. Does the mission reflect current requirements, desires, and the environment in which the organization operates? C. Is there a consensus on what the vision and mission are? D. Does the mission support the vision? E. Does the long-range plan support the vision and mission? F. Is there agreement on the vision and mission?	• What is the mission? • Is there consensus on the mission among all of the work groups? • Who are the customers? • How is the mission communicated? • Is there a long-range plan? • Does the company realize it needs to change?	• Mission statement • What people say the mission is • What people say the mission means to them • What customers need and how the business responds	• Written mission statement • Written communications to staff • Customer satisfaction surveys • Market research • Stratified random survey of employees • Interviews
2. *Goals and objectives* A. Are the goals congruent with the mission? B. Are there clear expectations and business plans for each division, department, and other units that include revenue and cost in both absolute numbers and trends? C. Do the goals reflect the resources and operating specifics required to progress as a whole? D. Do they exist for each operating unit? E. Do people know what they are? F. Are they followed? G. Is there congruence between those who set objectives, plans, and budgets and those who are accountable?	• Do the goals and objectives of each department support the mission? • Do they agree with each other?	• Department goals and objectives • What people say their objectives are • How well resources match objectives	• Nominal groups • Business plans • Managers' objectives
3. *Rewards and consequences* A. What are the leader's values? B. Are those values known and shared? C. What is the organization's culture, and what specific behaviors does it support? D. Are those behaviors rewarded? E. What are the rites and rituals? F. Do conditions support what the organization says it values, such as commitment, innovation, compliance, teamwork, individualism, or entrepreneurship?	• What's important? • How are the values prioritized? • Are the values and rewards congruent with each other and with the company's mission, goals, and objectives?	• What does success look like? • What does the company measure? • What is a "good person" like? • What is rewarded? • How are people promoted?	• Values statements • Customer satisfaction surveys • Sociograms • Reward and recognition programs: documentation, awards, recipients

Figure 7.4. The Hierarchy Job Aid

1. Hierarchy Model and Questions	2. Hypotheses: What to Confirm	3. Data to Collect	4. How to Get Data
G. Do the company's policies support the values, mission, and vision? H. Are there consequences for non-performance or violation of policy? I. Are those consequences known? J. Are the consequences acted on?	• What are the consequences of nonperformance?	• Who are the heroes?	• Focus groups
Efficiency			
4. *Organizational and job structures* A. Are jobs clearly defined? B. Are jobs given needed responsibility? C. Are positions, responsibilities, and reporting effective and efficient? D. Does structure aid communication, decision making, and accountability? E. Are tasks grouped efficiently? F. Is the span of control effective? G. Is each unit of command appropriate?	• What is the formal organizational structure? • What are the formal job descriptions and responsibilities? • What are people's concepts of the organizational structure and their own jobs? • Who has what authority to make what decisions? • Does the organizational structure match the market? The mission?	• Organizational charts • Job descriptions • People's perceptions of the organization and their own job • Decision referral up the chain • Location map and location decision-making process	• Job descriptions • Focus groups • Asking people to draw the organization, define their job responsibilities, describe who can make what decisions • By listening in on phone calls to see how customer problems are resolved • Site selection criteria and processes
5. *Work processes, procedures, and practices* A. Could tasks or processes be automated? B. Are processes well designed? C. Are duties assigned in ways that are effective and efficient? D. Do procedures exist, and are they followed consistently? E. Are resources used wisely? F. Do management practices support development, innovation, and commitment? G. Do people get feedback and information when they need it? H. Does nonperformance have consequences? I. Are those consequences carried out?	• What are the formal processes and procedures for getting work done and handling customer complaints? • How is the work actually done? • What information is available at what points in the work process? • What are the consequences for not following the formal process? • How do customers react to the processes and procedures?	• Formal processes and procedures • Actual processes and procedures • Information flow • Feedback, discipline, and reward actions • Customer praise and complaints	• Policies and procedures handbook • Observations of performers in all job functions • "Silent shopping" • Forms • Customer complaint letters and log

Figure 7.4. The Hierarchy Job Aid, *cont'd.*

1. Hierarchy Model and Questions	2. Hypotheses: What to Confirm	3. Data to Collect	4. How to Get Data

6. *Documentation and standards*
  A. Are procedures and practices documented?
  B. Are they accessible and usable?
  C. Do they reflect desired practice?
  D. Are there standards?
  E. Does standardization support innovation, compliance, and commitment?
	• Do the documents and standards match the work processes and procedures?
	• Do the same standards work for each location?
	• Are the standards used?
	• Can the standards be changed?
		• Documents from multiple locations
		• Employee use of standards documents
			• Documents
			• Observation
			• "Silent shopping"
			• Interviews

7. *Job aids, signage, and labels*
  A. Do job aids, signs, and labels exist?
  B. Are they used?
  C. Is intelligent, exemplary performance captured in a usable form?
  D. Do job aids, signs, and labeling support the desired and required performance?
	• Are there job aids?
	• Are they used?
	• Are there any that are needed that are not there?
		• Job aids from multiple locations
		• Employee use of job aids
			• Job aids
			• Observation
			• "Silent shopping"
			• Interviews

Resiliency and Capability:			

8. *Physical facilities and space*
  A. Is space adequate and used well?
  B. Do the space and layout facilitate work flow?
  C. Do the space and layout aid communication?
  D. Do the technology and systems support the required work processes?
  E. Are work conditions safe?
  F. Do environmental conditions (temperature, light, noise) support the required work processes?
  G. Do environmental conditions support health?
	• How does the computer system support desired processes and procedures?	• Computer system capabilities and use
		• Space use per employee
		• Facilities and space use studies
		• Safety records
		• Summary of health records and claims
			• Documentation
			• Observation
			• Interviews

9. *Training and development*
  A. Are skills maintained?
  B. Are skills developed?
  C. Are skills and knowledge adequate for required and desired processes?
  D. Are innovation and self-empowerment supported?
	• What skills do people in each job have on hiring, get from initial training, get from coaching and feedback, get from follow-up or advanced training?	• Training curriculum and courses for all employees
		• Employee evaluation reports and development plans
			• Documents

Figure 7.4. The Hierarchy Job Aid, *cont'd.*

1. Hierarchy Model and Questions	2. Hypotheses: What to Confirm	3. Data to Collect	4. How to Get Data
E. What methods are used for development (for example, coaching, cross-training), and do those methods support the desired and required performance?	• Do skills match job descriptions and work processes?		
10. *Resource capacity and sufficiency* 　A. Do people have the emotional, physical, intellectual, and economic capacity to achieve the desired and required performance? 　B. Are there support systems and processes in place to offset, reduce, or remove deficiencies in capacity? 　C. Are support systems sufficient for the desired and required performance? 　D. Do values conflict with requirements of the job or the desired outcomes?	• Whether they've done capacity studies • How turnover, absenteeism, and injuries compare to industry standards	• Workers' compensation claims • Absenteeism • Turnover • Employee complaints	• Exit interviews • Insurance records • Turnover, absenteeism records

Figure 7.4. The Hierarchy Job Aid, *cont'd.*

Goals and Objectives

Next, confirm that the goals and objectives employees are working toward support the vision and are not in conflict with the stated mission. Your hypothesis should be that they are *not* in harmony and are probably in conflict. Look for evidence to prove yourself wrong. For example, it is not unusual for short-term objectives to be so demanding that no resources are left to work on the longer-range goals. Examining the congruence between goals and objectives is similar to confirming congruence between vision and mission. Ask people what their goals and objectives are, how these goals and objectives relate to the company's vision or mission, and what they are currently working on. Then compare the answers. Another hypothesis is that the goals most closely aligned with the vision and mission are not funded or have very limited funding. Then find out what programs are actually budgeted and which ones directly support the goals and objectives.

Values, Incentives, Rewards, and Policies

The next step is to look for evidence that the accomplishments and behaviors that get rewarded are what people have been told will be rewarded and that they support the stated goals and objectives. Again, your hypothesis should be

1. Hierarchy Model and Questions	2. Hypotheses: What to Confirm	3. Data to Collect	4. How to Get Data
Congruency and Clarity			
1. *Vision and mission*			
2. *Goals and objectives*			
3. *Rewards and consequences*			
Efficiency			
4. *Organizational and job structures*			
5. *Work process, procedures, and practices*			

Figure 7.5.
The Hierarchy Worksheet

1. Hierarchy Model and Questions	2. Hypotheses: What to Confirm	3. Data to Collect	4. How to Get Data
6. *Documentation and standards*			
7. *Job aids, signage, and labels*			
Resiliency and Capability			
8. *Physical facilities and space*			
9. *Training and development*			
10. *Resource capacity and sufficiency*			

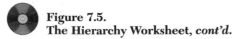

Figure 7.5.
The Hierarchy Worksheet, *cont'd.*

that what actually gets celebrated and recognized does *not* support the goals and objectives. Find out what the criteria are for merit increases, how people are tapped for coveted assignments, who has access to the leaders, and who gets mentioned in the company newsletter. These may in fact be the people whose results and behaviors conflict with the goals and guiding principles of the organization: people whose behaviors are just the opposite of what the organization says it wants. Find out when awards are announced, who won them in the last round, and what the criteria were for winning. You want to confirm that the criteria used were consistent with what the organization professes it values and its goals. Check who has been featured in the company newsletter. Investigate whether the company's HR policies support what the organization says it values, where it says it is going, and how it says it is going to get there. Look for congruency between the first three elements in the hierarchy.

FIELD NOTES: AGREEING ON GOALS

The call centers are Deborah's main customers. She and her department are responsible for helping call center managers get what they need to be successful. Deborah was unclear about how the call centers' performance would be evaluated in the coming year. She used the hierarchy to guide her in finding out if senior managers had clearly stated their goals for the centers and if they agreed on those goals. Her hypothesis was that they were not in agreement and were probably not even clear in what they expected. She decided to interview each vice president separately. She thought this would allow them to speak more freely, and it would give her an opportunity to compare their responses and check her hypothesis.

She met with the vice president of sales first. In answer to her question about what his goals were for the call centers in the coming year, he replied, "The big change is that every call center manager will have full profit-and-loss accountability in the coming year, and they will be evaluated in terms of sales. My plan is to have more contests to reward managers who achieve their sales goals." He also mentioned that two call center managers had been promoted, and he wanted more call center managers like them.

In her effort to get corroborating evidence that senior management was in agreement with these goals, she asked the vice president of operations what he understood the call centers' goals would be in the coming year and what criteria the company had used in promoting the two managers. He answered, "I'm not sure why they were promoted. The turnover rate at one of their centers was at least 30 percent. One goal is to implement an electronic support system for customer service representatives in every center. Our major goal is customer service; we want to be number one in customers' eyes when it comes to service."

Deborah then interviewed the senior vice president of finance and asked what initiatives had been budgeted or funded to support call center performance in the coming year. He answered, "The only initiative under consideration is the electronic support system for customer service reps. I want to know what the costs will be to maintain the system, however, and how the return on investment will be determined. Without a clear business case that shows the return on investment, funding will not be approved."

She also asked about call center managers' having profit-and-loss accountability. He answered, "That's not going to happen. We can't track costs by center. We can't even link revenue to a particular center. We don't have the systems to support something like that. The subject hasn't even been brought up for discussion, and it won't be."

Deborah begins to suspect the vice presidents were not in agreement about the company's goals for the call centers. She also suspected that their lack of agreement has resulted in mixed signals to the call center managers. Her next step was to interview the call center managers to get their understanding about what the goals were and how their performance would be measured.

FIELD TECHNIQUES: GETTING EVIDENCE OF EFFICIENCY

Once you have evidence of congruency, you can shift your focus to issues of efficiency. In fact, you might want to extend your investigation to efficiency issues even if you have evidence there is a lack of congruency, if only to find out if the lack of congruency is having a negative impact on efficiency.

Organizational and Job Structures

While you are determining if the first three elements are congruent, you can also get people to describe how the business or unit you are studying is organized: who reports to whom, who is responsible for what, and why work is structured as it is. Ask people to describe how customer calls are routed, who makes the final decisions, and who has sign-off authority, for example. Your hypotheses are that people are unclear, unsure, or do not agree on the answers and that the existing structure hides redundancy and lack of accountability. Ask enough questions to determine:

- The functions, roles, and responsibilities of each department, unit, and so on

- The customers of each function, division, and so on

- The outputs (deliverables or products) of each function, division, and so on

Just as you did for the first three elements, compare everyone's answers. Again, look for evidence of a shared understanding of the organization's structure and how the organizational units relate to each other.

Work Processes, Procedures, and Practices

This element addresses work processes, procedures, and practices, also referred to as work rules, whether for a discrete task or a job. Your hypothesis should be that processes are poorly designed, resulting in waste and unnecessary costs. Ask people to tell you how they do their work, and then watch them to confirm how many resources they actually require, if and where technology plays a role, how many interactions they have with others, and how many approvals they have to get and at what points in the process they have to get them. Check work records (such as job tickets and time sheets) to find out how long each task took and where cycle times were significantly longer than actual time at task. Look for evidence that work processes are well designed, do not result in rework, and use resources wisely.

Documentation and Standards

Easily accessible, user-friendly, and accurate documentation contributes to efficiency. Standards improve interfaces, allow flexibility, and result in lower costs because they permit economies of scale. When you are watching work get done, pay attention to what documents are used, when, and by whom. Ask where documents and work records are kept; those that are not readily accessible are probably not used. Notice if documents are well worn and personalized by bent corners. Just like the other elements in this section, do not believe they exist or are useful until you see them and have corroborating evidence to that effect.

Job Aids, Signage, and Labels

Check to see if there are visual and auditory cues that help people perform complex, infrequent, or critical procedures accurately. Notice if job aids, signs, and labels are well placed and designed in a way that helps people work quickly and smartly. Look for evidence that cues support efficiency by keeping people on task and on the right task. Your hypotheses should be that cues are lacking, unintelligible, and inconsistent, and as a result there are errors, rework, and added cost.

FIELD NOTES: THE SEARCH
FOR OPERATING INEFFICIENCIES

Russ, the HRD manager for a large medical equipment manufacturer, was asked to identify the training needs of the CSRs. It seemed the number of callbacks (customers who call a second or third time because they got the wrong information the first time) was too high.

Russ knew that the customer service center handled all customer requests about how to operate, repair, and install medical equipment. They also answered questions about delivery status, part status, and billing. The company had manufactured four product lines for over sixty years, and it had recently acquired a new line of diagnostic equipment. Customers (medical technicians who worked in hospitals, laboratories, and medical clinics) called a toll-free number that appeared on the equipment. The CSR who answered knew what line the customer was calling about based on the number dialed. The CSR was expected to confirm the customer was capable of safely dismantling and removing parts no matter what the product.

Russ's operating hypotheses were that the design of the CSRs' job (handling all lines, all models, and all types of requests) resulted in inefficiencies and waste, the equipment manuals the CSRs used did not support their need for fast and accurate information, and there were no consequences for giving out incorrect information. He asked to observe CSRs taking calls and to interview a few of them. He asked how CSRs were evaluated and learned:

- They were evaluated based on call volume and average call time.
- Large digital clocks positioned around the room displayed the average call time for the center.
- The CSRs had to be familiar with four different product lines, as well as multiple generations (models) of each line (sixty years' worth).

Russ asked some of the CSRs how they got the information they needed about older models. He was shown where the manuals were kept for every model of every line. He noticed that:

- The manuals were at the far end of a large room.
- It took at least one minute to get there.
- There were hundreds of manuals, all with the same white covers, with the year printed in small blue type on the spine.
- The CSRs were not allowed to remove the manuals from the area. They had to look up the information there, return to their desk, and resume the conversation with the customer.

Russ began to suspect the punishment for giving customers the wrong information (or making it up) was less painful than exceeding the average call handling time.

FIELD TECHNIQUES: GETTING EVIDENCE OF RESILIENCY

The final three elements in the hierarchy are about investment. You need to find out if the organization invests in its people, facilities, systems, and technology so that it can handle rapid change, growth, and market challenges. Not investing delays costs and limits the organization's ability to respond to changes in the marketplace or advances in technology. It can also erode employee and customer loyalty and relations.

Physical Facilities and Space

Shift your attention to how the design and maintenance of the company's buildings and equipment support performance. Be skeptical, just as you were when investigating the other elements. Pay attention to buildings, parking lots, bathrooms, cafeterias, closets and lockers, and so on. Look for dirt, disrepair, poor lighting, rooms, and graffiti. Confirm that the physical environment has adequate lighting, noise control, air quality, water, electricity, temperature control, and space to support the work that is done there. Pay attention to how the work space is arranged: Does it allow for easy access, noise control, and adequate room to support the required tasks and interactions. Check preventive maintenance records, OSHA reportables, and EPA reportables. Appropriately designed physical space will not guarantee that the company will get the desired performance, but it will increase the odds of getting it. The desired performance is more difficult to attain when the physical space is inappropriately designed or inadequate. Also remember that the physical space communicates a lot about what the organization values.

Training and Development

Look for evidence that people's skills and knowledge are maintained, and find out who is eligible for training. Your hypotheses should be that few, if any, employees get training, that it is hard to get training, and that training is not linked to any business initiative. Assume there is no strategy for keeping people current.

Ask to see the training budget, determine how many people have development plans, and ask about how many people have had development discussions with their supervisors. Find out how developmental needs are identified, if training records are kept, and how training programs are evaluated. At the same time, look for evidence that what was planned actually happened, that training and development are linked to the organization's business strategy, and that the training department can substantiate the value it adds.

Resource Capacity and Sufficiency

The last element in the hierarchy is about validating there are enough resources and that those resources have the capacity (emotionally, physically, and intellectually) to perform well. Find out if there are excess resources and to what degree those excess resources increase fixed costs. Your hypothesis should be that when it comes to resources, there are not enough, there are too many, or they are inappropriate for the task. You want to verify that the right amount of resources (systems, space, people, and equipment) exist to do the required tasks and that those resources have the capability to do the task. Look for and ask about what is not getting done (and whether it matters), how much work is outsourced (and whether it matters), how people compensate for the lack of resources, what they put at risk to do so (human or physical assets or customer service, for example), and how much time is spent on task.

Look for clues that indicate resources are insufficient: for example, preventive maintenance does not get done because production lines are operating around the clock, people do not get trained because no one is qualified to fill in for them while they train, vacation time goes unused but the trend in sick leave is up; or exit interviews show an increase in the number of people leaving the organization because they felt overworked or abused. Again, look, ask questions, and check records.

FIELD NOTES: THE SEARCH FOR A
DEFICIENT INVESTMENT IN RESOURCES

Mike, who is in charge of performance consulting at his company, worked at corporate headquarters. His department supported the product managers responsible for developing the supply chains for the system worldwide. A long-term supplier was in financial trouble, and the supply company's president was asking Mike's company for interim financing until he could turn his company around. Mike was asked to find out more about what was happening.

The supply company's president told Mike that morale was low, productivity was down, and employee theft was up. Mike suspected that if these statements were correct, something in the supply company's environment had changed because it had been known in the past for being efficient and having a conscientious workforce. Mike asked to visit the supplier's facility to get a better understanding of the problem.

When Mike pulled into the employee parking lot, he noticed the grounds were littered, curbs in the parking lot were crumbling, the lawn had bare spots, and the employee entrance door was filthy. While in the building, he went to the restroom, which was foul smelling, had a broken toilet, and lacked paper towels. Mike suggested that he and the facility manager have lunch in the employee cafeteria but was told the professional staff never ate there. He asked to visit the plant floor, and while he was there, he noticed that some of the forklift drivers did not wear safety belts, the aisles were dirty, one production line was not running, and a number of light bulbs were burned out.

Mike began to formulate some hypotheses: that the president had not reinvested earnings back in the business; that this had resulted in increased cost of operations, which eroded profits; and that there were no incentives to reinvest.

Mike next began his search for corroborating evidence. He reviewed the operating budget for the plant and the plant manager's bonus plan. Later he compared the budget and bonus plan to industry standards for similar plants. He began to suspect that because the president had not invested in the firm for some time, it could no longer operate cost effectively.

Kelly's company asked her to find out why employee turnover was high. She asked if the problem was across all jobs and departments or isolated. HR told Kelly that the highest turnover was among nonexempt staff corporatewide and among professional staff in information systems (IS). Kelly asked to see any exit interview data that HR had on file. A summary of the data indicated that the subjects felt there was no opportunity for advancement; lack of training came up frequently too.

Kelly began to hypothesize that the lack of training contributed significantly to the turnover problem and that the money saved by not supporting training actually shifted costs to other areas, such as the cost of recruitment and training new employees. She reviewed the training budget and discovered there was no budget for nonexempt workers because they were not eligible for training. She also discovered that very little was budgeted for IS. When she interviewed some of the IS staff, they told her that they couldn't afford to stay with the company because of the lack of training. If they stayed too long, they felt they could never compete on the outside. Kelly decided to continue her investigation of the implications of not investing in human resources, particularly into the cost of turnover, recruitment, and training new employees.

FIELD TECHNIQUES: DEVELOPING YOUR CLIENTS' SKILLS IN ASSESSMENT

Needs assessments are difficult, which is why I want my clients involved in them. Clients bring a deep understanding of the organization. I bring discipline, objectivity, and a fresh perspective. We do a better job together than singly. I use the job aid version of the hierarchy as a way to coach the client, particularly in working with me to create hypotheses and get the data. I use the worksheet to document what we want to find out, our hypotheses, the data we want, and how we will get the data. Documenting the process helps me measure and improve my efficiency. It helps the client participate, explain the process to others, get cooperation, and build a case for change. It also gives the client a model for future projects. Here are some guidelines for working with your client to assess the client's needs:

1. Show the hierarchy (Figure 7.3) to your client

2. Explain each element and what the concept of the hierarchy is designed to accomplish.

3. If you want to join with your client in designing a needs assessment, use the job aid (Figure 7.4) to get ideas about what to ask, possible hypotheses, and how to get the data.

4. Come up with some working hypotheses concerning why a performance gap exists or where gaps might exist.

5. Come up with a list of methods to prove your hypotheses right or wrong.

6. Decide how you will get the evidence.

7. Decide who will be involved in the process, how they will be involved, and when.

STAYING DISCIPLINED AND SETTING YOUR OWN STANDARDS

The hierarchy is only a tool to help you take a disciplined approach to needs assessments. It is not a performance checklist on which you sign off after checking each element in sequence. In practice, you might come across information about facilities before you learn anything about the direction of the work unit simply because you have to walk through the work area. Or your client might direct you to improve processes already identified as inefficient or to provide training because of errors due to the lack of skills. Just because you start with what you discover first or where the request directs you to begin doesn't mean you should overlook the importance of confirming congruency in the company's vision, mission, goals, and rewards. You can't improve processes unless there is agreement on what those processes are expected to accomplish and the company rewards people for being efficient. Job skill training will not compensate for conflicting directions from management or inefficient work procedures.

Improving performance is an iterative process. You should not try to improve every process immediately, but strive to improve your ability to measure, be more efficient, and link what you do to the goals that the organization considers most important. Every project is an opportunity to improve. If you set a goal to do every project perfectly, you will fail. What is important is to question the value of each project so as to avoid doing the wrong ones.

The hierarchy is designed to help you consider all the variables that support performance and all that impede it. When you find corroborating evidence, you get the information you need to develop your business case for doing what it will take to improve performance. Your recommendations may be for management to define and agree on where they are going, to start rewarding the behaviors and results that support their vision, to redesign work processes so they do not add unnecessary costs, and to invest in the resources required to accomplish the vision.

Decide at the beginning how rigorous you need to be in your process. Rigor, in this case, means defining your questions up front, carefully recording responses, and consistently engaging people in the same way. You might even pilot-test your data-gathering methods to confirm they work the way you expect them to. How rigorous you need to be depends on:

- The degree of confidence you have in your information (and the degree of confidence you need in order to defend your findings before management)

- The kind and amount of risk associated with acting prematurely on your conclusions

- The extent to which you want to periodically replicate your process to determine the reliability of your findings or evaluate the effectiveness of your interventions

- The extent to which you want to generalize your conclusions (broaden the area of application)

- The extent to which your processes, results, and actions have to withstand outside scrutiny, such as from a regulatory agency or collective bargaining unit

Here are two standards I follow.

- *Use more than one method to collect evidence, and get it from more than one source.* You need corroborating evidence from more than one source. If you interview people, for example, also check their work records. If you send out a survey, combine it with direct observation. The reason to use more than one method is to control any bias you may have introduced by how you asked questions, how you chose to include people, or how you conducted the study. The primary sources of bias are administrative error, questioning error, and sampling error (see Figure 7.6).

- Follow the guidelines in Figure 7.6 to control bias.

Source of bias	How to control bias
Administrative error	
Administrative error happens when:	How to control it:
• You do not ask people the same questions.	• Write out what you are going to say to introduce an interview, explain the purpose behind the study, and explain how people were selected to participate.
• You ask the questions in a different sequence.	
• You give people different amounts of time to answer.	• Stick with the script. This does not mean you have to memorize it. It does mean you strive to be experienced in the same way by everyone.
• Your preamble to your questions is emotionally laden or changes from person to person	• Prepare your forms for collecting the data in advance. Record your findings as soon as possible. Preferably, record the data as you are getting it.
• Your recording of answers (also observations) is incomplete or inaccurate.	• Give yourself a trial run. Practice explaining the reason and the procedures.

Figure 7.6. How to Control Bias

Source of bias	How to control bias

Questioning error

Questioning error happens when the questions you ask:

- Are unclear or misleading
- Are not relevant to the topic
- Fail to adequately cover the subject
- Focus on the inconsequential or irrelevant aspects of the topic
- Solicit opinions instead of the behaviors that lead to the desired performance

How to control it:

- Ask simple questions. Limit each question to a single topic.
- Avoid double negatives.
- Avoid indicating what other people said or thought before letting the person you are interviewing answer.
- If you are concerned that people will censor their answers, interview them individually and in private.
- Do a trial run to see if your questions elicit the quality of responses you are looking for.

Sampling error

Sampling error happens when you:

- Rely too much on one voice (audience).
- Fail to include other legitimately vested voices.
- Do not adequately sample the people, the documents, the work records, or the product or outputs of the task.

How to control it:

- Make sure you include all the relevant voices or populations. There are four categories of people whose voices should be included:
  —The people who are the subject of the investigation, usually called the target audience
  —The targets' bosses (the people who give the target audience direction and evaluate their performance)
  —The targets' customers or clients (the people who are recipients of the targets' output or benefactors of the outcome of the targets' performance)
  —The targets' suppliers (the people, processes, information, and systems the target audience relies on to perform their work)
- Sample all of your populations. You can pick everyone (a 100 percent sample) or select a smaller sample. If you sample (use less than the total), you can hand-pick people, use a convenience sample, or choose people randomly.
- Whether you pick the targets or they are nominated by someone else, they should be:
  —Knowledgeable (able to give you the information you want)
  —Credible (perceived as believable)
  —Capable (able to present a perspective that you can use to test the reliability of data gathered from other sources and in other ways)
- If there is variability in the target population, you can pick a stratified random sample.
- Remember that sampling applies to more than people. You pick places, situations, locations, documents, and types of things to investigate. The objectives for the assessment and guidelines for selecting a sample apply no matter what you are sampling.

Figure 7.6. How to Control Bias, *cont'd.*

FIELD TECHNIQUES: IDENTIFYING BARRIERS TO BECOMING A PERFORMANCE CONSULTANT

To increase your understanding of and proficiency in the process of identifying barriers to performance, practice on yourself. Think of your transition to performance consulting as an intervention, and use the scorecard to link your contemplated services to your client's needs. Follow these steps:

1. Meet with your colleagues, team, supervisor, and key clients. Build a scorecard to identify how adding performance consulting to your services will benefit the organization.

2. Identify the initiatives and performance gaps your becoming proficient at performance consulting will affect.

3. Assess how much success you will have to demonstrate to justify your investment (in time and dollars) in becoming a performance consultant?

4. Apply the hierarchy to identify barriers to and opportunities for adding performance consulting to your services. Confirm that you, your colleagues, your supervisor, and key clients have the same understanding of what performance consulting is. Then follow these steps:

   • Develop your hypotheses concerning what the barriers and opportunities are. For example, is one barrier a lack of understanding of performance consulting or something else? Is one barrier an unwillingness to reward or reinforce the behaviors of following a consulting process, measuring your own effectiveness, developing processes for identifying causes to poor performance, and so on? Do your colleagues, supervisor, and key clients agree on what performance consulting is or even share a similar understanding of what it can contribute? What do they think you will do differently from what you do now? Do you think the behaviors of a performance consultant will be rewarded? How about your results?

   • Share the model consulting process, the suggested measures of efficiency and effectiveness, your vision and mission, your list of products and services, and the model operational definition from Chapters One and Two, and ask them what they think these mean.

   • Ask them which behaviors they think will be rewarded.

   • If possible, get corroborating evidence that supports or refutes your hypotheses about what you think will be the barriers and opportunities.

   • If you discover the group does not share the same understanding, help everyone come to a shared understanding of what performance consulting is and what it can contribute.

5. Confirm that the way your department or work group is structured, the processes you use, your documentation and standards, and your job aids support your being efficient.

- You will now have a model consulting process, a model needs assessment process, and job aids for evaluating your processes and doing performance consulting. Again, develop your hypotheses concerning the adequacy of these processes and the need for other processes, documentation, and so on.

- Decide how will you get the data to measure how efficient you are today and what interferes with or supports your being efficient. You can begin to measure your efficiency and see if it improves over time.

6. Confirm how much of an investment you have already made or plan to make in your professional development and in the development of your processes, standards, and performance aids to support this new role.

    - Develop your hypotheses as to how much agreement there is to the amount invested to date and the amount needed in the future.

    - Decide how you will get the data to find out what the investment has been to date and what it will be in the future.

    - Decide how you will get the data you need to confirm what the groups will accept as evidence that you are capable of providing performance consulting.

7. Plan how you will use the scorecard and hierarchy on a client's project.

8. To practice developing hypotheses, think of some organizational unit, like a work group, a team, or department, and ask yourself the following questions:

    - What are your assumptions about how clear the unit's vision, mission, and goals are and to what degree its people are in agreement? How does this clarity (or the lack of it) affect performance?

    - What behaviors and results do you think get rewarded? How does what gets rewarded affect performance?

    - What do you know about the unit's work processes? Are they well designed? How do they affect performance?

    - Are there standards? Is the documentation accurate and accessible? How do these affect performance?

    - Do job aids exist? So people use them? Do people create their own? How does the adequacy (or inadequacy) of the job aids affect performance?

    - What do you know about the facilities? Is the space designed to support the work people do?

    - Who gets trained, and why? Who doesn't get trained, and why?

    - Do people fill time by looking busy? Are they overworked? Do they have what they need to be effective?

These questions should help you realize that you already know a lot about your client. Developing hypotheses is not that hard. Once you have some idea about what you want to confirm, you and your client can decide how to get the data you need about what is or is not true and the effect on performance.

SUMMARY

Performing needs assessment should become a natural part of doing your business. You are always in a position to question, confirm, and verify that people share the same vision and goals, that job procedures support efficiency, and that people have the skills and knowledge they require. There is always time to find out why accidents, errors, and waste are increasing rather than assuming you know the answers. There is time to find out if the people and the organization can support a new structure. Jumping to conclusions wastes time and resources.

If Lisa had used the hierarchy, she would have known to confirm whether the bank president and his management team were clear on and in agreement with the bank's vision, mission, and goals. Her hypotheses would be that they were not in agreement on their vision, they were unclear about their goals, and the behaviors they rewarded did not support accountability or performance. Another hypothesis might have been that the president's goals for the bank had changed and were no longer aligned with the bank's publicized vision and mission statements, or that the president was unable to explain how the bank's new practices aligned with its vision and mission. She could have interviewed the president privately to learn more about his expansion goals and determine if the bank's lending practices had really changed or if only a few loans had fallen outside its stated goals.

What Lisa discovered when she had people describe the organizational structure of the bank should have led her to still another set of hypotheses: that changes in the bank had disrupted old reporting relationships, managers were being undermined by the executive vice president, and as a result, they did not have a managerial job under this structure; and that the managers were comfortable with the arrangement because it meant they were not accountable for anyone's performance, including their own. She could then have found out how managers were chosen for the job, how their performance was evaluated, and whether there were consequences for poor performance. In her process of creating a training program, she could have begun to get the president to better understand his responsibility for supporting performance.

WHERE TO LEARN MORE

Dillard, J., and Reilly, R. *Systematic Interviewing: Communication Skills for Professional Effectiveness.* Columbus, Ohio: Merrill Publishing, 1988. This book is full of examples and guidelines.

Hale, J. *Standards for the Training Function*. Downers Grove, Ill.: Hale Associates, 1996. Accompanying these standards are checklists and surveys for evaluating the adequacy of processes used to identify client needs, demonstrate leadership, manage capital assets, and measure results.

Hale, J. *Performance-Based Evaluation*. San Francisco: Jossey-Bass/Pfeiffer, 2003. Chapters Nine (on sampling), Ten (on how to design and conduct interviews, surveys, observations, and document checks), and Eleven (how to analyze qualitative and quantitative data) are particularly useful. The book has over forty-four tools on a CD.

Payne, S. *The Art of Asking Questions*. Princeton, N.J.: Princeton University Press, 1980. A classic with lots of examples.

Rossett, A. *First Things Fast: A Handbook for Performance Analysis*. San Francisco: Jossey-Bass, 1998) and *Training Needs Assessment* (Englewood Cliffs, N.J.: Educational Technology Publications, 1987). Both books are useful guides on how to identify the causes of performance problems.

Stewart, C., and Cash Jr., W. *Interviewing: Principles and Practices*. (6th ed.) Dubuque, Iowa: Wm. C. Brown, 1991. This is full of guidelines and learning activities.

Chapter 8

Interventions

*I*n this fieldbook, the term *intervention* refers to any program, communication, or event intended to improve organizational and people performance. Organizations implement changes and adopt programs in the hope of improving productivity and performance. Those changes and programs frequently require a major investment in time and dollars. The changes companies implement and the programs they fund redefine work and work relationships. They affect people's lives. Consider the following situations.

FIELD NOTES: EXAMPLES OF INTERVENTIONS

- A bank opened an elementary school (K–8) on site.
- An insurance company installed an expert system for claims handling.
- A direct sales merchandiser decided to certify its product trainers.
- A multinational company installed an intranet so all of its sites could more efficiently communicate with each other.
- A manufacturer organized its production line employees into self-managed teams.
- A field office required all employees to attend a sexual harassment class.
- A retailer met with its distributor and paper bag manufacturer to standardize packaging sizes.
- A restaurant chain set criteria for determining the salary level of key jobs.

What these situations have in common is that the organization did something to solve a business problem. It is unclear, however, what the chosen solution was expected to fix, change, or improve in these situations. The goal may have been to reduce costs, shorten cycle time, retain employees, avoid fines, or improve customer confidence. Whatever the reason, the actions were not arbitrary. These companies planned their actions and committed resources. What they may or may not have had was a process that helped them fully understand the consequences of their actions and measure the results.

A BRIEF HISTORY OF INTERVENTIONS

The term *intervention* has been traditionally used by members of the counseling profession to mean a purposeful confrontation to get individuals to accept responsibility for their actions and change their behavior. The term was adopted by professionals in training and development when Barry Booth and Odin Westgaard first used it at a national conference in 1979. The term soon appeared in professional journals, referring to solutions other than training (more specifically job aids) to improve performance. The term *intervention* is still the performance consultant's word, not the language of our clients. Our clients do not talk about interventions. They talk about initiatives, programs, and strategies to solve problems, increase productivity, and reduce costs. The client's intent is to accomplish a goal—for example:

- Increase stockholder returns
- Improve market position or share
- Increase productivity
- Improve product performance
- Improve people performance
- Improve financial performance
- Achieve regulatory compliance

In the late 1980s, I conducted a research project to identify what companies were doing to improve performance. It was this research that got me to think less about specific interventions and more about what stimulated or triggered the need for the change and thus the intent behind the change. I learned that companies implement changes in response to a combination of business need, poor productivity, poor employee morale, the availability of new technology, and social pressure. I also noticed the role that the popular press, and later the mass media, played in influencing the types of interventions management sponsored.

That research has been helpful to me in a number of ways. I discovered that most interventions are initiated in response to a major event or real need.

Some were implemented because of the influence of a strong, popular personality. Therefore, when I'm hired after the client has already decided on an intervention, I still want to identify what drove the decision. Was it the results of a needs assessment? The desire to take advantage of a new technology? Or did someone just want to join in on the managerial fad of the day? I can't measure the effectiveness of a program unless I know the stimulus and the intent behind the particular solution. If the client has not decided on a course of action, I want to understand the problem well enough to recommend the appropriate solution.

Here is a brief overview of some significant events and people who influenced the business world's ideas about how to improve managerial and organizational effectiveness. My intent is to encourage all of us to question what affects performance and how best to improve it. Understanding why organizations chose certain interventions in the past will put us in a better position to recommend the same or a more appropriate intervention in the future.

Big business as we know it came about during the early twentieth century. The relatively new oil, steel, railroad, and meatpacking industries had two problems: very high turnover and the need to coordinate the efforts of more people than they ever had had to deal with in the past. Organizations turned to the leading thinkers of the day. Management was impressed with the work of Frederick Taylor, a mechanical engineer who later became known as the father of scientific management. Taylor, along with Frank Gilbreth (who refined the use of time and motion studies) and his wife, Lillian Gilbreth (who earned a doctorate in psychology from Brown University), were studying how jobs and tasks were designed. Rather than focus on how to reduce turnover, they used time and motion studies to reduce jobs to a few discrete tasks so people could be trained in hours instead of days to do the work. (Task and job redesign remains a popular intervention today; however, the goal has gone beyond that of reducing training time to improving efficiency.) At about the same time, management theorists began to define the job of the supervisor versus that of the worker.

Organizational theorists also began to propose ideas about how to structure, or organize, large businesses to improve efficiency. The concepts of vertical and horizontal integration were introduced, and they are still debated today. Vertical integration occurs when companies own or control everything in a supply chain, from raw material production, to manufacturing, to marketing and distributing finished products. An example is a cardboard box company that owns the forests, the lumber yard, the paper mills, the plant that manufactures the cartons, and the distribution centers that get them to stores that use them. Horizontal integration occurs when a company owns or controls the market in one segment of a supply chain (owning every forest or every paper mill, for example).

The result of vertical and horizontal integration in the early twentieth century was the emergence of monopolies. Today we see organizations creating holding companies, franchises, and joint venture partners as ways to control markets. Increasing numbers of companies are outsourcing functions such as human resources, payroll, accounting services, and customer and technical service call centers. They are also outsourcing manufacturing, sales, and technical support to third-party after-market firms. Among those they outsource functions to are independent companies located in other countries in order to capitalize on lower labor costs, access to skilled workers, and proximity to emerging markets. Partially as a result of the practice of outsourcing, global organizations have become federations or conglomerates of separate but mutually dependent businesses engaged in all aspects of the supply chain, from supplying raw materials to after-market support.

Organizations still wrestle with finding their optimum structure and size, particularly in response to the information and communication revolution, which has led to flattened organizations by shifting decision making to lower levels and outsourcing more functions. Advances in information and communication technologies have made much of traditional management philosophy, originally reforms in their own right, dysfunctional. And older management theories have not caught up with the idea of businesses as learning organizations; the older financial models are still wrestling with the concept of a knowledge economy or how businesses are making the transition to a service economy. Today CEOs of companies in the knowledge industry must understand how profoundly uninformative and misleading the balance sheet is. Restructuring and reorganizing are still commonly used interventions to solve business problems.

It was about the time of the stock market crash of 1929 that organizations began to shift their attention to what motivates workers. There were riots in Washington, D.C., in 1932, sit-down strikes in Detroit in 1937, and unemployment ranging from 12 to 15 percent during the Great Depression. Elton Mayo conducted a landmark study from 1927 to 1932 at the Western Electric Company and concluded that workers respond to the total work situation and that attitudes toward work and their social relations are important.

There was also increasing attention to the role of managers. Dale Carnegie's book, *How to Win Friends and Influence People*, published in 1936, was outsold only by the Bible. Chester Barnard, an executive with American Telephone & Telegraph Company, wrote *The Functions of the Executive*, a leading book in 1938, on the role of management. He was the first to distinguish between effectiveness (goal accomplishment) and efficiency (without harmful consequences). He also stressed the role of management as the vehicle for communication, the conduit of ideas and information. The Hawthorne studies, done between 1927 and 1931, were published in 1939, the same year the plight of the migrant farmworker was popularized in Steinbeck's *The Grapes of Wrath.*

The threat of war in 1941 accelerated the search for better ways to increase productivity. The U.S. government, together with big business, launched the "training within industry" program. This program, created in anticipation of U.S. entry into World War II, was designed to address growing labor unrest by training supervisors in what was called pragmatic human relations. It was also designed to train civilian and military supervisors how to lead and motivate. The program was framed around two assumptions: that it takes a strong leader to motivate workers and that the most important skill is the ability to persuade. One hundred speech teachers were trained at Harvard University to teach the program. The primary text they used to train both military officers and civilians was Monroe's *Principles of Speech,* which was published in 1935. This book was the primary text used to train military leaders until the mid 1950s. Every officer was subjected to Monroe's "motivational sequence," which combined traditional rhetoric with modern psychology. The belief that communication skills are key to leadership persists today.

Technologies that were by-products of the war (such as mainframe computers in 1944 and transistors in 1948) would later profoundly alter how and where work is done. The introduction of direct-dial telephones in 1951 changed the way organizations communicated. At the same time, another technology was evolving that would shape the workplace of the future. This technology grew out of search for ways to change the physical workplace in order to improve productivity. The husband and wife team, Charles and Ray Eames, began their experiments with molded plywood in 1941. Synthetic fabrics, furniture, and flooring were developed in the 1940s and 1950s. Molded plywood and synthetics resulted in stackable, modular furniture. The concept of the "office house" premiered in 1943. Furniture systems and suspended ceilings were introduced in the 1950s. The rising cost of health care and new work-related injuries and illness such as carpal tunnel syndrome, lower back injuries, and increasing breathing disorders continues to force companies to experiment with new ways to design work space and equipment. The American with Disabilities Act of 1992 forced organizations to redesign facilities to allow greater access to all people. In 1997 the American Society of Interior Designers published a major study on how to improve productivity through better lighting, space layout, furniture design, and carpeting. Today organizations invest significant resources in designing work space and equipment in the hope of reducing costs and improving performance.

The idea of lifelong learning gained momentum in the mid-1960s when junior colleges started to offer adult continuing education programs and professional societies offered professional development programs. The civil rights movement and the protests of the 1960s and 1970s fueled a more aggressive investment in managerial training and triggered the introduction of coaching and counseling in the workplace. The economic downturn in the early 1970s brought with it the realization that lifelong employment may not be possible. Companies introduced the first career counseling and preretirement planning programs in the early 1970s, signaling a shift in responsibility for job security from the organization to the individual. The twenty-first century continues to see health and fitness programs moving into the workplace, along with employee assistance programs.

The space race started in the 1950s, and when it was announced on nationwide television that the National Aeronautics and Space Administration had adopted zero defects as its standard, the business world began to pay more attention to standards. Japan began to establish itself as a dominant force in the automobile and electronic industries in the 1960s. The Baldrige Award was created in 1986 by President Reagan, and the ISO 9000 Standards were published that same year. Soon popular books about Total Quality Management (TQM) and reengineering increased our understanding of how standards, well-designed processes, measurement, teams, and leadership can affect performance. Today organizations are practicing the principles of 5S (sift, sort, simplify, standardize, systemize) and Six Sigma to reduce waste and improve work processes.

Companies continue to experiment with many of these same ideas to improve performance. Especially with globalization increasing, companies are changing their structures, reengineering their processes, and using new technologies to redefine where work is done, introducing programs and incentives to motive workers, redesigning the workplace, and experimenting with theories about management and leadership.

The programs that organizations implement to improve performance are done at many levels. Figure 8.1 lists examples of what organizations do at the individual, work group, department, division, and societal levels to improve performance.

Because performance consultants come out of HRD, organizational development, training, quality assurance, and other staff functions, they are more likely to get involved in interventions at the individual, work group, team, and department levels. Nevertheless, they may be part of a team working on a major initiative that can affect a whole division or company.

FIELD TOOLS: THE FAMILY OF INTERVENTIONS JOB AID

I find it helpful to classify the different types of interventions in "families." Otherwise the list of all the interventions that organizations could possibly implement would be long and unmanageable. I initially settled on thirteen families, but for this edition have expanded the list to fifteen, sorted into five groups. Each family of interventions has a unique label (see Figure 8.2) that quickly communicates the purpose or reason for the intervention. The label tells you what a specific activity or program is supposed to accomplish. It helps me identify the appropriate action or set of actions to improve performance, stay focused on what I'm trying to accomplish, and not overlook supporting interventions. The labels do something else as well: they help me establish credibility because I have a method for sorting, comparing, and selecting the most appropriate intervention. I use Figure 8.2 as a job aid and share it with clients.

Figure 8.1. Interventions at the Individual, Work Group, Department, and Division Levels

---

Interventions designed to improve individual performance

- Redesigning a job or workstation to accommodate physical limitations
- Allowing a flextime work schedule
- Permitting job sharing
- Providing personal financial or family counseling through an employee assistance program
- Installing electronic performance support systems

Interventions designed to shape or improve work group and team performance

- Adopting agile manufacturing practices
- Making cross-training available
- Implementing self-directed work teams
- Offering diversity training
- Holding competitions
- Building identity through department slogans or uniforms

Interventions designed to improve the performance of whole departments and divisions

- Adopting uniform standards
- Replacing traditional compensation structures with job banding
- Creating vision and mission statements
- Installing intranet and e-mail systems

- Giving business units accountability for profit and loss

Interventions to improve the performance of major divisions, subsidiaries, and even whole companies

- Selling off a product line, plant, or division
- Buying or merging with another division or company
- Decentralizing and centralizing staff functions
- Consolidating functions
- Reengineering major cross-functional processes, such as order-to-ship processes
- Outsourcing functions
- Adopting a new logo or corporate name

Interventions designed to improve society as a whole or specific groups

- Engaging in political and social advocacy to push for the enactment of laws and influence judicial and legislative actions
- Providing health care services
- Providing emergency care, including medical services, housing, and transportation
- Volunteering time and expertise to provide educational, health care, and social services
- Donating cars, clothing, housing, money, toys, medical equipment, unused frequent flyer miles, and the like to people in need

Group	Families (Labels)	Examples
Information focused	1. Interventions that *define:* Activities that specify or clarify the vision, mission, purpose, process, products, services, market position, roles, relationships, responsibilities, outcomes, expectations, and so on	Holding sessions to create vision statements; confirming market direction and market niche; mutually setting performance goals
	2. Interventions that *inform:* Activities that communicate goals, objectives, expectations, results, discrepancies, and so on	Producing internal newsletters; holding debriefing sessions; giving feedback
	3. Interventions that *document:* Activities that codify information (to preserve it and make it accessible)	Setting up libraries; creating manuals, expert systems, job aids, and decision guides
Consequences focused	4. Interventions that *reward:* Activities and programs that induce and maintain desired behaviors, eliminate undesirable behaviors, and reward desired outcomes	Holding public ceremonies and annual recognition events; paying for performance
	5. Interventions that *measure:* Activities and systems that provide metrics and benchmarks so people can monitor performance and have a basis to evaluate it	Developing a scorecard; tracking means and variance in performance over time
	6. Interventions that *enforce:* Activities that actualize consequences and achieve compliance	Policing, reviewing, double-checking, suspending, removing, withholding pay
Design focused	7. Interventions that *organize:* Activities that change the structure of or arrange business units, reporting relationships, work processes, jobs, and tasks	Reengineering processes; merging functions; reorganizing responsibilities
	8. Interventions that *standardize:* Activities that systematize or automate processes and standardize tasks, tools, equipment, materials, components, or measures	Adopting ISO 9000 and ANSI standards; implementing uniform standards; adopting common guidelines, procedures, tools, equipment, and language
	9. Interventions that *(re)design:* Activities that result in useful, easy-to-use, safe, and ergonomically designed environment, workplace, equipment, and tools	Building in safety features; designing for ease of installation, service, maintenance, and upgrading
Capacity and capabilities focused	10. Interventions that *reframe:* Activities and programs that generate new paradigms so people can experience new perspectives, find creative solutions, integrate new concepts in their behavior, and manage change	Facilitating challenging assumptions; engaging in dialogue; entering into new alliances; brainstorming; creating alternative futures
	11. Interventions that *counsel:* Activities and programs that assist individuals singularly or collectively to deal with work, personal, career, family, and financial issues	Offering on-site day care, preretirement seminars, on-site physical fitness centers, and employee assistance programs
	12. Interventions that *develop:* Activities and programs that expand skills and knowledge	Offering training, coaching, and structured on-the-job experiences
Action focused	13. Interventions that *advocate:* Activities intended to raise awareness and provoke action (personal, organizational, social, and political)	Conducting sit-ins; marching; convening in mass; using billboards and other media to promote a point of view and call for action; fundraising; setting up user councils
	14. Interventions that *serve:* Activities that offer assistance	Helping to rebuild a home; providing medical help; donating equipment and supplies; offering expertise
Congruence focused	15. Interventions that *align:* Activities and programs that work toward congruency of purpose, practice, and consequences	Setting up cross-functional teams; eliciting customer (internal and external) feedback; ensuring that hiring criteria match job requirements

Figure 8.2. The Families of Interventions

FIELD TOOLS: THE IF-THEN TABLES FOR INTERVENTION

The if-then tables for interventions shown in Figures 8.3 through 8.8 are meant to be used more with your team than with your client. Use them to decide what to do, as a reminder of what you want to accomplish, and to help you think about what you will use as evidence of success.

Information-Focused Interventions

Interventions that belong in the first three families are about information (see Figure 8.3). They are the most important group of interventions because:

- They are valuable in their own right. They are frequently the only things you need to do to improve performance.

- They support most, if not all, of the other interventions.

- When they are not done well or are overlooked, they can greatly reduce the effectiveness of the other interventions and even cause them to fail.

Interventions that fall in the first three families are more likely to draw on your interpersonal and facilitation skills. They require you to be politically savvy, remain impartial unless you have relevant information to share, stay focused so the group does not get off track, and challenge the assumptions of the group. Here are explanations and examples of interventions from the first three families that deal with information.

Interventions That Define. Interventions in this family are used to gain clarity. They are meant to contribute definition and dimension; help people find out what they agree or disagree about regarding their sphere of responsibility; where they are going as an individual, work group, or company; and what they are about, that is, their mission. Here are examples of this type of intervention:

- Creating vision and mission statements that clarify a group's purpose, goals, and expected deliverables

- Developing team charters that clarify why a team was created, who its customer or sponsor is, what it is expected to accomplish, and when it is expected to accomplish it

- Developing job descriptions that define responsibilities, roles, accountability, and so on

- Developing documents of understanding with contractors and suppliers to ensure a shared understanding of expectations

Family	If you have evidence that:	and	then decide
1. *Interventions that define*	People are unclear, disagree, or have different expectations; there are conflicting objectives; or people do not have a shared understanding:	You believe you can help, and it would be a benefit for people to better define and come to consensus about what they mean, expect, require, hope to accomplish, and so on; and it is feasible to facilitate a session to arrive at a shared understanding.	• Who needs to be involved in the session • Who will contact the people • Who will present the problem and explain why resolution is important • Who will facilitate the session • When you will do it • What process you will use • What the end product will look like • How you will measure success
2. *Interventions that inform*	Information has changed, the people have changed, or the people are uninformed and the consequence is poor performance; or people don't get the information they need.	There is agreement on what information people should have to perform their jobs; there is agreement on the amount of detail the information should contain; and there is agreement on who needs to know what.	• Who should be involved • Who will contact those who should be involved • How best to get them the information they need • Who will do it • Who else should be involved • When it will be done • What resources it will require • How you will measure success
3. *Interventions that document*	Information is not accessible over time or is too complex; job aids, manuals, help screens, and other devices are lacking or inadequate, inaccurate, or hard to access.	You agree that the variance in behavior is undesirable and can be reduced with accessible information; you agree to document the information in a form that makes it easily accessible and facilitates consistent interpretation or compliance.	• How to best codify the information so it is available in a form people can use • Who else needs to be involved • Who will arrange for their involvement • How you will test usability • How you will measure the effectiveness of the documentation

Figure 8.3. Interventions Job Aid: Information-Focused Interventions

Recommend these types of activities when people are unsure, are in disagreement, or have different expectations because of dissimilar experiences, knowledge, or motives.

Interventions That Inform. Interventions in this family make sure that the people who need to know do know. It is not enough just to define the purpose, responsibilities, and other attributes; the information has to be communicated as well. Calling staff meetings, broadcasting employee announcements, and sending memos, faxes, and e-mails are examples of activities intended to inform. Recommend these types of activities when either the information has changed or the people have changed.

Interventions That Document. Interventions in this family make information continuously accessible. In many cases, it is not enough to communicate information just once. It is important that people be able to retrieve and reference information as they need it. Job aids, help screens, contracts, process flowcharts, procedural manuals, diagrams, and if-then tables are examples of interventions designed to make information retrievable and accessible. Recommend activities and programs of this type when information is complex and documentation can help reduce variance in performance.

Your consulting and needs assessment processes should enable you to estimate the cost of getting, communicating, and codifying information and to compare that cost to the cost of doing nothing or something else. The operational definition worksheet (Figure 1.7), the product portfolio worksheets (Figures 2.3, 2.4, and 2.5), and the process or task performance worksheet (Figure 3.9) are tools for clarifying, gaining consensus, and helping make information available.

FIELD NOTES: CULTIVATING AGREEMENT

Deborah knew that the vice presidents were not in agreement on either the goals for the coming year or what they expected of call center managers. She met with the vice president of sales and explained what she had discovered. She suggested that they meet with the vice president of operations and the senior vice president of finance to discuss everyone's goals and expectations. Deborah offered to facilitate the meeting, since she wanted everyone to have an opportunity to speak and experience firsthand just how far apart they were. During the meeting, she planned to share the call center managers' experience with how the vice presidents' lack of agreement affected the performance of the centers. The managers could cite examples of false starts and conflicting objectives, and they could put a dollar value on the waste. She could then begin the process of bringing the vice presidents to agreement. Deborah knew that without clarity, there could be no agreement. And gaining agreement on the goal was key to coming up with criteria for measuring call center performance.

Consequences-Focused Interventions

The activities and programs that fall within the next three families of interventions deal with consequences. Like the interventions in the information-focused group, these also work together; however, they cannot be implemented effectively without first achieving the outcomes targeted by the first group of families. Consequences-focused interventions also require skill in facilitation, as well as expertise in defining and measuring performance (see Figure 8.4).

Family	If you have evidence that	and	then decide
4. *Interventions that reward*	Current incentives either reinforce the wrong behaviors or ignore the desired behaviors; or there are few incentives for people to do better, more, or differently.	You have identified and agree on what behaviors or outcomes you want the incentives to reinforce; you have identified the appropriate incentives; you agree on the procedures and criteria for receiving the incentive or reward; and you agree to stop incentives that undermine the desired behaviors or send contradictory messages.	• What behaviors you want to reward and how • What behaviors you want to stop rewarding and how • Who needs to be involved • How you will involve them • Who will arrange for their involvement • When you will do it • What rewards to use • What rewards to eliminate because they reinforce behaviors that support competing or incompatible goals • How to link rewards with behaviors and outcomes • How you will measure the effectiveness of the measures
5. *Interventions that measure*	People don't know what criteria are being used to judge productivity, performance, and value, and they could better control their own performance if they knew what the criteria are; measures of good performance are lacking; or measures are inappropriate.	You agree to make public what is being measured, what metrics are being used, and who is doing the measuring; you agree to identify ways people can do their own measuring.	• What you want to measure • What the measures should be • What metrics you want to use • What is required for people to measure their own performance • How the new measures will be implemented • Who needs to be involved • Who will arrange for their involvement • When you will do it • How you will measure the effectiveness of the effort
6. *Interventions that enforce*	Consequences for poor performance or unacceptable behavior are hidden or not enforced.	You agree there should be consequences for good and poor performance; you agree to identify why consequences are not being enforced, whose needs are being met by keeping them hidden, who should support the actualization; and put in a process for enforcing them.	• What you think the consequences should be • Who should be responsible for making the consequences real • Who else needs to be involved • Who will arrange for their involvement • When you will do it • How you will measure the effectiveness of the change

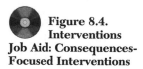

Figure 8.4.
Interventions
Job Aid: Consequences-
Focused Interventions

Interventions That Reward. The interventions in this family encourage and reward the behaviors and results that benefit the organization. Bonuses, merit increases, gifts and gift certificates, award banquets, plaques, tickets to major sports events, and dinners are examples of incentives designed to reward the behaviors and accomplishments the organization values. Recommend these types of activities and programs when current incentives reinforce the wrong behaviors or ignore desired ones.

Interventions That Measure. Interventions in this family compare actual behaviors or results to some identified standards, criteria, or expectations. Measuring emphasizes the organization's commitment to meeting its expectations and goals. What organizations measure, when they measure, and the measurement criteria they use make public what the organization thinks is important. Measures tell people how the organization will weigh behaviors or results when it makes decisions about money, promotions, and resources; therefore, it is especially important that what is measured is not just what can be easily counted but what is meaningful. Examples of uses of measures and measuring include:

- Signs that display expected call-handling times and flash actual average times

- Reports that show the difference between planned and actual performance in such areas as turnover, cycle time, fixed costs to variable costs, percentage of yield, number of accidents that cause lost time, and sales

- Capturing evidence of managers' commitment to giving employees feedback and developing their capabilities through quarterly reports that show which managers did and did not conduct performance reviews and enroll people in developmental activities

Recommend activities that measure when the information they provide will help people monitor their own performance or compare it against a standard.

Interventions That Enforce. Interventions in this family carry out the consequences. It is not enough to reward and measure; consequences, good and bad, need to be actualized if they are to be effective. Promises and threats produce cynicism when they are not made real. Some examples of this type of intervention are:

- Recognizing employees who meet goals and withholding bonuses from those who do not

• Celebrating supervisors whose crews worked accident free and holding them accountable for time lost to accidents

Recommend that your client always enforce rules and standards, since compliance and achievement reduce costs, increase customer satisfaction, and ensure safety.

Your consulting and needs assessment processes should enable you to determine the cost of interventions that reward, measure, and enforce the desired results and compare that cost to the potential gains. You can use the examples of standards and measures (Figures 2.1 and 2.2) and the tools in Chapters Nine and Ten to facilitate discussion of and eventual agreement on what measures are appropriate.

FIELD NOTES: ENFORCING WORTHY MEASURES

Kelly was asked to join a team charged with coming up with better incentives for the company's insurance agents. Although the agents were meeting their goals, management thought the company's cash flow could be improved. Also, an audit of the property and casualty line showed some major exposures for the company. Kelly and the team met with agents, finance, and sales to find out just what the problem was. They discovered that agents' bonuses were based on the dollar volume of policies sold. Extra incentives were given during the fourth quarter of the fiscal year (the fiscal year ended in October). As a result, 60 percent of the business happened during the last quarter (August to October), 60 percent of that happened during the last month in the fourth quarter (October), and 60 percent of that happened during the last week of October. This sales pattern had a substantial effect on the company's cash flow. There were other problems as well. Agents who sold property and casualty insurance were encouraged to sell as many policies as possible. This meant they would try to sell every home on the block and every small business in the mall. This was fine except when major disasters—tornados, fires, floods, and violent storms—occurred. Major disasters tend to damage every building on the block or in the mall, which results in significant losses for the company. Kelly and her team began to suspect that agents targeted their sales to customers whose policies expired during the fourth quarter and relied heavily on referrals for new business.

Kelly and her team knew the way agents were compensated and rewarded partially contributed to the company's cash flow and exposure problems. The team decided to recommend developing an incentive package that would reward agents for increasing the company's cash flow by bringing in business throughout the year and turning down a certain percentage of business so the company's overall risk was lessened. In addition, the incentive package should not punish agents when their fourth-quarter sales were down from past years.

Because the ability to get new business depended on a policy's expiration date, this would require either designing policies with nontraditional expiration dates or helping the agents identify potential customers with expiration dates throughout the year. Kelly and the team met with finance to determine the feasibility and cost implications of a package designed to help the agents change their approach so business would be less cyclical. Kelly's solution incorporated defining and gaining agreement on the problem and criteria for a new incentive package and changing the incentive package so it better supported the needs of the company.

Design-Focused Interventions

The interventions that fall into the next three families are about design—specifically, the design of relationships, work, and physical things. Like the interventions that address consequences, these too should be performed after or in conjunction with those that deal with information. These interventions may require you to join with other experts such as industrial engineers and interior designers; however, your expertise in job and task analysis and the development of performance checklists will be uniquely valuable. If you do work with other experts, your skill in facilitation and keeping the group focused will come into play. Also, having some external status will help you establish credibility with the other experts. These interventions are summarized in Figure 8.5.

Interventions That Organize. Interventions in this family address the design of organizations, functions, duties, jobs, and tasks. Their goal is to provide a structure or sequence that enhances efficiency without sacrificing due diligence or safety. Examples of interventions that organize are outsourcing functions, decentralizing or centralizing functions, reengineering processes, redesigning jobs, and combining tasks. Recommend these types of interventions when the current structure is inefficient, results in redundancy, adds excess cost, overly burdens cycle time, or hides accountability.

Interventions That Standardize. Interventions in this family address the design of equipment, materials, procedures, and work space. Their goal is to achieve consistent performance, allow for interchangeability, or increase product flexibility and longevity. A common example is when manufacturers of different brands adopt industry standards that allow customers to interchange parts; in such cases, consumers can mix and mingle components from products built at different times. Another example is when standardization allows for automation; in this case, procedures and work protocols are standardized

Family	If you have evidence that	and	then decide
7. *Interventions that organize*	The current structure is inefficient, results in redundancy, adds excess cost, overly burdens cycle time, and hides accountability.	You agree that the way tasks and jobs are structured adds costs, reduces morale, and interferes with service; you agree to either propose a new way to restructure work or create a task force to redesign the way work gets done.	• What changes to the structure you want to make • How will you do it • What process you will use • Who needs to be involved and what they will do • How you will get them involved • Who will be affected by a change in structure and how • What the new structure will look like • How you will measure the effectiveness of the change
8. *Interventions that standardize*	Deviation in equipment, materials, specifications, procedures, common practices, and so on add extra costs, result in low yields, and cause variance in the quality of work.	You agree the lack of standardization is adding unnecessary costs; you agree to standardize whatever is causing most of the deviation; or you agree to do a feasibility study or cost-benefit analysis to answer the question of whether standardization is appropriate.	• What should be standardized • What process you will use to develop the standards • Who is in the best position to do it • What kind of a business case you need for the change • Who will prepare the business case • Who will facilitate the development, testing, and implementation of the new standards
9. *Interventions that (re)design*	The current work space, equipment, tools, or materials encumber, result in non-value-added activity, or put health and safety at risk.	You agree the way equipment, materials, tools, and work space are designed add time, costs, or errors or reduces morale; you agree that a feasibility study or cost-benefit analysis on redesigning the thing or space should be performed.	• How the current equipment, materials, tools, or work space are affecting costs today and in the future • Who needs to be involved • Who will arrange for their involvement • Who will own the project and facilitate changes • How you will measure success

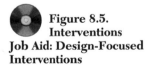

**Figure 8.5.
Interventions
Job Aid: Design-Focused
Interventions**

so that the same tasks can be automated. Examples of interventions that standardize include:

- Requiring all production runs to produce the same volume of product
- Using the same packaging sizes for multiple products
- Requiring production workers to follow the same line setup procedures
- Adopting standard labels and icons

- Designing new technology to work with older technology
- Applying the same formatting rules to documents and training materials
- Using an automated answering system to handle customer calls
- Installing process controllers to monitor and run production lines

Recommend interventions that standardize when deviation adds extra costs, results in lower yields, or causes variance in the quality of work.

Interventions That Redesign. Interventions in this family address the design of physical things to enhance safety and reduce injury. Physical things include space, equipment, tools, and materials. These interventions call for changes in lighting, furnishing, fixtures, finishes, and fabrics and the reconfiguration of space, computer screens, and keyboards. Recommend interventions that redesign work space, equipment, tools, and materials when the current design results in non-value-adding activity or endangers people's health and safety.

Your processes should enable you to determine the cost of reorganizing, standardizing, and redesigning relationships, tasks, procedures, workplaces, or equipment and compare that cost to the anticipated gain.

FIELD NOTES: REDESIGNING MANUALS
AND WORK PROCEDURES

Russ knew there had to be a better way for the CSRs to get information about different equipment models. He knew that the manuals were located too far from the CSRs' call stations and that it was time-consuming to locate the specific information required to answer a customer's question. He suggested putting together a small team of CSRs to identify ways to make the information more accessible.

The team first identified the equipment and models most frequently asked about. Next, they created job aids with the information that CSRs needed to reference most frequently. The team also recommended standards for the manuals, specifically the use of icons, labels, and colors to help speed up the process of finding information. The team recommended as well a different set of procedures for the least-asked-about equipment and models. The new procedures allowed the CSRs to note the exception and offer to call the customer back after researching the question. They also recommended establishing a different standard call-handling time for questions about these models. Then the team compared the cost of handling the current number of callbacks with the cost of implementing these changes to see if the number of callbacks would go down enough to justify the change. Russ's solution incorporated defining and getting agreement on the most used information, agreeing on a design, and creating a job aid (documenting what was agreed to) so the information was more easily retrievable, and agreeing on new work protocols.

Capacity- and Capability-Focused Interventions

The next three interventions are about enhancing people's capacities and capabilities (see Figure 8.6). Just like the interventions that deal with consequences and design, these too must be performed after or in conjunction with those that focus on information. These interventions in particular require superior interpersonal skills and skill in creating dissonance and staying focused. Expertise in designing instructional programs may also be required

Interventions That Reframe. Interventions in this family consist of events or messages that produce a new mental image for people. They are performed to help people look at problems in a new way, gain a new perspective, or redefine a situation so that they can solve their own problems. Reframing is done a lot but is rarely recognized as an intervention. Creating a new paradigm is an example of reframing. New paradigms help people let go of old ways of doing

Figure 8.6. Interventions Job Aid: Capacity- and Capability-Focused Interventions

Family	If you have evidence that	and	then decide
10. *Interventions that reframe*	Old attitudes about work are preventing innovation or growth.	You agree that strategies are needed for breaking up old models, letting go of the past, and coming up with new possibilities; people are stuck or keep applying the same solution with no results, or there is resistance to change.	• What opportunities are available to get people to let go • Who you want to involve • How you want it done • When it will start • How you will measure success
11. *Interventions that counsel*	People are preoccupied with or distracted by personal and career issues, and this is limiting productivity or adding unnecessary costs.	You agree people are preoccupied with themselves, their future, their family; their behavior interferes with others' work or calls into question their effectiveness; you agree to recommend programs or services designed to help people take action and feel more in control.	• What resources are available • Who you want to involve, and what they will do • How you want it done • When it will start • How you will measure success
12. *Interventions that develop*	Current performance is suffering or future performance will suffer because people lack skills and knowledge.	You agree people's skills are out of date; people need cross-training so they can be redeployed; there is a need to develop people for the future; you agree to recommend programs designed to build and reinforce the skills and knowledge required for today and tomorrow.	• Who needs development, why they need it, and when they need it by • How to best fulfill the need • How to best develop and deliver the program • How you will measure the development achieved the desired results

business. Turning a disadvantage into an advantage is another example. Board, electronic, and team games, that distort time, relationships, and location, or impose different social rules can be examples of reframing. Photographs and drawings done from an unusual vantage point enable people to see things in new ways. Organizations use reframing activities when they want to rechannel people's energy toward new possibilities. Therapists use them when they want to help patients develop new mental models that support emotional growth and constructive relationships. Recommend these types of interventions when old attitudes and frames of reference prevent growth.

Interventions That Counsel. Interventions in this family help people deal with family, financial, career, and health issues. Some examples are employee assistance programs, on-site fitness centers, on-site day care services, smoking cessation programs, and preretirement and financial planning seminars. Recommend interventions from this family when people are preoccupied with personal and career issues that distract them, reduce productivity, and increase costs.

Interventions That Develop. Interventions in this family improve or expand people's knowledge and skills. Examples are training programs, mentoring programs, job swapping, cross-functional teams, community college programs, continuing education courses, conferences, and seminars. Recommend interventions from this family when people's lack of skills and knowledge adversely affect their current or future performance.

Your consulting and needs assessment processes should help you determine the cost of increasing people's capacity to perform and deal with personal and business issues and compare that cost to the anticipated gain.

FIELD NOTES: BUILDING COMMITMENT AND REFRAMING A RELATIONSHIP

Mike returned from visiting the supplier's plant. The dirty, rundown conditions he saw and poor employee morale indicated either that the company was misusing money or the owner was not sufficiently reinvesting in the company. Mike shared his observations about the supplier with his management, particularly about the condition of the plant, quality of the cafeteria, and operating budget. He recommended that before his company lent money to the supplier, it should reframe its relationship with the supplier. He recommended requiring the supplier to implement some specific performance goals:

- Reinvest an agreed-on amount of money in the business.
- Use the reinvestment to upgrade the plant and equipment.

- Fund training for employees.
- Do a morale survey to establish a baseline measure that can be used later to determine if improvement had occurred.
- Agree to on-site visits.
- Make quarterly progress reports.

In exchange, Mike's company would guarantee the supplier a minimum amount of business over the next five years. Mike also suggested that the two companies set product performance standards and financial performance goals. If the supplier did not meet those standards or goals within a specified amount of time, the supplier would lose the business. Mike recommended his company determine how much improvement the supplier must demonstrate, and by when, to make a loan worthwhile. Mike's solution was a combination of defining new performance standards and making the consequences of not meeting those standards clear. Finally, he recommended a significant redefinition of his company's relationship with the supplier that spelled out expectations, measures, and accountability. The recommended changes were so significant that they constituted a reframing because they changed how both companies viewed their relationship.

Action-Focused Interventions

These interventions are about engaging in activities that stimulate or enable others to act (see Figure 8.7). Similar to interventions that deal with capacity, capability, design, and consequences, these too should be performed after or in conjunction with those that focus on information. These interventions require superior skills in diplomacy, tact, and persuasion. An understanding of how to use group pressure, guilt, shame, and other psychological appeals is helpful.

Interventions That Advocate. Interventions in this family are designed to get individuals and groups to support goals by committing funds, resources, time, and the like. Maybe you've witnessed social groups appealing to elected leaders or public opinion through sit-ins, marches, advertisements, and blogs. Businesses, especially large, decentralized ones, find it difficult to get functional leaders to commit resources to major initiatives, such as committing to a standard technology or work procedure. The problem is especially difficult when the organization is a federation of firms that must work together as a collective to be competitive in the marketplace. The individual leaders may have

Family	If you have evidence that	and	then decide
13. *Interventions that advocate*	Key constituents or stakeholders are unwilling to act, commit to support, or change their behavior despite being informed of consequences of nonaction.	Failure to act, support, or change could undermine the success of an effort or potentially put at risk life, safety, image, power, or assets; appeals to ego, public image, or status have not been tried; the use of public or peer pressure might be effective; getting commitment requires people to break ranks or go against their peers; or effectively confronting a manager whose style is to intimidate requires a great deal of skills.	• Who specifically needs to act and how • How to appeal to those whose support is required • What psychological, social, and personal appeals you might use • How to make public or create public awareness that support is lacking and the consequences • How to set up structures that protect potential supporters and adopters • How you will measure success • Who individually or collectively has the skills to effectively confront managers
14. *Interventions that serve*	People lack the resources to intervene on their own behalf.	You know people with the required resources, expertise, and interest to serve.	• How to communicate the need for service • How to schedule and organize the service • Whether anonymity is desired • What has to be in place to ensure the safety and effectiveness of the server and recipient • How you will measure the success or effectiveness of the action

**Figure 8.7.
Interventions
Job Aid: Action-Focused
Interventions**

different priorities, values, and perceived understandings of the need to act. The techniques that organizations use to get leaders and senior managers to act include:

- The creation of user or customer councils where leaders have to respond to their stakeholders about emerging market needs and new demands

- Reporting how leaders rank in comparison to their peers on specific variables like earnings compared to investment in development, safety records, and customer and employee retention

- Participation in industry studies requiring participant organizations to reveal their practices, which are then compared to an industry standard or industry peer, and made public

FIELD NOTES: USING PEER PRESSURE AND APPEALING TO EGOS

Carol knew that simply telling executives that the company needed better employee practices would not be enough. Telling them about the increased incidence of occupational suicides, job-related accidents, and job disability due to job stress was not enough either. She knew, though, that the executives were very competitive and status conscious and decided to devise a way to get them to report their progress on adopting a suite of behaviors they identified as necessary for reducing job stress.

After briefing the executives on the economic impact of the increased deaths, accidents, and turnover tied directly to management practices, she persuaded them to identify and commit to a set of behaviors they believed would improve the situation. They then set personal goals for adopting those behaviors, committed to holding each other accountable, and agreed to report their progress at the regularly scheduled quarterly executive meetings. She also persuaded the president to set aside time on the agenda for this, increasing the odds that the executives would be prepared with their reports. Each executive was asked to report his percentage of goal accomplishment, and the results were put on a chart for everyone to see. Carol gambled that their egos would pressure them to make a serious attempt at meeting their commitments.

Jeff was charged with improving the performance of field technicians who worked for independently owned dealerships throughout the world. His company could build the training, create the assessments necessary for certification, and even hold contests to reward those who achieved it, but the company had no authority over the technicians. His success depended on his ability to convince dealers to commit the funds required for technicians to participate in the training and certification.

He began with an appeal to the more successful dealers, and together they decided to set up a dealer council to provide direction and set priorities on what products most needed training and certification. The plan was for the council to meet semiannually to discuss participation in the training and certification and compare it to key metrics on a scorecard such as technician productivity, customer satisfaction scores, and equipment utilization. Jeff and the dealers who devised the plan counted on peer pressure and the competitive nature of using a scorecard to get participation. Dealers in each market were asked to elect a representative. Within a short time, it was considered an honor to be elected to the council and participate in the training and certification. Jeff used the council to recognize dealers whose scores improved after participation in the training. He also used the council to recognize technicians who achieved certification.

Interventions That Serve. Interventions in this family are intended to provide resources to individuals and groups who might usually be capable of helping themselves but due to extenuating circumstance cannot. These types of interventions are usually done in response to political, economic, or environmental crises such as wars and natural disasters. Some examples are the tsunami that hit Sri Lanka, India, and neighboring countries; the earthquake in Pakistan; and Hurricane Katrina. Each left hundreds of thousands of people homeless. Other examples of service providers include Habitat for Humanity, which builds homes for the homeless, the Heifer Foundation, which gives people livestock along with training so they are self-sufficient, the Red Cross, which provides emergency food and shelter, and Doctors Without Borders, which sends doctors into war zones to provide medical help. Extenuating circumstances happen to businesses as well, necessitating employees to help in ways beyond their normal work. Some examples of these types of interventions at the organizational level include:

- Loaning skilled workers to industry partners in response to a major disaster
- Asking workers to supplement teams because of a shortage of skilled help due to an excessive demand for work as the result of a market demand or a natural disaster

Your consulting and needs assessment processes should help you determine the effort required to encourage others to act and provide service.

FIELD NOTES: COMING TO THE RESCUE

When the New Orleans airport was destroyed by Hurricane Katrina in 2005, leadership from area airports met to decide how they could help. The Houston, Dulles, and Atlanta airports developed a disaster response plan and decided they would take turns sending equipment and skilled workers for ten to twenty days at a time to do whatever was necessary. As a result, the New Orleans airport was one of the first facilities restored to functionality after the hurricane.

Congruency-Focused Interventions. The last family of interventions is about congruency. Like the interventions that deal with consequences, design, capability, capacity, and action, these too are done after or in conjunction with those that precede it. Like the other interventions, you will use your expertise in assessment and measurement and your skill at facilitation (see Figure 8.8).

Family	*If you have evidence that*	*and*	*then decide*
15. *Interventions that align*	Current messages, behavior, consequences, systems, structures, or environment do not support the organization's goals.	You agree that what people say is not what they do, what the organization wants, or how people get the work done is not in keeping with the organization's values or public image; you agree to identify what is out of alignment and recommend ways to bring it into alignment.	• What is out of alignment • What it will take to bring it back into alignment • Who needs to be involved • How to get them involved • Who will facilitate the session to get buy-in • When it will be done • How you will measure success

Figure 8.8. Interventions Job Aid: Congruency-Focused Interventions

Interventions That Align. Interventions in this family help ensure that an organization's goals, practices, consequences, and resources are all supporting the same vision and mission. Sometimes programs that seem to be appropriate, on track, or working successfully may actually be counterproductive over time. The result could be wasted investment because programs are aborted or abandoned when the company realizes they drain resources, shift costs, or undermine other initiatives. An example is an intervention that is designed to promote the values of openness and honesty but is implemented in an environment that punishes people for being candid. Another example is work groups that claim to encourage critical debate to avoid mistakes but actually chastise people who offer criticism for not being team players. The result is that communication is accomplished through innuendo and the rumor mill.

Recommend interventions that better align values and norms with goals when rhetoric and behavior do not support each other. Your processes should allow you to compare the cost of operating under conflicting goals, practices, and so on with the cost of bringing them into alignment.

FIELD NOTES: CERTIFICATION

Russ and the team assigned to support the new product line at the medical manufacturer decided they wanted a program (an intervention) that improved the reliability of diagnostic equipment by ensuring field technicians were competent to install and service the equipment, and would earn customer confidence (the intervention's measures of success). The team decided that if the company certified the field technicians (the specific intervention) they might accomplish both goals. Field technicians install and commission the equipment; they also do preventive maintenance and repairs. The equipment performs diagnostic tests for doctors. Because doctors use the results of these tests to prescribe treatments, the performance of the equipment is critical.

The decision to develop a certification program put into motion a series of smaller yet supportive interventions. First the team had to do a job analysis (*define* the job and the criteria for judging proficiency). In the process, the team discovered wide variances in preventive maintenance practice across geographical zones. The team brought together engineers, zone directors, and technicians who shared their practices and agreed to a common set of procedures (*standardization*). To be certified, technicians would be required to demonstrate competence and consistent performance (based on *established measures*). The criteria used to judge competence and consistent performance were level of customer satisfaction (measured by ratings on customer satisfaction surveys), productivity (measured by noting the number of installations within a period of time, the efficiency of the installations, and the average time spent on the installation), troubleshooting skill (measured by using problem simulations), and adherence to procedures (measured by direct observation of the task at a client site). The technicians' performance was documented and communicated informally to technicians and zone managers. Technicians had six months to meet the criteria. Those who did were given special recognition (a reward); those who did not were offered the opportunity for remediation (development) or placement in another job (enforcement). The team then looked at the training given to new employees. The training did not adequately explain customer expectations or provide practice in the procedures and troubleshooting. The team then recommended that the training be modified to match the criteria of the certification (alignment).

FIELD TECHNIQUES: USING THE INTERVENTIONS IF-THEN TABLES

You can use the if-then tables (Figures 8.3 through 8.8) to facilitate discussions about what other elements might be affected by implementing a major intervention. Use them to drive discussions about what else has to change for the intervention to work. The tables can help you evaluate an intervention after it has been implemented and identify why an intervention failed or met with resistance. Here are some guidelines for using tables:

1. Go over the table row by row. For each problem or "if" statement, ask if this describes your situation. If it does not, write your own problem statement, complete the "and" section, and then list what you think you should do.

2. If appropriate, discuss with your team what you want your solution to accomplish and how you might judge which actions are more likely to yield the greatest benefit.

3. Use the table with your team to identify the kinds of activities or programs that will help in your situation.

4. Identify what else has to change or be in place for your recommendations to be successful.

5. Identify how you will measure the effectiveness, cost benefit, or success of the intervention.

FIELD TOOLS: THE HIERARCHY-INTERVENTIONS MATRIX

The matrix in Figure 8.9 summarizes for you, your team, and your client, on one page, the relationship between the hierarchy and the interventions. The columns contain the elements of the hierarchy you examined during your needs assessment, and the rows are the families of interventions.

As the matrix shows, more than one intervention is almost always necessary to produce long-lasting results. Use the matrix to help you decide what needs to be done and in what order to do it. Here are some guidelines for using the matrix:

1. Compare what you decided would be the appropriate combination of interventions from the if-then table with what the matrix indicates.

**Figure 8.9.
The Hierarchy-
Interventions Matrix**

If one of the elements in the hierarchy is a cause of a performance problem, then one or more of the interventions marked in that column can help eliminate the problem.

Families of Interventions — *Elements of the Hierarchy*

Interventions that . . .	Vision and Mission	Goals and Objectives	Rewards and Consequences	Organizational Job Structures	Procedures and Processes	Documentation and Standards	Job Aids and Signage	Physical Spaces	Training and Development	Resource Capacity
Define	X	X	X	X	X	X	X	X	X	X
Inform	X	X	X	X	X	X	X	X	X	X
Document	X	X	X	X	X	X	X	X	X	X
Reward			X							
Measure		X	X	X	X	X	X	X	X	X
Enforce		X	X	X	X	X	X	X	X	
Organize				X	X			X		
Standardize					X	X	X	X		X
(Re)Design					X	X	X	X		
Reframe		X	X							
Counsel										X
Develop					X				X	
Advocate	X	X	X							X
Serve										X
Align	X	X	X	X	X	X	X	X	X	X

2. Remember that performance problems are caused by a series of interdependent variables, not just one factor.

3. Because most performance problems are the result of a number of smaller breakdowns, the solutions must be done in combination if long-term change is your goal.

4. Discuss with your team how a single large intervention (like implementing new technology, reengineering a major process, or establishing a certification program) might accomplish most, if not all, of your goals.

5. Discuss what has to be done for your intervention to produce lasting results.

6. Decide what would be a reasonable course of action.

7. Decide who needs to be involved, in what ways they need to be involved, and when they need to be involved.

8. Define everyone's roles and responsibilities.

9. Use this information to build a project plan for designing, implementing, and evaluating the intervention.

FIELD TECHNIQUES: ELIMINATING BARRIERS TO BECOMING A PERFORMANCE CONSULTANT

To gain practice identifying the best combination of interventions, use the if-then tables to come up with an action plan to support your own transition—for example:

1. Information-focused intervention

   • Define performance consulting. What will you do to gain agreement and understanding among your colleagues and clients as to what performance consulting is and how it will be done in your organization?

   • Inform others of your intent and services. How will you communicate your vision and mission to staff, clients, and colleagues? Will you develop a flowchart like Mike's (Figure 1.10) or use something else to document your vision, mission, goals, and processes?

2. Consequence-focused intervention

   • Consequences. What are the consequences of your success or failure?

   • Measure results. Will you measure your performance in terms of how efficient and effective your processes are, how satisfied your customers are, or your ability to measure your results? Will you use the kinds of measures Mike wants to use (Figure 2.2) or something else?

3. Design-focused intervention

- How have you decided how to organize your department or your projects?

- What standard procedures and processes will you adopt?

- Will you redesign any elements of your work space or equipment to support the new role?

4. Capacity- and capabilities-focused intervention

- Would reframing your new role help your clients understand it and be better able to work with you in new ways?

- Do you or any of your colleagues want additional development or training? If so, what would be the topic or skill? Do you think development would be valuable?

5. Action-focused intervention

- Whose commitment do you need? How will you get it?

- Are there opportunities to provide service that would allow you an opportunity to build credibility?

6. Congruence-focused intervention

- How will you align your vision, mission, processes, measures, and practices so that all your resources are concentrated on the same goal?

SUMMARY

Organizations are always going to do things to shape human performance and improve business results. They can do it with or without a process. As a performance consultant, you offer them a process that allows them to set measures, identify resources, identify barriers, and take control. You can use that same process to help them fully understand the implications of their actions and be successful.

WHERE TO LEARN MORE

There are a number of publications on different types of interventions. You are encouraged to learn all you can if you want to develop special expertise in a particular type of intervention such as designing jobs, reengineering processes, developing leaders, and developing job aids. You are also encouraged to develop relationships with experts in your organization who may specialize in rewards and recognition, interior design, industrial design, and other topics.

In addition to reading what others have written about Taylor and the Gilbreths, I found it enlightening to read their writings myself. This way I could draw my own conclusions about the importance of their work.

Clark, R., and Estes, F. *Turning Research into Results: A Guide to Selecting the Right Performance Solutions.* Atlanta, Ga.: CEP Press, 2002. Every performance consultant should have command of the insights and ideas explored in this well-written and well-researched book.

Hale, J. *Performance-Based Certification: How to Design a Valid, Defensible, Cost-Effective Program.* San Francisco: Jossey-Bass/Pfeiffer, 2001.

Hale, J. *Outsourcing Training and Development: Success Factors.* San Francisco: Jossey-Bass/Pfeiffer, 2006.

Chapter 9
Measuring Results

*S*ometimes people have trouble measuring because they are unclear about what it is they want to accomplish by doing so. Some people simply don't know how to measure. Nonetheless, managers keep asking for better measures so they can decide which programs to fund and support. All of us are being asked to prove that our programs are worth the investment. Here are some examples.

FIELD NOTES: MEASURING RESULTS

- A large data processing firm wanted to certify its resellers. The resellers had asked for the certification. They claimed that being "brand certified" would give them a competitive edge. Senior management wanted to know how the payoff would be measured.

- A company decided to require quality training for all employees. The company had seven field offices located in three states. The training was scheduled to last from one to one and a half days. The training manager wanted to know how success would be measured.

- The HR vice president got his company to support a corporate university because a benchmarking study had found that employees were attracted to and more inclined to stay with companies that have aggressive employee development programs. The company also bought, at the vice president's insistence, a new computer system so HR staff at corporate headquarters could transfer information to field HR staff. In the past, they had relied on phone calls and faxes. Senior management now wants the vice president to show the return on investment.

In each of these cases, people wanted support for their program or intervention. What they hadn't figured out was how to measure its worth or effectiveness. Measurement, when done well, helps people make better decisions about where to direct resources, what programs to fund, and if they should invest more (or less) in current programs. Our role as performance consultants is to help clients develop better measures and measuring systems.

EXPERIENCES FROM THE FIELD: ABOUT MEASURING

I've learned that my clients and I do not share a common language or understanding of evaluation. For example, clients frequently use the words *evaluation* and *measurement* to mean the same thing, but at other times they use them to mean completely different things. By listening and questioning, we can help our clients define what they want to evaluate and why. Here is how I use these and related terms:

- *Evaluation* is the act of judging something or placing value on it. To learn what your clients value, observe what they pay attention to. For instance, if a client keeps talking about something or repeatedly raises a particular issue, that subject is important to him or her. Our job as performance consultants is to use our questioning and active listening skills to find out what makes a subject important to our clients.

- *Measuring* is the act of comparing. When clients talk about needing to improve performance, they are motivated by the difference between current performance and some standard or goal they want to obtain. They would not know that their current performance needed improvement if they had not compared it to something and found it lacking in some way. Measuring is done by gathering information about a situation, activity, or process and then comparing the information against criteria that define a desired standard. As performance consultants, our job is find out if our clients have considered sufficient information and to determine what criteria should be used as a basis for comparison.

- *Criteria* are the gauges or yardsticks people use to weigh, rank, or value what it is they are comparing. The criteria may be stated, unspoken, or assumed. For example, when people say "the training worked," they are measuring the program or intervention they are referring to (in this case, training). What such statements leave unclear is the criteria they are using. The criterion might be that the participants liked the training or that after the training was complete, a performance problem went away. When you hear "The safety program fell short of what we wanted" or "People don't get it," those making the statements are basing their conclusions on some criteria. Our job is to ask questions to find out what information people are using as the basis for their conclusions—what they are using to judge adequacy. Commonly used criteria are time, speed, quantity, weight, accuracy, purity, consistency, earnings, costs, savings, compliance, satisfaction, appearance, appropriateness, and performance.

- *Metrics* are units of measure. They allow for precision and exactness. For example, if the criterion is speed, the metric used might be seconds to the fourth decimal point (as in Olympic swimming and running competitions). For some other purpose, the metric for speed might be days, weeks, or even months. The metric for weight might be grams or tons. When product performance is measured by sales volume (the criterion), the metric could be tens of thousands of dollars. If the criterion for product performance changes from sales volume to customer satisfaction, the metric might be the number of customer complaints over a six-month period.

Measuring can be the impetus for formal needs assessments (described in Chapter Seven), it can influence the process of identifying appropriate interventions (as described in Chapter Eight), and it can affect how a program gets evaluated (the focus of this chapter). What is most important is that everything gets measured for a reason. Here are some examples.

FIELD NOTES: TRANSACTIONS, NEW ACCOUNTS, AND THE PERFORMANCE APPRAISAL FORM

A retailer decided to launch a promotion. The retailer hired a public relations (PR) firm to design the campaign. They agreed that the PR firm would receive a bonus if the promotion was a success, and the store owner agreed that the criteria for measuring the promotion's success would be the number of transactions (cash register sales) recorded during the campaign. This criterion provided only a partial picture of the promotion's effects, however. Promotions often encourage customers to buy items priced at or below cost; therefore a high number of transactions may or may not mean that the store is making money. In fact, it may only be breaking even, or possibly losing money. Transactions by themselves do not give an accurate picture of financial success. Thus although the criterion of number of transactions met the PR firm's needs, it may not have met the store owner's needs. If the store owner's objective was to grow the business, to increase profits, or to build customer loyalty, the owner would not know whether the promotion had met his objectives. Other criteria were needed.

A bank had a $5 million merchandising budget to attract new customers and encourage current customers to buy additional products, such as mortgage loans, auto loans, and certificates of deposits. Merchandising is used to attract customers to other products or services at the point of sale, in this case, the bank. The merchandising budget was for signs, banners, window decals, fliers, and lobby displays.

One of the bank's products was free checking with no minimum balance for three years. To determine the return on investment of the merchandising effort, the bank asked its branch managers to track the number of new checking accounts opened over a one-month period. Free checking is a loss leader, however; customers who want free checking usually have low-balance accounts, which makes them the most costly accounts to service. Banks therefore lose money on free checking accounts. Measuring only the number of new free checking accounts does not accurately measure the return on investment for the merchandising campaign.

The HR director for a municipal government developed a new performance appraisal process. The municipality's employees were all unionized, and the union had negotiated that performance measures and salary could not be linked. The HR director wanted to prove there was nevertheless a benefit to adopting a new performance appraisal process and convinced management that a new performance appraisal form would have value and increase productivity despite the union contract. The director suggested that they measure the form's effectiveness based on how many managers used it. However, the number of managers using the form has no bearing on productivity. Other criteria were needed before HR could prove that the cost to develop the form and train managers how to use it was worth the investment.

These stories illustrate two common measurement problems: insufficient criteria and inappropriate criteria and metrics:

- *Insufficient criteria.* In each case, only one criterion (the number of transactions, new checking accounts, and managers who used the process) was used. Other measures the retailer might have used were the number of add-on transactions (transactions for items that were not part of the promotion), the margin (profit) that resulted from those other transactions, and how much the overall sales volume changed. The retailer could then have compared these measures to the cost of the promotion, which included the costs of advertisements and printed collateral materials and the amount of time it took sales clerks off the floor to be briefed on the promotion. In the case of the new appraisal process, the HR department could have measured whether performance had improved, how the process affected development, or if it reduced turnover.

• *Inappropriate criteria and metrics.* In each of these cases, the only thing that was tracked was volume over a period of time. None of these measures tracked if costs were eliminated, avoided, reduced, or shifted to other parts of the organization, and as a result, management got a distorted picture of what happened. For example, new checking accounts may have been opened, but if the balances were low, the cost of servicing those accounts was not recovered, thus increasing overall costs. The bank should have used other criteria that are better indicators of business results.

FIELD TECHNIQUES: GETTING MORE THAN TWO SOURCES OF MEASURES

It takes more than two sources of measures to get an accurate picture of what is working and how well it is working. Therefore, find out:

• Whose needs are being met by the current mode of measurement

• Why the client chooses to use certain criteria and metrics

• How the picture would change if different criteria or metrics were used

• What other criteria or metrics could be added that would give a more accurate picture of the situation

• How you can capture the information you need in a reasonable and cost-effective way

---

FIELD NOTES: MEASURING THE SUCCESS OF A BLENDED LEARNING SOLUTION

Before she joined the firm, Deborah's department had contracted with a vendor to develop a Web-based component for training new employees. The company asked Deborah to prove the investment in the component was worth it. Deborah learned that the new training program was nine weeks long, that on average eight hundred to nine hundred new employees were trained annually, and that forty-five full-time trainers were dedicated to delivering the training. The initial investment for the Web-based component was $1.2 million. The promise made to management was that the Web-based component would shorten the time required for training new employees. What had happened instead was that the length of the training got longer by two weeks, not shorter.

Deborah knew that the length of the training program was only one measure of its success. A second measure could be the overall cycle time it takes to bring a new employee to proficiency. A third measure could be how the Web-based component affected the indirect costs of the center. Deborah began her search for the other measures. She learned that:

- The training course was now longer because more content had been added. In the past, the content covered by the Web-based component had been left to supervisors to cover once an employee was released to his or her job.
- In the past, it had taken on average another fifteen weeks beyond the training period to bring a new employee to proficiency.
- Proficiency was measured in terms of average call-handling time and order accuracy.

After the company added the Web-based component to the training course, new employees achieved the standards for order accuracy and call-handling time within seven weeks. This meant that the overall cycle time had dropped from twenty-four weeks (nine weeks of class time plus fifteen weeks of on-the-job training) to eighteen weeks (eleven weeks of class time plus seven weeks on the job). Achieving order accuracy faster reduced the cost of rework due to errors (an indirect cost), and the supervisors' time to coach the new employees was reduced by half (an indirect cost). The reductions in cycle time and indirect costs proved the value of the Web-based component. If Deborah had looked only at how the Web-based component had affected the length of the class, she would have had a distorted picture of the impact it had.

MEASUREMENT: THREE PHASES

Measurement should occur at three points during the life cycle of an intervention (see Figure 9.1). First, the results of the measurement activity are used to create a business case for supporting an intervention. Once an intervention is approved, measurement is done to ensure it is workable. After an intervention is implemented, measurement is done to determine the results or impact.

The Business Case

When measurement is done before an intervention is agreed on or funded, the result is a business case that describes the need for an intervention and presents an argument for action. The information in the business case should come from more than one source, such as through observations, interviews, or surveys. The business case describes the current condition (also known as the *baseline*) and what is to be gained if action is taken (the intended results). Ideally it should contain the leading and lagging indicators of success. *Leading indicators* are interim results or behaviors that predict ultimate success, such as the rate of adoption by the target audience and trends in consumer survey data. This information is essential to the next phase of measurement activity. *Lagging indicators* are the results that occur at the end of an agreed-upon period of time, such as the annual turnover rate, healthcare costs, or dollar volume of sales.

Phase I: Analysis	Phase II: Design and Development	Phase III: Implementation and Maintenance
Purpose: To determine the scope of the need	Purpose: To increase the odds an intervention will produce the desired results	Purpose: To determine the degree to which an intervention fulfilled the goals set during Phase I
Output: A business case with: • An argument for an intervention • A call to action • Baseline measures • The goal and expected gain or benefits • Leading and lagging indicators of success • Project milestones	Output: Recommended corrective action based on a formative evaluation of the intervention and its components: • Usability • Compatibility • Feasibility • Workability • Status at milestones • Progress against leading indicators	Output: A summative or confirmative evaluation of an intervention's results: • Outputs • Outcomes • Fallout

Figure 9.1.
When Measurement
Occurs and Why

Formative Evaluation

Measurement should happen during the design and development of an intervention and its components to confirm the project is on track and to identify the need for corrective action. Measurement at this time is called *formative* or *in-process* evaluation. It includes tests of usability, compatibility, and feasibility. During the design and development phase, assumptions were made that need to be confirmed: for example, how easy it is for the user to use the intervention or its components compared to what was intended and if the interface between the intervention's technologies works as intended. Measurement at this phase increases the odds that an intervention will be successful.

Summative or Confirmative Evaluation

Measurement should occur once an intervention is launched and at predetermined times thereafter to measure the results and confirm the intervention is working as planned. Measurement at this time also identifies any unintended consequences (good and bad), such as adoption by people beyond the target audience or an increase in indirect costs by a user group. As a performance consultant, you are in an ideal position to show the purpose, benefits, and outputs of measuring during all three phases.

FIELD NOTES: GETTING SUPPORT FOR MEASURING

Carol wanted her program to reduce stress in the workplace by changing the behavior of senior managers. But the organization had no history of even measuring needs, much less results. Instead, action occurred once a sponsor declared a need. Carol determined to use this program to do a more formal measurement effort. To begin, she wanted to develop the business case that would document health care and related costs associated with the managers' current behaviors. She wanted to use the business case as a technique to persuade the president, the executive HR vice president, and the senior executive team to identify and agree on the baseline measures, what the leading indicators of success would be, and how they wanted to confirm the program was working as intended. She began by explaining to the president, the executive HR vice president, and the medical director when, why, and how she thought the measurement should happen and what the benefits would be. They used the opportunity to suggest leading indicators, ways to get the data by leveraging other data-gathering efforts, and what she should do if she found the program was getting off track. Daring to explain the when, whys, and how of measuring such an important initiative set a new precedent for Carol and her team.

HOW TO SELECT CRITERIA

One of the hardest parts of measuring anything is knowing what to use as criteria. When should the criterion be money? When should it be time? When should it be compliance, customer satisfaction, volume, or something else? As a performance consultant, your goal is to identify sufficient criteria to corroborate the results. You want an accurate picture of the situation. Following are discussions of some possible measurement criteria.

Costs

All interventions affect costs in one or more ways. They can eliminate costs, reduce costs, avoid costs, or shift costs to someone else or to a later time. An intervention affects costs if it:

- Saved time (time is money)
- Eliminated activities such as checking work fewer times or reducing the number of steps in a process (activities consume resources)
- Improved product performance such as lengthening the shelf life or reducing the amount of maintenance required
- Improved processes, such as eliminating the need for checking, waiting, or handling, or resulted in products and services that deviated less from standard

• Increased human productivity (for example, increasing the unit of work per hour)

I pay particular attention to whether the intervention shifted costs. This happens when the intervention increases the number of activities to be performed by others (such as forcing them to do more checking, take more steps to do their work, wait longer, use more resources, or do work they would not ordinarily have to do). Shifting costs also happens when others are forced to use more resources or more expensive resources than they have in the past.

Another consideration is the cost of the intervention itself. What did it cost to develop, and what did it cost to implement? Be sure to include both direct costs (such as consultant or vendor fees or any resource dedicated to the project) and indirect costs (for example, administrative and management time). How do these costs compare to the cost of the problem? What other costs did the intervention affect?

Satisfaction

Next, I think about how satisfied all the vested parties are with the results of the intervention—the consumers, internal customers, management, and the employees performing the job. As a criterion, satisfaction is more than how happy people are; it includes how they feel about the intervention, how it was developed, who was involved, and how it was implemented. Another component of satisfaction is how confident the vested parties are that the program will fulfill its promise. A third component is image. In this case, you find out how strongly people want to be associated with the intervention. If the intervention is popular, more people will want it known that they played a role in its identification, development, or deployment. If it is unpopular, they will disassociate themselves from it.

Rate of Adoption or Use

Interventions work only if people do them, use them, or embrace them as part of doing business. Consider measuring who is using the intervention, how many are using it, and how often they are using it.

Goal Accomplishment

Behind every intervention there should have been a need to satisfy, an issue to resolve, an opportunity to seize, or a problem to be avoided. The criterion then becomes what the client will accept as evidence the intervention achieved its purpose.

FIELD TOOLS: THE COMMON MEASURES, CRITERIA, AND METRICS JOB AID

Figure 9.2 mirrors the first four columns of the scorecard introduced in Chapter Seven for needs assessment. It contains a more detailed list of what commonly gets measured, the criteria used, and possible metrics. Use it with your team and client to come up with more ways to measure what happened, what changed, and what still needs attention. Add any criteria and metrics you would like so that it meets your needs. Discuss what might be a feasible way to measure the project you are working on.

FIELD TECHNIQUES: GETTING EVIDENCE

When clients have difficulty coming up with measurement criteria, I ask them what they will accept as evidence that the program worked, the problem was solved, or the situation improves. This seems to be an easier question to answer than, "What criteria do you want to use?" Evidence is made up of the behaviors and results that have to be present or absent for people to believe changes have been made.

FIELD TOOLS: EVIDENCE WORKSHEET

Figure 9.3 has examples of evidence for each intervention. Figure 9.4 is a worksheet you can use to list what you and your client will accept as evidence that your intervention has worked.

To use the worksheet, think about the kinds of projects or programs you are working on. Then:

1. List what you will take as evidence that your project or program has been successful.

2. Be sure to list corroborating evidence (this is analogous to having more than one measure or set of criteria).

3. Discuss how different people might want different evidence depending on how they see the situation.

4. Discuss what might be a feasible way to get the evidence you are looking for.

FIELD TECHNIQUES: GETTING TO THE OBVIOUS

Clients sometimes assume the right people know what is being measured, how it is being measured, and why. These are dangerous assumptions. Subordinates in particular are inclined to behave as if they understand even when they don't. It takes courage to ask questions, especially if someone of higher status has the answers. One of the benefits to being a consultant is that you are expected to ask questions. Ask open-ended questions that elicit information, clarification, or additional insight. Stay away from closed questions, except to confirm your

Key Measures: what organizations pay attention to and value	Criteria: things commonly used to measure performance	Metrics: what gets counted, weighed, and so on	Ways to get the information or metrics
Customer satisfaction	Perceptions and opinions; complaints and returns; referrals	Ratings of how strongly the opinion is held; number of incidents; cost to resolve problems	Focus groups; rating scales on surveys; customer service numbers
Employee satisfaction	Morale; grievances; turnover and retention	Mean score on survey; number of incidents per year; percentage within x months; cost to recruit	Surveys; focus groups; interviews; exit interviews
Market share	Actual compared to potential or competition	Dollar amount or percentage of sales; number of units sold; cost to increase service	Market research; industry indexes
Productivity	Time at task; units produced; calls received; process versus cycle time	Percentage of time; number and average per time; average call-handling time; size of gap; indirect cost to achieve	Time sheets; production records; worksheets
Product performance	Cost; recalls; variance; customer opinion; unscheduled service; waste	Dollars or cents per unit; number per unit or model; standard deviation; ratings; number, percentage, or ratio; direct and indirect cost of waste	Finance; statistical process control (SPC) data; focus groups; service calls
People performance	Yield; waste; time at task; attainment of objectives; cost of supervision; rework	Ratio or percentage; percentage of time; percentage of achievement; ratio of managers to employees; direct and indirect cost to achieve	SPC data; time sheets; plans; budgets
Financial performance	Fixed costs; variable costs; margin; rate of growth; cost of sales; cost of service	Ratio; percentage or dollars per unit	Daily reports; actual dollars versus budgeted dollars; sales analyses
Compliance	Formal filings; incidents; reportables	Quantity, dollar value; rate per 1,000 hours; number of incidents	Quality control reports; complaint calls; citations
Growth	Training; succession plans	Number trained; dollars per employee; training that meets individual development plans; retention (dollars, number, or percentage)	Actual versus budget; changes in the database

Figure 9.2. Measures, Criteria, and Metrics Scorecard

	Intervention	Example
Information focused	1. Interventions that define: what you did to achieve clarity	An operational definition exists and is used; mistakes and rework have decreased.
	2. Interventions that inform: what you did to make sure people have the information they need when they need it	Incidents of errors and misunderstandings are down; the cost to go back and clarify or correct is down.
	3. Interventions that document: what you did to make information accessible and retrievable over time	Documents are used and have reduced cycle time for harder and less frequent tasks.
Consequences focused	4. Interventions that reward: what you put in place to make sure behaviors and results that are desired get rewarded and celebrated	Cost shifting has decreased; margins are up; complaints by employees about being treated unfairly are down.
	5. Interventions that measure: what you put in place to ensure that behaviors and results are measured according to valid criteria	A sufficient number of people have used the measures to improve processes or performance, and this has positively affected costs, service, and so on.
	6. Interventions that enforce: what you put in place to ensure there are positive and negative consequences to actions and results	Enforcement is up and appropriate.
Design focused	7. Interventions that organize: what you did to change the structure of work relationships	Cycle times and costs have decreased, and satisfaction has increased.
	8. Interventions that standardize: what you did to automate and standardize tasks, processes, and so on	Costs and cycle time have changed positively.
	9. Interventions that (re)design: what you did to make space, equipment, and materials safe, easy to use, and so on	Time lost to accidents, sick leave, and absenteeism have decreased; productivity is up.
Capacity and capabilities focused	10. Interventions that reframe: what you did to help people see new possibilities and move forward	Less time is spent rehashing old issues; more time is spent on tasks that contribute.
	11. Interventions that counsel: what you did to help people deal more effectively with personal issues	The number of people who use the services is up; there is less absenteeism and tardiness.
	12. Interventions that develop: what you did to keep people current and prepared for the future	Number of people prepared has increased; bench strength for the future is greater; turnover is lower; job satisfaction is higher.
Action focused	13. Interventions that advocate: what you did to stir others to action	More people changed their behavior in ways that were promoted by the intervention; more people publicly endorsed programs.
	14. Interventions that serve: what you did to help others	People volunteered service to those in need and donated goods and services.
	15. Interventions that align: what you did to keep promises and practices in harmony with each other and between purpose and practice	Customer surveys show less dissonance or disagreement between what is said and what is done.

Figure 9.3.
Examples of Evidence

Intervention	If you have evidence that:	What will you recommend?	What will you accept as evidence that things have improved? What metric will you use?
1. Defining	There is disagreement about goals, no shared understanding, or conflicting objectives.		
2. Informing	People are uninformed, and the consequence is poor performance; people don't get the information they need.		
3. Documenting	Documentation (job aids, manuals, help screens, and so on) is lacking, inadequate, inaccurate, or hard to access.		
4. Rewarding	The wrong behaviors are celebrated; desired performance is overlooked; there are few incentives for people to do better, do more, or to do things differently.		
5. Measuring	Measures of good performance are lacking or inappropriate.		
6. Enforcing	There are no consequences for poor performance.		
7. (Re)organizing	The way jobs and tasks are structured adds costs, reduces morale, or interferes with service.		
8. Standardizing	Lack of standardization is adding unnecessary costs.		
9. (Re)Designing	Equipment, materials, tools, or work space add time, add costs, increase errors, or reduce morale.		
10. Reframing	People are stuck, applying the same solution with no results, or resist change.		
11. Counseling	People are preoccupied with themselves, their future, or their family; people's behavior interferes with others' work or calls into question their effectiveness.		
12. Developing	People's skills are out-of-date; there is little opportunity to develop skills for the future.		
13. Advocating	People make promises but fail to carry them out; programs are aborted or only partially implemented.		
14. Serving	People have the resources and time to help others facing extenuating circumstances, and the help would enable others to meet goals or resume a previous level of self-sufficiency.		
15. Aligning	People's practices are not congruent with what the organization says it values; the amount of resources assigned to a program or initiative does not match the professed priorities of the organization.		

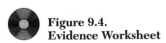

Figure 9.4.
Evidence Worksheet

understanding of a point or to get directions. Here are some examples of open-ended questions:

- "What made you notice there was a problem?" Ask this to find out what they pay attention to, what they value.

- "What makes you think the situation needs improvement or is not up to par?" Ask this to find out their reason for seeking a change and to determine if they are acting on firsthand or secondhand information.

- "What exactly has changed?" Ask this to find out what they track and if it is the same as what they pay attention to and value. If the answers are the same, the client is on track.

- "Can you think of a time when it [whatever is being measured] was okay? What was different then?" Listen for whether the answer is the same as for the previous question or if they are using other criteria. Again, this indicates whether the client "has a clue."

- "What would have to be different for you to change your opinion of the situation?" Ask this to find out what criteria the person is using.

- "What will you take as evidence things have improved?" Again, you are trying to get at all of the criteria.

- "How much do things have to improve? How will you know when the change is enough?" Ask this to find out the metric. Do things have to change 1 percent or 100 percent?

A good consultant is willing to ask tough questions instead of politically correct questions. You want clients to reflect on and question their own thinking. This is important because:

- What clients pay attention to and what they want to measure might not give them an accurate picture of performance.

- The criteria and metrics being applied might not be appropriate; they might even be misleading.

- More than one criterion is necessary to get an accurate picture of performance.

FIELD NOTES: CRITERIA FOR PERFORMANCE IMPROVEMENT

Mike, who heads his company's shared services department, had to prove that centralizing word processing, financial analysis, and performance analysis had not only been cost-effective but had more effectively driven costs out of the system. He had already studied the effects of the intervention on one supplier and could place a value on what the system had gained in that case. Now he had to prove that combining these services and following a consulting process had allowed him to drive costs out of the system better.

Mike set up two sets of criteria to evaluate his department's effectiveness. The first set gauged how well everyone on his staff modeled the principles they espouse. Mike wanted evidence that his group was respected and was used as consultants to other departments on initiatives to improve the system's performance. The second set concerned his staff's ability to deploy and institutionalize performance improvement initiatives worldwide that would drive costs out of the system and improve product quality. In the past, the company had insisted that its suppliers measure their processes and outputs, but had never done so itself. The company had also invested in new programs on a regular basis, only to never implement them. Mike and his staff were putting in place processes for measuring results and holding other departments accountable for implementing the programs they supported. Measures that Mike would accept as evidence of his department's worth included the number of strategic projects his team had been asked to work on, how often his team had been invited to participate on strategic teams, whether the team's client had adopted their recommendations, and lower costs that could be linked directly to their interventions.

Kelly's department was making the transition from delivering training to performance improvement. She knew she would have to prove the value of this move. She and her staff began by making sure that this change in mission had supported the company's mission and goals. Next, they identified the criteria and metrics they would use to evaluate how this change affected the company. Their criteria were their ability to measure how efficiently they did their work and whether what they did improved performance as measured by criteria selected by the client. In the past, the department did not have a process for measuring results.

 **FIELD TECHNIQUES: MEASURING YOUR RESULTS**

To gain practice measuring, think of becoming a performance consultant, adding consulting services to your repertoire, and positioning yourself as an expert in performance improvement. Next, think what the impact might be on yourself, your department, or your organization using the measurement principles discussed in this chapter:

1. What will you accept as evidence that adding performance consulting was worth the investment in time and money?

2. What will you use as criteria: cost, satisfaction, adoption, goal accomplishment, increased outputs, better outcomes, greater consistency of products, or something else?

3. If you choose cost, which costs do you want performance consulting to affect?

- Whether you are an internal or external consultant, start with your internal costs (your cost of doing business, or overhead, which is a fixed cost). What was this cost in the past? How will adding consulting services enable you to reduce your fixed costs: by outsourcing services or by being more efficient?

- How will adding consulting services increase your output? Your fixed costs may remain the same, but if you increase your billable hours or increase the amount of time you have available to consult because you are more efficient, the ratio of fixed costs to outputs will be more favorable.

- What do you want the effect to be on your direct or variable costs? Do you want it to enable you to reduce the use of costly outside services such as consultants and vendors, which will reduce your direct variable costs? If your costs are less than those of consultants and you can bring the same level of expertise to the project, it may be more cost-effective for you to do the work. This could reduce your direct costs.

- Will the change reduce turnover in your department? What does it cost to recruit competent performers?

- If you are an external consultant, what costs do you want it to reduce?

4. If you choose satisfaction as a criterion, whose satisfaction will you measure? Your own? Your staff's or colleagues'? Your management's? Your clients'? Your consultants' and vendors'?

5. If you choose adoption or deployment as a criterion, will you count the number of instances clients use your performance consulting services or the proportion of time spent on consulting versus other services?

- Will you count the number of times you are called in early to facilitate defining the problem, evaluating the scope of the problem, and selecting the team to work on the problem?

- What will you accept as evidence that your services are valued and being used appropriately?

6. If you choose goal accomplishment as a criterion, what was the goal for becoming a performance consultant and adding consulting services? What will you take as evidence that you are achieving your goal?

By now, you should understand that assessment, analysis, and evaluation are closely related. They all involve some element of measurement.

SUMMARY

If the large data processing firm described at the beginning of this chapter wants to evaluate the cost benefit of certifying its resellers, it first has to answer a few important questions: Does having a certified reseller shorten the sales cycle, thus reducing the cost of sales? What is the average length of the sales cycle now? What is the cost of sales? What does it cost now to recruit and train a reseller? Does the certification reduce the cost of recruitment? Does it contribute to retention?

The company that wants to roll out quality training to all employees should first ask what it wants to change as a result of the training. Is the training intended to help everyone reduce the cost of their work processes? Is it intended to make all staff more customer oriented? If so, how will that be demonstrated? What impact will it have on the company's ability to compete, increase market share, retain profitable customers, or retain high-performing employees? The criteria it might use to measure the impact of the training might be reducing the cost of expansion, avoiding the cost of winning back customers it had lost to the competition, and reducing the cost of recruiting and retaining high-performing employees.

To prove the cost benefit of setting up a corporate university and investing in an electronic information system, the HR vice president should find out the current cost of recruiting, training, and retaining qualified HR staff worldwide. Other information that would provide a basis for comparison is the gap in skills and knowledge of HR staff because of the company's inability to communicate efficiently with them. Another piece of information is how satisfied HR's customers are with the department's performance and how much of that satisfaction is due to HR's being qualified or informed.

Measuring begins with getting information on how current performance affects cost, satisfaction, and goal accomplishment. Once you know this, you can get information about what changed as a result of the interventions. You want to know if the intervention improved performance. The evidence you need is how the intervention affected cost, satisfaction, adoption, and goal accomplishment. If you do not have any information about current performance, you can measure performance after the intervention, but you need to be clear as to what you and your client will accept as evidence of worth and value.

WHERE TO LEARN MORE

Becker, B., Huselid, M., and Ulrich, D. *The HR Scorecard: Linking People, Strategy, and Performance.* Boston: Harvard Business School Press, 2001. This is a must-read book for better understanding ways to demonstrate the value of your work. It has an excellent discussion on leading and lagging indicators.

Brown, M. G. *Keeping Score: Using the Right Metrics to Drive World-Class Performance.* New York: AMACOM, 1996. This is an excellent book on how to measure and metrics to drive performance.

Hale, J., and Westgaard, O. *Achieving a Leadership Role for Training.* New York: Quality Resources Press, 1995. The book describes how to apply the Baldrige criteria and ISO 9000 principles to managing the function of training and performance improvement. It has numerous examples of criteria and ways to measure performance.

Chapter 10

Measuring People Performance

*E*very day, managers are asked to evaluate their staffs' performance. Management wants better measures so they can decide who to promote and how to reward performance fairly. HR in particular wants better methods for linking compensation to performance.

FIELD NOTES: PERFORMANCE REVIEWS

Merit reviews were coming up, and people would soon find out what their salary increases would be. The compensation department had set guidelines limiting what people could receive. It was an emotional time for managers, who were left with the burden of reconciling performance with the merit budget policy.

A professional association outsourced its training to contractors. The association used a two-part process to evaluate these instructors: first the instructors evaluated other instructors, and then students evaluated the instructors. The result was that every instructor received the most positive evaluation possible every time. The association struggled with how to get a more accurate evaluation of the instructors.

The lack of adequate measures results in managers' having inadequate information to evaluate people's performance fairly and accurately. The irony is that we all measure one another all the time. In the work situation, however, the criteria may not be clear. Worse, the criteria may be inappropriate, misleading, or insufficient. Measures communicate what the organization values. They tell people what is important and what is expected. Therefore, an important part of our job as performance consultants is to help our clients find and fairly apply good measures of behaviors and results.

More often than not, what people say they measure and what they actually measure are not the same. The most frequently overlooked criteria concern those that are noticed only when they are not done or done poorly, shift costs to others or to a later time, or destroy relationships.

Administrative duties, for example, often are noticed only when they are not done or are done poorly. Furthermore, they do not usually earn a person extra points even when they are done well. But poor performance in this area shifts costs to the manager or to administrative staff. Late, incomplete, or inaccurate paperwork by one group actually shifts costs to another group, whose own work gets delayed.

Not communicating what all the criteria are misleads employees. Other examples of criteria that get overlooked are:

- *Safety.* People do not get extra points for being safe or driving safely. However, they may get punished for being unsafe, doing things unsafely, or having an accident.

- *Honesty.* People rarely get extra points for being honest. However, they may experience negative consequences if they misrepresent something, such as work records, product performance, or expenses.

- *Professional demeanor,* which includes social skills and the ability to rapidly establish credibility. People do not usually get evaluated higher because they dress well, speak well, or possess social graces. However, they may be overlooked for plum assignments, promotion, or rewards if they lack professional demeanor.

- *Quality of relationships,* that is, the relationships required to gain cooperation, access to information, or sponsorship of one's ideas. It is assumed people will get along. However, when people insult others or somehow erode a long-standing relationship, someone else has to come in and soothe hurt feelings. Again, the consequences are added unnecessary costs.

- *Ability to handle ambiguity and lack of certainty.* For some jobs, people are presented with the same variables day after day. Other jobs require people to work with a great deal of ambiguity and uncertainty over what might happen next. For example, they may have to work with people from different cultures, with different social norms, and with different business protocols.

FIELD NOTES: EVALUATING SALES REPS

Steve was the sales training manager for a medical equipment manufacturer where Russ worked. He worked with Russ to devise ways to reduce costs and improve people performance. The vice president of sales asked Steve to help develop a better way to evaluate sales representatives' performance. In the past, they had evaluated sales reps only on how skilled they were at the sales call process and how often they followed this process. The process was a proven approach to consultative selling. It was well documented and every rep had been trained in it. Each sales manager went on sales calls with his or her reps two to four times a year to evaluate how well each rep followed the process. They recorded their evaluations on a quarterly review form where they were asked to rate how often the reps used the process, using a five-point scale ranging from "Never" to "Always."

When the vice president of sales met with Steve, he did not talk about the validity of specific metrics, criteria, or measures. He was concerned only with whether all sales managers were using the same criteria to evaluate the reps. He thought that basing evaluations on the sales call process would reduce the variance in the managers' ratings. This proved not to be the case, however. A rep who was evaluated highly by one manager could be rated as poor by another manager on the same criterion. Steve decided to talk to the sales managers individually to find out how they used the sales call process to evaluate performance. Here is what he concluded and reported to the vice president of sales:

- *The criterion used to evaluate the reps was inappropriate and insufficient.* It was inappropriate because it did not take into account how much time the customer was willing to spend with the rep, the relationship the rep had established with the customer, what the rep and customer agreed to during the previous visit, or how the customer felt about the product. It was insufficient because it was only a single variable and gave a limited picture of performance. Steve told the vice president that there might be other activities they could measure that contribute as much, if not more, to results than following a sales call process. Additional criteria Steve suggested included territory management, number of customer calls, product knowledge, and customer satisfaction with the product.

- *There was a mismatch between the criterion and the metric.* The sales managers could not honestly say if a rep followed the process 100 percent of the time. They observed each rep for only one or two days a quarter. During the visit, the manager and rep would jointly call on four to eight customers. Therefore, managers could judge performance based only on what they saw. To draw a conclusion about what happened the rest of the time, they had to rely on what the rep told them.

- *There were hidden criteria.* The sales managers were applying other criteria in evaluating reps that were not universally known or agreed to by the other managers. For example, one or more of the managers considered a combination of (1) the number of sales calls made weekly, (2) whether sales reps worked with reps from other departments to ensure a coordinated effort, (3) product knowledge, (4) whether the reps completed paperwork on time, (5) how well they controlled expenses, (6) the reps' driving record, and (7) achievement of the company's sales goal. Not all of the managers considered these same criteria or even applied them consistently across all reps.

Steve also concluded that the sales managers' performance was not evaluated in terms of evaluating, coaching, and developing high performers. Therefore, instead of focusing on how to evaluate the reps, Steve recommended a series of interventions aimed at improving the sales managers' ability to evaluate the reps' performance more fairly and consistently:

- Rewarding the sales managers for consistently using agreed-on criteria
- Measuring the sales managers' compliance with applying the criteria
- Measuring the sales managers' skill at coaching, developing, and evaluating reps
- Defining and documenting the criteria for evaluating sales managers' performance

Steve recommended that the vice president of sales meet with his zone managers (the sales managers' bosses) to:

- Jointly determine what they expected of the sales managers
- Jointly determine ways to measure sales managers' performance
- Agree on the criteria and metrics
- Agree on how to share their expectations and criteria with the sales managers

---

FIELD TECHNIQUES: SELECTING USABLE CRITERIA

One of the more difficult aspects of evaluating people performance is identifying and getting agreement on the criteria. The first step is to find out the reason for the evaluation. Once you have that, you can help develop the performance criteria. Figure 10.1 list some common reasons for evaluating performance and gives examples of possible criteria.

Figure 10.1. Reasons and Criteria for Evaluating Performance

Reasons	*Possible Criteria*
To determine developmental needs	• Growth • How long it takes a person to achieve proficiency • The cost of development
To assess level of competence	• Level of productivity • How well work relationships function • Work or project cycle time • The cost to raise the level of competence
To determine bonuses or merit increases	• Goal accomplishment • What it cost to achieve the goal • The impact on others of achieving the goal
To assess readiness to take on more responsibility	• Quality of the work produced • The time to produce at the current level • What might be put at risk if more responsibility were added

Once I know how the client wants to use the criteria, I can facilitate the process of identifying what criteria to use. I use the nominal group technique (NGT) early in the consulting relationship to identify hidden criteria and help the group come to consensus on what they will use as evidence of adequate performance. The NGT has a couple of advantages over other group processes. It limits the influence of people with higher status and the more vocal members of the group. The process gives everyone an equal chance to contribute. You can even analyze the results statistically by computing the mean (average) number of points and the standard deviation. Answers that receive points that are one or more standard deviations above the mean are considered significant. Figure 10.2 has directions for conducting a nominal group session.

Once I have what the client expects, I can develop a worksheet to document and communicate the criteria. I find it helpful to separate quantitative measures from qualitative measures. Quantitative measures are similar to productivity in that they include things like frequency and volume (they can be counted easily). Qualitative measures include customer satisfaction, product knowledge, and reasoning—factors that require some type of scale to measure them. For the qualitative measures, I use a combination of Likert scales and behavioral descriptions similar to what Mike used to evaluate his consultants (Figure 2.2). Just like conducting a nominal group session, the process of documenting the quantitative and qualitative measures results in clarity and helps achieve consensus. Figure 10.3 has guidelines for developing people performance worksheets.

**Figure 10.2.
Directions for
the NGT**

1. Explain the purpose of the meeting (that is, what you want the group to accomplish).

2. Present the question (you may have a series of questions, but ask only one question at a time).

3. Ask everyone to silently generate a list of answers to the question. Recommend that they keep their answers short, and avoid compound answers.

4. Once everyone is done, ask each person to share one answer at a time. Record everyone's answers on flip chart paper, and hang each page where everyone can see it. Keep going around the table until everyone has exhausted his or her list. Ask everyone to withhold their comments and questions until all of the responses are listed.

5. Once all of the answers are listed, the group may choose to combine those that are alike. However, don't let them combine answers to make compound or complex statements.

6. Ask each person to silently pick five answers from the whole list that he or she feels are the most important.

7. When everyone has picked five, ask them to rank the five, from 1 for least important to 5 for most important to the question.

8. Read each answer one at a time, and ask how many points everyone gave to that answer. Record the number of points next to the response. When all of the points are recorded, read aloud the responses that received the greatest number of points. These are the ones the group considers the most important.

**Figure 10.3.
Guidelines
for Creating People
Performance Worksheets**

1. Separate the quantitative evaluation criteria from the qualitative criteria.

2. Create a separate worksheet for each set of criteria.

3. Label and date each performance worksheet.

4. Make enough rows on each worksheet to list the names of all the people being evaluated.

5. For both worksheets, create enough columns for all of the criteria, plus a column for comments. If appropriate, include a key indicating what information goes in each column.

6. For the qualitative worksheet, add columns to record performance ratings. Create rating scales for each factor. The scales can be behaviorally anchored or based on performance checklists. Remember to add a column for comments.

7. If appropriate, develop a set of instructions on how to fill in the worksheet, what criteria to use for the ratings, and how to interpret the information.

FIELD NOTES: EVALUATING SALES REPS

Steve learned from his interviews that the sales managers, their bosses (the zone managers), and the vice president of sales were in agreement on using the performance criteria to:

- Identify the reps' developmental needs
- Determine which reps were worth investing more time in and which were too costly to support
- Determine which reps might be considered for a management position
- Determine bonuses and merit increases

The zone managers were not in agreement on how to evaluate the sales managers, however, so Steve decided to use the nominal group technique to get the zone managers to identify and rank the criteria they use to evaluate sales managers. The zone managers, the vice president of sales, the head of consumer products, and two sales managers participated. The results of the exercise are shown in Figure 10.4.

The vice president of sales assigned a team to develop worksheets the zone managers could use to evaluate the sales managers. The team consisted of Steve, two of the zone managers, and the two sales managers who participated in the nominal group session.

Figure 10.4.
Performance Criteria
for the Sales Managers

The question: What factors should be considered when evaluating a sales manager's performance?

Responses, in the order of importance	Points awarded
1. Number of shared expectations sessions done and agreed to	26
2. Ability to give regular, focused, specific feedback	15
3. Number of developmental plans that meet needs	14
4. Performance (compared with objectives)	8
5. Unbiased quantitative and qualitative analysis	7
6. Knowledge of business factors affecting territory	7
7. Ability to immediately verbalize each rep's strengths and weaknesses	4
8. Product sales volume	3
9. Number of observations	3
10. Consistency between verbal and written feedback	2
11. Soliciting feedback from reps	0
12. Staying on top of administrative duties	0
13. Having clear goals	0
14. Exit interview data	0
15. Including regular feedback on field observation forms	0
16. What I see happening in a coaching situation	0
17. Business acumen	0
18. Making realistic evaluations	0
19. Initiating relationships with counterparts in other departments	0
20. Confronting negative behavior	0
21. Giving consistent messages to reps	0

The process of using the nominal group technique and developing the worksheets helped the zone managers clarify what they valued. Steve was able to facilitate discussions about what behaviors they attend to and how they interpret those behaviors. Then Steve worked with his team to come up with the metrics for each of the criteria. The metrics would be behaviors that would give evidence of adequate performance. The zone managers could use these worksheets when they met with sales managers to talk about expectations. The worksheets also served as models for other worksheets the sales managers could use to evaluate reps' performance.

The first worksheet had the quantitative measures. Steve wanted to raise the zone managers' awareness of which reps the sales managers spent time with and what effect that had on performance. He used the qualitative worksheet to define the behaviors and results for evaluating the sales managers. The sales managers were rated separately on eight factors. A five-point rating scale was used, with 1 the most favorable and 5 the least favorable. A rating of 2 on the scale meant the sales manager met expectations. The worksheets are reproduced in Figures 10.5 and 10.6.

Figure 10.5.
Quantitative Measures
Summary Worksheet

Sales Manager names	1. Number of reps		2. Number of joint calls			3. Number of plans		4. Sales by product family: actual versus goal								5. Turnover	6. Comments
								Z		X		M		Q			
	f	p	l	m	h	d	s	a	g	a	g	a	g	a	g		
1																	
2																	
3																	
4																	
5																	
6																	
7																	
8																	
9																	

f = full product line, p = partial product line; l = low performer, m = medium performer, h = high performer; d = developmental, s = strategic, a = actual, g = goal

1. Number of reps: Record the number of reps who report to each sales manager and how many of those reps represent the full product line versus a more limited line of products.

2. Number of days spent doing joint sales calls: Record how many days each sales manager spent jointly calling on customers with low-, medium-, and high-performing reps. Pay particular attention to:
   • Whether the joint sales calls were 1 or 2 days in length.
   • How the joint sales calls are distributed across low, medium, and high performers. It may be appropriate to have fewer 2-day joint calls depending on the performance or developmental needs of the rep. However, the distribution should become less skewed over time. If distribution remains skewed, find out why. Rate the effectiveness of working directly with the rep during calls on the qualitative measures summary worksheet.

3. Number of plans: Record the number of developmental and strategic plans each sales manager has for his or her reps. Developmental plans are designed to improve skills that lead to better performance; strategic plans are designed to build business. Rate the quality and appropriateness of those plans on the second worksheet.

4. Actual versus goal: Record the year-to-date sales for products Z, X, M, and Q compared to the goal.

5. Turnover: Record the amount of turnover each sales manager has experienced. This gives a basis for discussing the reasons behind the turnover. Reducing turnover by 20 percent is a corporate objective.

6. Comments: Use this column for notes regarding necessary action steps, explanations, or overall ratings.

JC: Joint sales calls led to changes in behavior that improved business results.	*DP:* Plans meet reps' individual and business needs, and were achieved.	*PO:* Objectives are current, appropriate, aligned with the business needs, and met.	*KP:* Knows the products; is considered an expert; knows the competition and the field of therapy.
1. Extra calls led to significant improvements in reps' performance.	1. Reps are consistently high performing, and all have strategic plans.	1. All reps met objectives, which had a positive effect on the business.	1. Selected to instruct new sales managers and reps in the products.
2. Did 100 percent (all reps) or per plan, distribution is fair.	2. Have plans for all reps or per objective all plans meet needs.	2. Reps met objectives appropriate to their level of experience.	2. Completed all product training priority assessments at 85 percent.
3. Did 90 percent, or distribution skewed for this quarter.	3. Have plans for 90 percent or less, or only 90 percent of plans meet needs.	3. 90 percent of reps met objectives.	3. Completed all product assessments at 85 percent except for one major product.
4. Did 80 percent, or distribution skewed for more than one quarter.	4. Have plans for 80 percent or less, or only 80 percent meet needs.	4. 80 percent of reps met objectives.	4. Completed all product assessments at 85 percent except for two major products.
5. Did 70 percent or less, or distribution skewed for more than two quarters.	5. Have plans for 70 percent or less, or only 70 percent meet needs.	5. 70 percent of reps met objectives.	5. Has not completed any product assessments.
RFF: Feedback is consistently regular, frequent, specific, timely.	*UQQ:* Evaluations are based on corroborated facts.	*KBF:* Knows business factors affecting the territory.	*AM:* Administrative practices don't affect others negatively and are current.
1. Exceptional skills inspired and led to business results.	1. Bases analysis on all variables and customer feedback.	1. Regularly shares local market factors and plans to address them.	1. Suggestions on administrative processes produced enhancements, efficiency.
2. All get regular, frequent, specific, timely, and constructive feedback.	2. Bases analysis on objectives attainment, quality of sales call process, and call activity.	2. Initiates relationships with other sections and counterparts.	2. Administrative duties performed on time and accurately.
3. Confronts negative behavior sometimes and gives specific feedback 70 to 90 percent of time.	3. Bases analysis on the quality of sales call process and call activity, but not on objectives.	3. Knows roles and goals of customer, division, and territory well.	3. Has to be reminded about 30 percent of time to get reports in or to do them correctly.
4. Feedback has some action steps for improvement with time lines or is not specific or relevant to issue.	4. Bases analysis on call activity or sales process alone.	4. Focuses efforts on processes alone; ignores or doesn't identify market factors.	4. Reminded more than 30 to 50 percent of time; others can't meet their expectations.
5. Written and verbal feedback are not consistent.	5. Bases analysis on gut instinct and experience alone.	5. Relies excessively on feelings or past knowledge.	5. Reminded more than 50 percent of time.

Figure 10.6. Qualitative Measures Summary Worksheet

Period covered: _____										
1. Manager's name:	2. Ratings								3. Average Rating	4. Comments
	JC	DP	PO	KP	RFF	UQQ	KBF	AM		
1										
2										
3										
4										
5										
6										
7										
8										
9										

Ratings Key: JC: joint sales calls; DP: development plans; PO: performance against objectives; KP: knows the products; RFF: regular, frequent feedback; UQQ: unbiased quantitative and qualitative analysis; KBF: knows business factors affecting the territory; AM: administrative management.

Ratings: Rate each sales manager on a scale of 1 to 5, from most to least positive. See attached form for the behavioral anchors for each factor.

Average rating: Total the ratings for all eight factors and divide by eight to get the average rating.

Figure 10.6. Qualitative Measures Summary Worksheet, *cont'd.*

EXPERIENCES FROM THE FIELD: EVALUATING THE JOB

Sometimes there is more to be gained by evaluating a job than by evaluating a person's job performance. Every job has dimensions. Those dimensions are the inputs to the job and the processes used to produce the expected outputs and outcomes (see Figure 10.7).

Once I identify the inputs, processes, outputs, and outcomes, I can measure them. Examples of the types of measures you can use for each of these dimensions are in Figure 10.8.

Identifying how to measure these dimensions helps when hiring and assigning people to a job. When the right people are hired or assigned, the need for a lot of interventions goes away. Knowing the dimensions also helps you determine what to use when measuring the effect of an intervention. Figure 10.9 is a job aid you can use to evaluate a job.

**Figure 10.7.
Dimensions
of a Job**

1. Job *inputs:* the requests, information, and people demanding that a job be performed. The criteria used to measure inputs are volume, complexity, clarity, and maturity. Measure inputs to determine:
   - The complexity of a job or task, the volume of work expected for it, the quality and clarity of direction given, what needs the job is expected to satisfy, and who depends on the outputs
   - How skilled people have to be at managing the inputs
   - How well an intervention improved either the inputs or people's ability to manage the inputs
2. Job *processes:* the procedures, systems, equipment, and technology used to perform the job. The criteria used to measure processes are response time, cycle time, efficiency, and cost. Measure processes to determine:
   - The effectiveness and sufficiency of the processes in terms of response time, cycle time, efficiency, and cost
   - How skilled people have to be at managing the processes
   - How well an intervention improved the processes
3. Job *outputs* (also called productivity measures): the products of the processes. The criteria used to measure outputs are volume, customers served, and worth. Measure outputs to determine:
   - How much work a person did and for whom the work produced worthy results
   - How well an intervention increased either the volume of outputs or the ratio of value-adding outputs to non-value-adding outputs
4. Job *outcomes:* the consequences of the outputs. The criteria used to measure outcomes are satisfaction, accomplishment, aftermath, cost, compliance, and image. Measure outcomes to determine:
   - The worth and worthiness of what a person accomplished
   - How well an intervention improved, enhanced, or increased the consequences of what was accomplished

FIELD TECHNIQUES: EVALUATING A JOB

1. Explain to the client that before you can recommend ways to evaluate a person's performance, you want to understand the person's job better.
2. Arrange to interview a few people currently in the job. It is even better if you can observe them in the job.
3. Start by asking people in the job what their typical tasks are. If there are a lot of tasks, ask if they fall into families or if they can be grouped under larger headings.
4. Once you have a sense of what tasks make up the job, ask what causes the person in the job to perform these tasks. Explain that you want to find out what or who creates a need for the job. If you observed the job, you should have seen some of the people or systems that signaled a need for the job to be performed.

Inputs	*Processes*	*Outputs*	*Outcomes*
Measures at this level are about *what* people in the job have to deal with:	Measures at this level are about *how* people do the task:	Measures at this level are about *how much* people did:	Measures at this level are about the *results* or consequences of what people did in terms of:

Inputs

Measures at this level are about *what* people in the job have to deal with:

- How much work is there?
- Is it routine or unique?
- What's the driver behind the request (personal, business, legal)?
- How clear, complete, or accurate is the information the person has to work from?
- Who generates the request? Who is the customer?

Processes

Measures at this level are about *how* people do the task:

- Does something cue the person to respond, and if so in what priority?
- Is the process mapped or defined?
- How long does it take to complete or carry out the request (cycle time), on average?
- How many resources are used to carry out the task (efficiency)?
- What does it cost to do the task or respond?

Outputs

Measures at this level are about *how much* people did:

- How much got done?
- How many requests were handled?
- Does what got done break out by customer or some other factor?
- How much was done of each type of request?
- How much time was spent on each type of request?
- Which customers were served? Which were not served?
- How were the results used?
- What effect did the results have on others?

Outcomes

Measures at this level are about the *results* or consequences of what people did in terms of:

- Feelings:
  - How confident in and satisfied are people with the results?
- Accomplishment:
  - Was the goal achieved?
- Aftermath:
  - Was there any unforeseen fallout?
- Compliance:
  - What regulations were met or not met?
- Money:
  - Were direct and indirect costs incurred or avoided?
  - What was the return on investment?
- Image:
  - How did goal achievement affect the status of the job, department, or person?

Figure 10.8. Examples of Measures for Job Dimensions

5. Ask the client to name the job processes. The more hesitant he or she is about the processes (or if he or she cannot think of any processes), the more likely it is that processes exist but have not been defined. This means it will be harder to evaluate an individual's performance.

6. Ask the client to describe the job's products and the effects of those products on others. Be sure to ask who uses the job's outputs, as these are the people who can help you come up with criteria for measuring the outputs and even the outcomes.

7. As you interview or observe (either individuals or a group), fill in the form (Figure 10.9). Once you feel you have a fair picture of the job, share the form with the people you interviewed to see if anything needs to be added.

Inputs	Processes	Outputs	Outcomes
What do people in the job have to deal with?	*How* do people do the task?	*How much* gets done?	What are the *results* or consequences of what got done?
Criteria:	Criteria:	Criteria:	Criteria:
• Volume	• Response time	• Quantitative measures	• Satisfaction
• Complexity	• Cycle time	• Customers serviced	• Accomplishment
• Clarity	• Efficiency	• Worth	• Aftermath
• Maturity	• Cost		• Cost
			• Compliance
			• Image

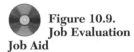

Figure 10.9.
Job Evaluation
Job Aid

8. Once you and your client are in agreement about the characteristics of the job, ask if there is anything about the job that could be changed to support improved performance.

9. Ask if the purpose of the intervention is to help people deal with the realities of the job or to change some aspect of it to eliminate the cause of poor performance.

10. Focus on those things that will be most likely to help people perform better if they are changed or improved.

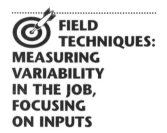

FIELD TECHNIQUES: MEASURING VARIABILITY IN THE JOB, FOCUSING ON INPUTS

Frequently job environments differ significantly for people with the same job titles. However, since the job titles, descriptions, and even salary grades are the same, people assume the jobs are the same as well.

Inputs are all the stimuli that cause a task to happen or a job to be done. Sometimes inputs are customer requests. Sometimes they are the outputs of another work group. Measure inputs to find out what people have to manage to do their job effectively. The criteria used to measure a job's inputs are volume, complexity, clarity, and maturity.

Volume

As a measurement criterion, volume concerns how much work the person in the job is expected to handle within a given time period. Work can be defined as requests, orders, or units. Here are some examples:

• For a medical doctor, volume is the number of office appointments, patients to see in the hospital, medical test results to be reviewed, patient consultations, and so on over the course of an hour, a day, or a week.

- For an HR generalist, volume is the number of employee complaints to respond to and investigate, the number of positions to fill, the number of terminations to process, the number of orientations for new employees to conduct, meetings to attend, and so on.

- For a building engineer, volume is the square footage of the building to be maintained, the number of floors and entrances to be monitored, and number of heating and cooling systems to be serviced, and so on.

Complexity

As a measurement criterion, complexity is about the number and variety of variables the person in the job has to handle. The opposite is simplicity. Having many customers adds some complexity. If those customers have different needs and expectations, the complexity is even greater. Complexity is also about how many inputs are routine compared to how many are unique—for example:

- For a medical doctor complexity increases as volume, variety, uniqueness, and gravity of patient diseases go up.

- For an HR generalist, complexity increases as the number of departments, management levels, employees, and services go up. It also increases as situations become more atypical.

- For a building engineer, complexity increases as the number of contractors goes up, the variety of equipment manufacturers increases, control systems become more sophisticated, and the need to comply with rigorous environmental standards goes up.

Clarity

As a measurement criterion, clarity concerns how much direction a person is given in the job. The opposite is ambiguity. Clarity increases with well-defined rules and procedures; it decreases when people have only broad guidelines. Like complexity, the need for clarity depends on whether the input is routine or not. The more atypical the inputs, the more the person has to use professional judgment in deciding what to do—for example:

- For a medical doctor, the procedures for treating some conditions are proven and quite straightforward. Others require more professional judgment.

- For an HR generalist, some procedures, such as enrolling new employees in the benefit program, are well defined and do not allow for any deviation. Other tasks, such as investigating harassment or drug abuse charges, may be less well defined and have only broad guidelines. They require greater sensitivity and judgment.

- For a building engineer, procedures for preventive maintenance may be well defined because the activity is routine. However, there may be only general guidelines for troubleshooting and decommissioning a system.

Maturity

As a measurement criterion, maturity concerns the length and functionality of relationships. Maturity increases as people gain experience in the job. It increases with the sophistication of customers and suppliers. It increases as people begin to trust one another's expertise and experiences—for example:

- For a medical doctor, maturity refers to how well the doctor functions with his or her staff. Maturity also refers to how long patients have had a relationship with the doctor.

- For an HR generalist, maturity refers to how well labor and management get along and to what degree employees and management rely on HR's expertise.

- For a building engineer, maturity refers to the engineer's relationship with suppliers and service contractors. It also refers to the engineer's relationship with the people who work or live in the building.

FIELD NOTES: EVALUATING INPUTS

Steve asked the sales managers to describe what reps do and how they do it. He discovered that although the reps all have the same job title they work in very different job environments. For example, some reps represent fifteen products; others represent only five. Some sell in what are considered friendly markets; others have hostile markets. Some had inherited well-established relationships with customers; others had to spend a significant amount of time doing cold calls with potential customers. Some are assigned concentrated geographical areas like big cities; others are given very large geographical areas like the state of Idaho.

The zone managers and the sales managers need to decide if they want to apply the same criteria to reps with significantly different job inputs. If they do apply the same criteria, they need to decide how the metrics might differ.

Russ, at the medical manufacturer, was asked to develop a curriculum for HR generalists. Management believes that the generalists lack skills. Russ met with some generalists and discovered that:

- Some are assigned to manufacturing plants, report to the plant manager, and run a one-person shop.
- Some work at regional offices, report to a vice president of HR, and work with specialists in compensation and benefits.
- Some work out of zone offices, reporting to a vice president of HR in the regional office but serving field sales and service personnel.
- Some spend from 10 to 30 percent of their time on non-HR duties such as managing the cafeteria, reinforcing security, acting as a receptionist, and coordinating large-scale meetings.

Different work environments require different criteria. The best way for Russ to improve the performance of generalists might be to help management establish fair and reasonable criteria for each work environment. Then he could conduct a skill gap analysis to uncover real deficiencies in skills and knowledge based on the new criteria.

FIELD TECHNIQUES: MEASURING EFFICIENCY, FOCUSING ON JOB PROCESSES

Processes are how a job or task gets done. They include all the procedures, systems, equipment, and technology used to perform the job or produce an output (idea, recommendation, product, and so on). You measure processes to determine if they support the required work cost-effectively. The criteria used to measure processes are response time, cycle time, efficiency, and cost.

Response Time

As a measurement criterion, response time is about how efficiently the process signals the person to respond. Response time is affected by how well or poorly the process communicates priority or urgency—for example:

- For a medical doctor, effective intake procedures identify patients in need of immediate medical attention.
- For an HR generalist, informal communication networks help identify problems before they escalate into more serious situations.
- For a building engineer, appropriate equipment sensors signal the need for maintenance before a major breakdown.

Cycle Time

As a measurement criterion, cycle time is how long it takes to complete a task. Cycle time goes up when the person has to wait for inputs or wait for work to get checked by someone else, and it goes up as more steps are added. Well-designed processes have minimal, if any, checking and wait time, and few non-value-adding steps—for example:

- For a medical doctor, efficient procedures for coordinating hospital admissions lead to more rapid treatment.
- For an HR generalist, procedures for investigating problems and submitting recommendations to management lead to quicker resolution of problems.
- For a building engineer, procedures that quickly restore a building system to full functioning lead to faster job outcomes.

Efficiency

As a measurement criterion, efficiency is about how well resources are used during the process. Resources include people, time, equipment, space, and materials. The more resources that are dedicated to rework and checking, the less efficient the process is—for example:

- For a medical doctor, reducing operator and equipment error reduces the need to redo tests.
- For an HR generalist, reducing the number of dead ends investigated before getting to what actually caused a complaint or situation leads to faster problem resolution.
- For a building engineer, grouping similar tasks to avoid repetitive activities leads to faster service.

Cost

As a measurement criterion, cost refers to the number of resources a process consumes. The more unnecessary resources are consumed (and the more expensive the resource), the greater the cost—for example:

- For a medical doctor, prescribing generic drugs appropriately and not running unnecessary tests reduces costs.
- For an HR generalist, outsourcing certain services can reduce costs if the services consume more resources when done internally.
- For a building engineer, using materials with longer shelf lives reduces the number of service calls.

FIELD NOTES: EVALUATING PROCESSES

While developing the curriculum for his company's HR generalists, Russ discovered that they spend most of their time on employee relations and staffing and recruiting. Employee relations and staffing and recruiting are processes. Because Russ defines his own job in terms of processes, he took the same approach to defining the generalists' jobs. He recommended that a team be set up to define these processes and measures be created to evaluate their effectiveness.

FIELD TECHNIQUES: MEASURING PRODUCTIVITY, FOCUSING ON JOB OUTPUTS

Outputs are what a person produces—for example, products, reports, ideas, recommendations, sales calls, and classes taught. Measuring outputs determines how much work people do, for whom they do it, and which activities lead to worthy results. The criteria used to measure outputs are quantity, customers served, and worth.

Quantity

As a measurement criterion, quantity refers to how much work was actually done compared to what was expected or what the process is capable of producing. When a process is capable of producing more than what is being produced, it is being underused. Underuse may be due to insufficient demand or the availability of other processes that accomplish the same results (this may be redundancy)—for example:

- For a medical doctor, the number of hours billed can be compared to the number of hours available. Fewer billed than available hours indicates insufficient quantity.

- For an HR generalist, the amount of paperwork completed can be compared to the amount that needed to be done.

- For a building engineer, the number of building systems serviced during a time period can be compared to the number that could have been serviced.

Customers Served

As a measurement criterion, customers served concerns who got served and who did not. Some customers demand so much attention that they prevent servicing other customers; not servicing customers may result in lost business—for example:

- For a medical doctor, it is important to attend to patients with urgent needs and still being able to attend to those needing more routine care.

- For an HR generalist, it is important to be able to service the home office staff without sacrificing the needs of the field staff.

- For a building engineer, it is important to meet the needs of every tenant in the building, as opposed to just some tenants.

Worth

As a measurement criterion, worth concerns the value of what was produced—for example:

- For a medical doctor, providing preventive treatment avoids more serious situations or complications.

- For an HR generalist, preparing programs that are proven to reduce the number of charges of harassment improves the workplace environment.

- For a building engineer, proper maintenance of building equipment and systems avoids breakdowns and possible damage to tenants' equipment, materials, and inventory.

FIELD NOTES: EVALUATING OUTPUTS

Chris, a performance consultant at Mike's company, headed the group that did financial analyses for product managers. In the past, Chris's group had been evaluated only in terms of customer satisfaction. Since the group members were now expected to evaluate their own processes and their ability to add value, they decided to start by looking at what they did, how much time they spent doing it, and which customers consumed most of their time.

Chris went back to her group's work records and found that 60 percent of their time was spent with U.S. product managers; half of that time was spent providing quick answers to financial questions (the financial help desk function). The other half was spent producing standard financial reports that Chris wasn't sure the U.S. managers really used. About 25 percent of the remaining time was spent on international issues and another 15 percent spent on global issues. All of their international and global work was strategic in nature (such as determining how to more effectively compensate dedicated suppliers or reduce packaging costs). They realized that what drove the help desk activities was the product managers' lack of skills and knowledge in financial analysis. They also believed that the help desk was not the best use of their time and had doubts about the value of some of their recurring reports. Chris went back to her mission and vision (see Figure 1.13) and used that information to establish goals and measures for her group and for each member of her group (see Figure 10.10).

Figure 10.10. The Finance Group's Measures

Goal No. 1: To increase our customers' awareness of our services. The criterion to measure our success is an increase in activities that directly support our vision and mission and our global strategic initiatives.

Goal No. 2: To increase our ability to influence and add value. The criteria to measure whether we increase our level and sphere of influence will be

1. The number of approved projects and activities that we identified as strategic and are supported by the supply chain managers.

2. The number of strategic initiatives in which we play a leadership role.

3. The number of relationships we establish with influential stakeholders that result in those stakeholders' supporting our vision and mission.

4. The ratio of time spent on help desk and routine matters compared to time spent on global strategic initiatives.

Goal No. 3: To measure the effectiveness and efficiency of our projects. The criteria to measure effectiveness and efficiency will be

1. Timeliness: How often was our work delivered on time, and how often was it timely enough to make a difference to the system even if the work was not perfect (the 80–20 rule)?

2. Customer satisfaction: How often did we meet customers' expectations, and to what degree did our work satisfy their needs?

3. Worth: What is our ability to provide evidence of our cost benefit to the system?

4. Implementation: How often were our recommendations actually implemented or acted on by the customer?

FIELD TECHNIQUES: DETERMINING REWARDS AND BONUSES, FOCUSING ON OUTCOMES

Outcomes are the consequences of doing or not doing the job. The consequences can affect customers, employees, and the organization. The criteria used to measure outcomes are satisfaction, accomplishment, aftermath (negative fallout), cost, compliance, and image.

Satisfaction

As a criterion, satisfaction concerns how satisfied customers, bosses, and other vested parties are in what was done and how confident they are that it will meet their needs—for example:

- For a medical doctor, it refers to patients' level of satisfaction with their treatment and level of confidence in their doctor's ability.

- For an HR generalist, it refers to employees' and management's level of satisfaction with staffing and recruitment, employee relations, compensation, benefits, and training.

- For a building engineer, it refers to tenants' and owners' level of satisfaction with the building in terms of flexibility, ergonomics, security, attractiveness, and how disruptions in utilities were handled.

Accomplishment

As a measurement criterion, accomplishment concerns the degree to which a goal or objective was achieved—for example:

- For a medical doctor, successfully treating a patient indicates accomplishment.

- For an HR generalist, getting managers to do annual performance reviews indicates accomplishment.

- For a building engineer, meeting an energy conservation goal indicates accomplishment.

Aftermath

As a measurement criterion, the aftermath of an intervention, action, process, and so on refers to any unexpected or undesirable consequences. Examples are shifting costs to other work units, damaging relationships, or putting something else at risk—for example:

- For a medical doctor, a course of treatment may have long-term negative consequences on a patient's health.

- For an HR generalist, dealing with the aftermath of a process might mean confronting emotionally laden situations without jeopardizing labor or management relationships.

- For a building engineer, an energy efficiency program might produce an uncomfortable environment for tenants, causing their productivity to suffer.

Cost

As a measurement criterion, cost is about the financial consequences of achieving or not achieving the goal. It is the financial impact on direct or indirect costs, fixed or variable costs, cash flow, return on investment, return on capital employed, profits before taxes, or other economic variables—for example:

- For a medical doctor, it could include the impact of the practice's management on fixed costs, direct costs, and profits before taxes.

- For an HR generalist, it could include the effect of staffing and recruitment practices on the cost of retention, recruitment, benefits, and salaries.

- For a building engineer, it could include the effect of preventive maintenance practices on direct costs and the market value of the property.

Compliance

As a measurement criterion, compliance concerns whether regulatory or organizational requirements were violated when accomplishing the goal—for example:

- For a medical doctor, compliance with medical state board requirements is essential.
- For an HR generalist, processes must comply with labor laws and the organization's guidelines.
- For a building engineer, building modifications must comply with Environmental Protection Agency and Occupational Health and Safety Agency regulations.

Image

As a measurement criterion, image concerns how accomplishing a goal affected community relations, industry standing, and the reputation—for example:

- For a medical doctor, image includes the doctor's professional reputation and community standing.
- For an HR generalist, image includes the HR's reputation and status in the organization.
- For a building engineer, image includes the engineer's technical and facility management reputation among tenants, owners, and peers.

HOW PERFORMANCE GETS TRANSLATED INTO MERIT REVIEWS

Another breakdown in measuring people performance comes when it is time for salary discussions and merit increases. The problem is complicated by compensation policies that limit the number (or percentage) of people who can get the maximum raise. Looking only at goal attainment is not enough. Managers need to consider all the factors: the inputs, process, and outputs. They should also pay attention to all of the criteria used to measure outcomes.

 **FIELD TECHNIQUES: FAIRLY APPLYING CRITERIA FOR MERIT REVIEWS**

One technique I recommend to clients is to create a list of questions the manager and employee both go over before conducting the merit review. Ideally, the list should be reviewed at the beginning of the annual pay cycle. The list should include the criteria the manager takes into account when deciding on a person's merit increase. What is helpful about the list of questions is the emphasis on outputs and outcomes, particularly worth, costs, and aftermath. The list makes public the behaviors and results that the organization values. It helps managers move the discussion from "I met my goals" to "at what cost?" Figure 10.11 has an example of the list of questions.

To create a similar job aid for managers and employees, meet with your team and clients to discuss what the real criteria are and should be for merit reviews. Make sure you discuss those often-overlooked, assumed factors such as cost, relationships, compliance, and teamwork. Then build your own merit review form. Ask managers to try it. Find out if and how it affected the quality and focus of their discussions with employees.

FIELD TECHNIQUES: MEASURING YOUR OWN PERFORMANCE

You should now have a thorough understanding of what the job of performance consultant is. You can begin by asking what the job purpose is. Is the position of performance consultant developmental? If the answer is yes, what position are you being prepared for? Is your goal to improve your competence? If the answer is yes, then what will you and others take as evidence that your competence has improved?

Develop your own quantitative and qualitative evaluation worksheets. Develop the supporting performance checklists or behaviorally anchored scales to evaluate your performance. Use the dimensions of a job (Figures 10.7 and 10.8) to describe your inputs, processes, outputs, and outcomes. Decide what becoming a performance consultant is supposed to accomplish and what you can do to become the best at performance consulting.

SUMMARY

Better criteria help managers and employees evaluate performance and identify ways to improve performance. Without criteria, judgments about performance are arbitrary and unfair. To help identify relevant criteria, examine the job. Start by identifying and evaluating the job's inputs to determine:

- The complexity of the job, the volume of work it is expected to handle, the quality and clarity of direction given to it, whose needs it is expected to satisfy, and who depends on the outputs

- How skilled people are at managing the inputs

- How much an intervention improved the inputs or people's ability to manage the inputs

Next, evaluate the job's processes to determine:

- If they are effective and sufficient in terms of response time, cycle time, efficiency, and cost

- How skilled people are at using the process

- How much an intervention improved the process

Here are some questions to help managers be more consistent in what they consider when determining merit raises. The manager should answer the questions before meeting with the individual. The intent is to get the manager to consider what was or was not accomplished, how important to the organization the accomplishment was, and the impact the person's actions and results had on resources and others' ability to perform. To complete this form, read each question while keeping in mind the staff person you are rating. The scale reflects a continuum, ranging from marginal performance, with opportunity for improvement, to high performance, where the person is meeting or exceeding expectations. Select the numerical position on the scale as appropriate. An example of the scale follows:

No	Somewhat	Not relevant	Mostly	Yes
1	2	3	4	5

Factors pointing to opportunities for improvement ↔ Factors indicating the employee met or exceeded expectations

Comments: _____

1. Did the person accomplish the objectives of the work plan (business volume, customer satisfaction, personal development, staff development, and so on)?

No	Somewhat	Not relevant	Mostly	Yes
1	2	3	4	5

Comments: _____

2. How difficult were the work plan's objectives to achieve, that is, were they stretch goals?

No	Somewhat	Not relevant	Mostly	Yes
1	2	3	4	5

Comments: _____

3. Did the person overcome barriers that interfered with the achievement of the objectives?

None	Minor ones	Don't know	Significant ones	Major ones
1	2	3	4	5

Comments: _____

4. To what degree did the person use unplanned resources to carry out the work plan?

Used a lot of unplanned resources	Used some	Don't know	Used very few	Used no unplanned resources
1	2	3	4	5

Comments: _____

5. Did the person use resources wisely when carrying out the work plan?

No	Not enough	Not relevant	Mostly	Yes
1	2	3	4	5

Comments: _____

6. How much did accomplishment of the objectives interfere with others' ability to accomplish their work plan?

A great deal	Somewhat	Not relevant	Very little	Not at all
1	2	3	4	5

Comments: _____

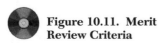

Figure 10.11. Merit Review Criteria

7. Did the person achieve the goals considered the top priorities of the work plan?

No	Somewhat	Not relevant	Mostly	Yes
1	2	3	4	5

Comments:

8. Was the person's work plan strategically aligned with the department's initiatives, and did the results contribute to the department's goals?

Not at all	Somewhat	Not relevant	Mostly	A great deal
1	2	3	4	5

Comments:

9. Did the person contribute to helping others accomplish their goals?

Not at all	Somewhat	Not relevant	A lot	Led to breakthroughs
1	2	3	4	5

Comments:

10. Did the person accomplish goals beyond what was on the work plan?

Not at all	Somewhat	Not relevant	Mostly	Led to breakthroughs
1	2	3	4	5

Comments:

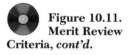

Figure 10.11.
Merit Review
Criteria, *cont'd.*

Evaluate the expected and actual job outputs to determine:

- How much work a person did and for whom and if that work led to worthy results

- How much an intervention increased either the volume or the percentage of outputs that led to worthy results

Finally, evaluate the outcomes of the job's outputs to determine:

- The consequences of what was or was not accomplished

- How much an intervention improved or enhanced the consequences of what was accomplished

WHERE TO
LEARN MORE

To learn more about the nominal group technique and controlling group bias, consult the writings of A. L. Delbecq and A. H. Van de Ven. They have done extensive research on controlling bias in decision making.

Fitz-enz, J. *The ROI of Human Capital: Measuring the Economic Value of Employee Performance.* New York: AMACOM, 2000. This book contains an interesting formula for valuing people's performance.

Shrock, S., and Coscarelli, W. *Criterion Referenced Test Development*. Washington, D.C.: ISPI, 1989. This is an excellent guide for learning about the use of scales to evaluate performance.

Ulrich D., and Smallwood, N. *Why the Bottom Line Isn't: How to Build Value Through People and Organization*. San Francisco: Jossey-Bass, 2003.

Index

A

ABC Manager's Primer Straight Talk on Activity-Based Accounting (Cokins, Stratton, and Helbling), 76

Accountability: assessing, 155; for development *versus* implementation, 24, 213; sustaining, 108–109

Accounting systems, 68, 76–77

Accuracy standards and evaluation, 37, 38, 41

Achieving a Leadership Role for Training (Hale and Westgaard), 216

Action-focused interventions, 176, 188–191, 196, 210–211

Active listening, 200

Activities: identifying cost drivers and, 66, 75–76; rating, for value, 75

Activity-based costing, 68, 76, 77

Adding value, 13, 94

Adler, A., 136

Administrative error, 162

Administrative performance criterion, 218

Adoption: rate of, 207; tracking, 104, 107, 110–111, 207, 214

Advocacy interventions, 176, 188–190, 210–211

Air quality, 120, 158

Alignment interventions, 176, 192–193, 196, 210–211

Alliance building, 18, 31, 35

Ambiguity: ability to handle, 218; in jobs, 230–231

American Foundation for Suicide Prevention (afsp.org), 111

American Quality and Productivity Council, 86

American Society for Training and Development (ASTD), 101; competencies list of, 11–13; performance consulting roles defined by, 11

American Society of Interior Designers, 173

American Telephone & Telegraph Company, 172
Americans with Disabilities Act, 173
Amortization, 63
ANSI standards, 176
Argyris, C., 136
Art of Asking Questions, The (Payne), 167
Assembly costs, 60
Assessment, scorecard evaluation of, 140, 142. *See also* Needs assessment
Automation standards, 183–184

B

Balanced scorecard, 139
Baldrige Award, 174
Bank case studies: hierarchy tool assessment in, 166; performance problem in, 137; results measurement in, 201–202, 203; work environment in, 115, 136
Barnard, C., 172–173
Barriers to becoming a performance consultant: eliminating, 195–196; identification of, 164–166
Baseline, 106, 204, 206
Becker, B., 215
Behavior: analysis of, 12, 126–127; dysfunctional, 128; group norms and, 127–132; principles of understanding, 128; reinforcing new, 106–107; stopping ruthless, 103–104; sustaining change in, 103–111
Behavioral descriptions, 221
Biases: consultant, 3–4, 7–8, 84; group, 241; in hierarchy tool, 162–163; in scorecard tool, 145; sources of, 162–163
Blaming, 137

Blended learning, 203–204
Block, P., 55
Bonuses, criteria for, 221
Books: on cost and cost management, 76–77; on credibility and influence, 101; on environment and performance, 136; as information source, 86; on interventions, 196–197; on measurement, 215–216; on needs assessment, 166–167; on performance consulting transition, 30–31, 55; on performance measurement, 241–242; on social systems, 136; on sustaining change, 111
Boyatzis, R., 116, 136
Brown, M. G., 215
"Brown suiters," 89–90
Business case, 204
Business competencies, 11–12
Business drivers, 41–42, 46
Business management costs, 59, 61, 70
Business practices, 70. *See also* Processes
Business understanding: acquiring, 86; as competency, 11
Byrd, R., 82, 101

C

Call center case studies: clarifying intervention in, 179; cost reduction in, 69; credibility and influence in, 87, 91, 95; hierarchy tool in, 154–155, 156–157; performance consultant job description in, 133–135; performance consulting transition in, 47–50; redesign intervention in, 185; scorecard tool in, 143–144; technology change in, 131; training results measurement in, 203–204

Capability assessment. *See* Capacity-and-capability-focused interventions; Resiliency and capability

Capacity-and-capability-focused interventions, 176, 186–188, 196, 210–211

Capacity studies, 151

Capital-intensive businesses, 59, 63, 64

Career counseling, 174

Carnegie, D., 172

Cash, W., Jr., 167

Causality, dramatizing, 104–108

Cause analysis: defined, 14, 138; in logic chain, 105. *See also* Needs assessment

Certification interventions, 192–193, 199, 215

Certified performance technologist (CPT), 5, 13–14

Change: in group norms, 127–132; in jobs and work environment, 117–127; in people, 126–127; sustaining, 104–111

Change (Watzlawick, Weakland, and Fisch), 101

Change agent role, 11

Change initiatives, needs assessment for, 138–139. *See also* Interventions; Needs assessment

Chartered Property and Casualty Underwriting (CPCU), 116

Cialdini, R. B., 101

Civil rights movement, 174

Clarity. *See* Congruency and clarity; Definition

Clark, R., 197

Client meetings: brevity in, 92–93, 95; process for, 38. *See also* Interviews

Clients: assessing and qualifying, 20–21, 96–99; cost classifications of, technique for determining, 64; getting performance consulting experience with, 53; hierarchy tool discussions with, 147, 160–161; observing, 89, 91; performance problem premises of, 138; process improvement for, 75–76; scorecard discussions with, 139–140, 142–144; sophistication level of, 21, 96, 99; understanding the business of, 11, 86. *See also Customer headings*

Closed questions, 208, 212

Code of conduct, 83

Cognitive dissonance, 31, 80, 89–90, 100, 186

Cokins, G., 76

Collaboration, 14

Collaborative Change (Gelinas and James), 104, 111

Comic strips, dissonance in, 89

Commitment, interventions for, 188–190, 196

Communication: of causality and logic, 105–108; interventions that inform with, 176, 178, 195, 210–211

Communication competencies, 31, 83. *See also* Interpersonal skills

Communication revolution, 172

Compensation, performance measurement and, 217, 238–239

Competence: contextual factors in, 116–117; criteria for, 221; zone of, 117

Competencies: for action-focused interventions, 188; for capacity-and-capability-focused interventions, 186; changes in group, 128,

130; for congruency-focused interventions, 191; for consequences-focused interventions, 179; for design-focused interventions, 183; for information-focused interventions, 177; for performance consulting, 11–13, 30, 31, 134–135
Competency identification skill, 11
Competent Manager, The (Boyatzis), 136
Competing Against Time (Stalk and Hout), 77
Complete Guide to Activity Based Costing, The (O'Guin), 77
Compliance criteria and measures, 209, 228, 229, 238
Conceptualization, 31
Confirmative evaluation, 205. *See also* Evaluation
Conflict: creating dissonance in cases of, 31, 80, 89–90, 100; impartial stance in, 93; information accuracy and, 91–92
Congruency and clarity: data collection on, 148–149; hierarchy tool assessment of, 146, 147, 151, 154–155; hypotheses for, 148–149, 151, 154
Congruency-focused interventions, 176, 191–193, 196
Conquering Organizational Change (Mourier and Smith), 111
Conscience, performance consultants as, 89–90, 105, 132
Consequence-focused interventions, 176, 179–183, 210–211. *See also* Rewards and consequences
Consultants: biases of, 4–5, 7–8, 84; performance consultants *versus* other, 6–8, 29; vendors disguised as, 84. *See also* Performance consultants
Consultant's Quick Guide to Grammar and Style (Ranshaw), 101
Consulting assignments, assessing potential, 20–21
Consulting process: defining one's, 19–28, 30; in global company case study, 23–28; measurement and evaluation of, 36–40, 41; phases of, 19–23
Consulting Process in Action, The (Lippitt and Lippitt), 55
Consulting proficiency evaluation, 36–40, 41
Continuing education, 174
Contractor relationships, 177
Conversations: facilitating, 8; about ongoing sponsorship, 109
Cooke, R., 76
Corroborating evidence: bias and, 162–163; for credibility and influence, 22, 80, 87–88, 90–91; in hierarchy tool, 145–166; need for, 146, 162; for performance consulting transition, 164–166; in scorecard tool, 139–144. *See also* Data collection; Evidence; Information
Coscarelli, W., 242
Cost-benefit analysis: as competency, 11; of development-related interventions, 187; of documentation-related interventions, 179; of interventions, 37; of performance consulting services, 26, 37, 41
Cost drivers, 58, 66–69, 75–76
Cost-effectiveness standards, 37, 38
Cost management: books on, 76–77; cost drivers and, 58, 66–69,

75–76; for performance consulting, 70–75; techniques and tools for, 66–70

Cost reduction: cost-shifting *versus*, 58, 66–67, 207; of fixed costs, 62, 74–75; job processes and, 233; measurement criteria for, 206–207, 209, 214; for noncompliance, 69; pricing and, 63; process improvement for, 70–76; techniques and tools for, 66–70; unnecessary cost drivers and, 67, 71, 75–76

Costs, 57–77; books on, 76–77; causes of, 58, 66–67, 68–69; classifications of, 58, 59–64; concepts of, 58–64; criteria of, 206–208, 209, 214, 233, 237; determining, in phase I, 21; direct, 61–63, 64, 207, 214; fixed, 62–63, 65–66, 74–75; hidden, 60, 66–67, 68–69, 74–75; identification of, 58; importance of understanding, 57–58; indirect, 61–63, 64, 207; infrastructure, 59; job outcomes and, 228, 229; job processes and, 233; long-term, 59; in manufacturing, 59–61, 62; of noncompliance, 69; pricing and, 63–64; sales, 57–58, 61, 67; shifting, 58, 66–67, 207; valuing of, 58, 61–62; valuing time and, 65–66, 74–75; variable, 62–63, 214

Counseling interventions, 176, 186, 187, 210–211

Courage, 80, 82–83, 100

Credentials, 90

Credibility and influence, 79–101; books on, 101; components of, 80, 100; courage and, 80, 82–83, 100; for design-focused interventions, 183; dissonance technique for, 31, 80, 89–90, 100; focus and, 17, 80, 93–96; group norms and, 133; impartiality and, 80, 93, 94–96; information and, 80, 81–82, 85, 86–92, 100; integrity and, 80, 83–84; interpersonal skills for, 80, 82, 83, 100; intervention labels for, 175; need for, 79; plan for strengthening, 100; political savvy and, 80, 88–89, 90–91, 100; presence and, 80, 92–93, 94–96; status and, 80, 90–91, 100; trust and, 80, 83–84, 87–88, 100

Criteria: adoption as, 207, 214; cost, 206–207, 209, 214, 233, 237; defined, 200–201; goal accomplishment, 207, 214; hidden, 218–220, 221; inadequate, 202–203, 217–220; for job evaluation, 226–238; in merit reviews, 217, 238–241; mismatch between metrics and, 219; overlooked, 218; for people performance measurement, 217–242; for performance consulting, 212–214; for performance improvement, 212–213; for sales managers, 223; satisfaction, 207, 209, 214, 236–237; selection of, for intervention results, 206–207, 208, 209, 213–214; selection of, for people performance, 220–226

Criterion Referenced Test Development (Shrock and Coscarelli), 242

Critic-doer-spectator continuum, 7–8

Critical mass, 104

Criticism, openness to, 82, 89–90

Critics, performance consultants as, 7–8

Cultural sensitivity, 83

Culture, group norms and, 128, 129, 130

Culture change, 115

Customer confidence, 41

Customer councils, 189

Customer identification, 45, 73

Customer satisfaction measurement, 41, 144, 207, 209, 236–237

Customers served, 234–235

Cycle time: assessment of, 156; efficiency standards for, 37; as job measurement criterion, 232–233; reduction of, 203, 204

Cynicism, 181

D

Dailey, C., 81

Data analysis: competency of, 31; phase of, 12. *See also* Needs assessment

Data collection: books on, 166–167; competencies of, 12, 31; for congruency and clarity, 148–149; for efficiency, 149–150; with hierarchy tool, 145–166; in phase II, 21–22; for resiliency and capability, 150–151; for results measurement, 204–206, 208–212; with scorecard tool, 139–144. *See also* Corroborating evidence; Information

Data reduction skill, 12

Dealer council, 190

Deductive thinking, 31

Definitional interventions, 176, 177–178, 210–211

Delbecq, A. L., 241

Delivery methods, describing, 46

Depreciation costs, 59, 62, 63, 75

Descriptive statistics, 22

Design: defined, 14; interventions focused on, 176, 183–185, 196, 210–211; measurement in phase of, 205; redesign and, 184, 185, 196, 210–211

Dessinger, J., 31

Development-related interventions, 176, 186, 187, 193. *See also* Training and development

Developmental needs criteria, 221

Deviation, 89–90, 91, 128, 132

Diabetes, 126–127

Diagnosis of concepts, 31

Dialogue, observing clients in, 89, 91

Dictionary of Occupational Titles (DOL), 9–11

Dillard, J., 166

Direct costs, 61–63, 64, 207

Disaster relief interventions, 191

Discounting, 89

Dissonance, 31, 80, 89–90, 100, 186

Doctors Without Borders, 191

Documentation: of change, 106; hierarchy tool assessment of, 150, 156, 157; interventions related to, 176, 178, 179, 185, 210–211; of performance consulting results, 95

Documents of understanding, 177

Doers, performance consultants as, 7–8

Drucker, P., 83

Dubner, S. J., 77

Dun and Bradstreet ratings, 86

E

Eames, C., 173

Eames, R., 173

Early adopters, 104

Earthquake relief interventions, 191

Ecology of Commerce, The (Hawkins), 77
Economies of scale, 156
Effective Executive, The (Drucker), 83
Effectiveness: efficiency *versus*, 173; standards of, 37, 38. *See also* Results; Results measurement
Efficiency: data collection on, 149–150; effectiveness *versus*, 173; hierarchy tool assessment of, 146, 149–150, 155–157; hypotheses for, 149–150, 155–157; measurement of job process, 232–234; theories of, 171
Efficiency orientation, 31
Efficiency standards and evaluation, 37, 39, 40
Ego appeals, 189
Electricity costs, 62
Elevator conversations, 92–93, 95
Employee assistance programs, 174
Employee satisfaction criteria, 207, 209, 236–237
Employees: characteristics of, 116, 118; isolating changes in, 126–127; morale problems of, 115, 159–160; motivational theories and, 172, 173; personal problems of, 176, 186, 187
Enforcement interventions, 176, 180, 181–183, 193, 210–211
Engineering jobs: measurement criteria for, 229–238; variability in, 121
Environment. *See* Group norms; Work environment
Equipment change, 120
Estes, F., 197
Evaluating New Methods of Measuring the Qualities Needed in Superior Foreign Service Officers (McClelland and Dailey), 81

Evaluation: defined, 14, 200; formative or in-process, 205; of jobs, 226–238; Kirkpatrick's levels of, 51–52, 58; measurement in phase of, 205; of people performance, 217–242; performance standards for, 36–40, 41, 54; of personal power, 84–85; of processes, 71; of product/service portfolio, 51–55; quantification and, 58; summative or confirmative, 205; of training, 76. *See also* Measurement; Performance measurement; Results measurement
Evaluators, performance consultants as, 11
Evidence of results: examples of, by intervention type, 208, 210–211; techniques and tools for getting, 208–213. *See also* Corroborating evidence
Evidence worksheet, 208, 211
Experience, status and, 90
Expert-facilitator continuum, 6–7
Expertise: perceived, 84; scorecard process and, 145
Experts: biases of, 3–4; for design-focused interventions, 183; performance consultants as, 6–7
External status, 80, 90–91, 100, 183

F

Face-saving, 92–93
Facilitation skills: for interventions, 177, 179, 183, 191; for performance consultants, 6–7, 8
Facility costs, 60, 62
Fact-finding phase, 21–22. *See also* Data collection
False economies, 75

Fatigue, 120

Feedback, competency of, 12

Field technician performance improvement, 144, 190, 192–193

Field work, 96

Fifth Discipline (Senge), 82

Financial impact measurement, 19

Financial performance measurement, 209

Findings-analysis phase, 22. *See also* Data analysis

First Things Fast (Rossett), 167

Fisch, R., 101

Fish bone diagram, 106

Fitz-enz, J., 241

5S, 174

Fixed costs: concepts of, 62–63; reducing, 62, 74–75; spreading, 65–66

Fixed direct costs, 62–63

Fixed indirect costs, 62–63

Flattened organizations, 172

Flawless Consulting (Block), 55

Focus, maintaining, 17, 80, 93–96, 177, 183, 186

Formative evaluation, 205. *See also* Evaluation

Freakeconomics (Levitt and Dubner), 77

Front-end analysis, 138. *See also* Needs assessment

Fuller, J., 55

Functions of an Executive, The (Barnard), 172–173

Furniture, 173

G

Gambit, 88–89

Gardner, R., 128

Gelinas, M., 104, 111

General and administrative (G&A) costs, 62

Geographic differences, 121, 122

Getting Things Done (Schaller), 82, 101

Gilbreth, F., 171, 197

Gill, J., 77

Global company case study, internal performance consultants in, 17–19, 23–28, 39–40

Global organizations, 172, 174

Goal accomplishment criteria and measures, 207, 214, 228, 229, 237

Goal setting, for transition to performance consulting, 29–30, 33–34

Goals and objectives, client: alignment of, 192; congruence of, 151, 154–155; hierarchy tool assessment of, 148, 151, 154–155; interventions and, 170; scorecard analysis of, 140, 141–142

Grapes of Wrath, The (Steinbeck), 173

Great Depression, 172

Great Game of Business, The (Stack), 77

Group bias, 241

Group norms: analysis and management of, 12, 127–132; organizational dynamics and, 116; performance and, 129–132; for performance consultants, 133; principles of, 128; social systems and, 127–128

Group process competencies, 12, 31

Growth measures, 209

Guide to Personal Risk Taking (Byrd), 82, 101

Guidebook for Performance Improvement, The (Kaufman, Thiagarajan, and MacGillis), 30

Guilt, 188

H

Habitat for Humanity, 191
Hale, J., 76, 111, 167, 197, 216
Handbook of Human Performance Technology (Pershing), 31
Harvard University, 173
Hawkins, P., 77
Hawthorne studies, 173
Health and fitness programs, 174, 187
Health problems, 126–127, 150, 173, 187
Hearsay and folklore, 87–88, 90, 145, 146
Heifer Foundation, 191
Helbling, J., 76
Hidden agenda, 84, 100
Hidden costs, 60, 66–67, 68–69, 74–75
Hidden criteria, 218–220, 221
Hierarchy-interventions matrix, 194–195
Hierarchy tool, 145–166; bias in, 162–163; congruency and clarity section of, 146; efficiency section of, 146, 149–150, 155–157; guidelines for using, 147, 160–163; job aid version of, 147–151, 160; purposes of, 139, 145–146; resiliency and capability section of, 146, 147, 150–151, 157–160; rigor in, 161–162; sections of, 146–147; for transition to performance consulting, 164–166; worksheet version of, 147, 152–153
Honesty criterion, 218
Horizontal integration, 171–172
Hout, T., 77
How to Win Friends and Influence People (Carnegie), 172
HR Scorecard, The (Becker, Huselid, and Ulrich), 215

Human Performance Technology (HPT) Standards, The (International Society for Performance Improvement), 5, 13–14, 30, 101
Human relations movement, 173
Human resource (HR) costs, 62
Human resource development (HRD): in information chain, 81; performance consulting-related competencies of, 11–13, 30; performance consulting transition of, 40
Human resource (HR) generalists, measurement criteria for, 229–238
Human resource (HR) programs, business drivers and, 42
Humor, 89
Hurricane Katrina, 191
Huselid, M., 215
Hypotheses: for congruency and clarity, 148–149, 151, 154; developing, 165–166; for efficiency, 149–150, 155–157; for performance consulting barriers and operations, 164; for resiliency and capability, 150–151, 157–160

I

If-then tables: for interventions, 177–194; for qualifying clients, 99
Illustrations, for demonstrating causality and logic, 105–108
Image: of intervention, 207; as job outcome, 228, 229, 238
Image management, 31, 35, 80, 92–93, 94–96, 101
Impact assessment, 31
Impartiality, 80, 93, 94–96

Implementation: accountability for, 24, 213; defined, 14; phase of, 22; sustaining change and, 104–111; tracking adoption and, 104, 107, 110–111, 207, 214. *See also* Interventions

Incentives, interventions in, 180, 181. *See also* Rewards and consequences

Indirect costs (overhead), 61–63, 64, 207

Industrial management theories, 171

Industry standards, 183

Industry study participation, 189

Industry trade associations, 86

Industry understanding, competency of, 12

Inferential statistics, 22

Influence. *See* Credibility and influence

Influence (Cialdini), 101

Information: action-focused interventions and, 188; for credibility and influence, 80, 81–82, 85, 86–92, 100; in hierarchy tool, 145–166; interventions focused on, 176, 177–179, 195, 210–211; job performance and, 120; measurement and evidence for, 210–211; problems due to inaccurate, 91–92; in scorecard tool, 139–144; sharing, 87; techniques for getting, 86–87, 90–91; trustworthiness of, 80, 84, 87–88, 100; verification of, 80, 87–88, 90–91, 100. *See also* Corroborating evidence; Data collection; Evidence

Information revolution, 172

Information search skill, 12. *See also* Data collection

Infrastructure costs, 59

Institutional memory, 105

Instructional design, 186

Instructor evaluation, 217

Insurance industry, 36, 95–96, 116, 182–183

Insurance School of Chicago, 116

Integrity, 80, 83–84

Intellectual competencies, 12, 31

Intellectual versatility, 12

Intelligences, multiple, 128

International product managers, job redefinition for, 124–125

International Society for Performance Improvement (ISPI), 84, 86; activities of, 5; certification by, 5, 13–14; self-assessment tool of, 30; standards of, 4–5, 13–14, 30, 95, 101; Web site of, 30

Interpersonal skills: for capacity-and-capability-focused interventions, 186; for credibility and influence, 80, 82, 83, 85, 100; development of, 83; for information-focused interventions, 177; as performance consulting competencies, 12, 31

Intervention Skills (Reddy), 55

Interventions, 169–197; action-focused, 176, 188–191, 196, 210–211; books on, 196–197; capacity-and-capabilities-focused, 176, 186–188, 196, 210–211; clients' language for, 94, 170; congruency-focused, 176, 191–193, 196; consequence-focused, 176, 179–183, 195, 210–211; defined, 138, 169, 170; at departmental level, 175; design-focused, 176, 183–185, 196, 210–211; drivers of, 170–171; examples of, 169–170, 174, 175, 176; families of, 175–196; hierarchy matrix for, 194–195; history and research on, 170–174; if-then tables for, 177–194; image or popularity of, 207; at individual level, 175; information-focused, 176, 177–179, 195, 210–211; job aids for, 175, 176, 178, 180, 184, 186, 189, 192; life cycle of, measurement during, 204–206; measurement of, 199–216; at organizational level, 175; at societal level, 175; tools for selecting, 193–195; tracking adoptions as, 104; at work group level, 175. *See also* Implementation; Results; Results measurement; Solutions

Interviewing (Stewart and Cash), 167

Interviews: books on conducting, 166–167; controlling bias in, 162–163; for job evaluation, 227–229; open-ended questions in, 208, 212

Investment: of clients, 147, 157–160; in performance consulting career, 165

ISO 9000 Standards, 174, 176

Iverson, K., 101

J

Jackson, S., 83–84

James, R., 104, 111

Job aid hierarchy, 147–151, 160

Job aid scorecard, 139–140, 142–144

Job aids: for evaluating jobs, 226, 229; hierarchy tool assessment of, 150, 156; as interventions, 185;

for merit reviews, 238–241; for results measurement, 208, 209; for selecting interventions, 175, 176, 178, 180, 184, 186, 189, 192

Job analysis: with hierarchy tool, 149, 155; in logic chain, 105; in manufacturing case study, 193; techniques and tools for, 121–125

Job descriptions: assessment of, 149, 155; characteristics and changes in, 122–123, 124–125; interventions that define, 177; for performance consultants, 133–135

Job security, 174

Job-specific training, 41

Job task analysis, 138, 183

Jobs: aftermath criterion of, 237; characteristics of, 118, 226; clarity of direction in, 230–231; complexity of, 230; compliance criterion of, 228, 229, 238; contextual descriptions of, 122–123, 133; cost criteria of, 233, 237; customers-served criterion of, 234–235; cycle time in, 232–233; dimensions of, 226–241; efficiency of, 232–234; evaluation of, 226–238; goal accomplishment criteria of, 237; group norms and, 130; image criterion of, 238; inputs to, 122, 226–232, 239; interventions that design, 183; isolating different conditions in, 123–125; job aid for evaluating, 226, 229; outcomes of, 226–229, 236–238, 241; outputs of, 226–229, 234–236, 241; performance and, 116, 118, 119–120, 121–125; processes of, 226–229, 232–234, 239; response time in, 232;

satisfaction criterion of, 236–237; variability in, 121–122, 229–232; volume criterion for, 229–230; work quantity criterion of, 234; worth criterion of, 235

Journals, 86, 170

K

Kaufman, R., 30
Keeping Score (Brown), 215
Kirkpatrick, D., 51–52, 58, 104
Kirkpatrick's levels of evaluation, 51–52, 58
Knowledge industry, 172

L

Labels, 150, 156
Labor costs, 60, 62
Lagging indicators, 204
Langdon, D., 101
Language: analysis of, 12; clients' *versus* consultants', 94, 170, 200
Late adopters, 104
Lawler, E., 136
Leading indicators, 204, 206
Learning, from other companies' experience, 81–82
Learning organizations, 172
Level 4 evaluation, 52, 58
Levitt, S. D., 77
Librarians, 86
Lifelong learning, 174
Lighting, 120, 150, 158, 173
Likert scale, 51, 221
Lippitt, G., 55
Lippitt, R., 55
Listening, 86, 89, 200
Literature review, 23, 30
Logic chains, 105–108

Logical thinking, 31
Logo, for performance consultants, 94, 96

M

MacGillis, P., 30
Management theories, 172–174
Managing Performance Improvement Projects (Fuller), 55
Mandated programs, 42
Manufacturing organizations: alignment intervention in, 192–193; costs in, 59–61, 62; hierarchy tool use in, 156–157; reframing supplier relationship in, 187–188; scorecard tool use in, 144; tracking in, 110; work environment problem in, 120–121
Market share, 209
Market support programs, 42
Marketing, of performance consulting services, 34, 95–96. *See also* Credibility and influence
Maturity: client, 96–99; as job criterion, 231
Mayo, E., 172
McClelland, D. C., 81, 116
Measurement: in analysis phase, 204, 205; books on, 215–216; for comparison, 200; of consulting performance, 36–40, 41, 54; definitions related to, 200–201; in design and development phase, 205; in evaluation phase, 205; existing information sources for, 110, 111; of financial impact, 19; focus on, in performance consulting, 8; getting practice in, 213–214; interventions related to, 176, 180, 181, 182–183, 195, 210–211;

in logic chain, 106; ongoing, 110–111; of people performance, 217–242; phase of, 22; reasons for lack of, 110; of results, 22, 36–40, 41, 106, 110–111, 199–216; and tracking adoption, 104, 107, 110–111, 207, 214; of training, 76, 199, 203–204, 215. *See also* Performance measurement; Results; Results measurement

Measures: documentation of, 106; identifying, with scorecard tool, 140, 141, 143–144; interventions related to, 176, 180, 181, 182–183, 195; of job dimensions, 226–229; multiple sources of, 203–204; of people performance, 217–242; of performance consulting proficiency, 34, 35, 36–40, 54; qualitative, 221, 224–226; quantitative, 221, 224. *See also* Criteria; Performance measurement; Results measurement

Mental models: for performance improvement, 104–105; reframing, 186–187

Merchandising, 201–202, 203

Merit reviews and criteria, 217, 221, 238–241. *See also* Performance measurement

Metrics: mismatch between criteria and, 219; in performance measurement, 217–242; in results measurement, 201, 203, 208, 209. *See also* Measurement; Measures; Performance measurement; Results measurement

Middle adopters, 104

Mission and mission statements: congruence of, 148, 151; evaluating clients', 146, 147, 148; inter-

ventions that define, 176, 177–178; for performance consulting, 28–29, 30, 33–34

Model-building skill, 12

Models for HRD Practice (ASTD), 101

Molded plywood, 173

Monopolies, 172

Monroe, A. H., 173

Monroe, M., 92

Moseley, J., 31

Motivation, management theories based on, 172, 173

Mourier, P., 111

Multiple Intelligences (Gardner), 128

Municipal government case study, 202

N

Nadler, L., 136

Name change, for performance consulting, 33, 55, 95

National Aeronautics and Space Administration, 174

National Society for Performance and Instruction, 4. *See also* International Society for Performance Improvement

Needs analyst role, 11

Needs assessment, 137–167; books on, 166–167; business case and, 204, 205; defined, 14; guidelines for, 160–161; hierarchy tool for, 139, 145–166; in logic chain, 105; measurement in, 204, 205; for performance consultants, 164–166; process criteria for, 138–139, 145; purposes of, 137–139, 166; scorecard tool for, 139–144

Negotiation competency, 12

New Language of Work, The (Langdon), 101

New Orleans airport, 191

New York Times, best-seller list, 86

Newspapers, 86

Noise, 120, 150, 158

Nominal group technique (NGT), 221, 222, 223–224, 241

Noncompliance costs, 69

Nonverbal communication, 83

Norms. *See* Group norms

O

Objectives-preparation competency, 11

Objectivity: for credibility and influence, 80, 93, 94–96; maintaining, 19, 31; perceptual, 31; social, 31

Observation: of clients' dialogue styles, 89, 91; competencies in, 11, 12, 31; of people at work, 120

Office house, 173

O'Guin, M., 77

101 Tips for Marketing Your Services (Ranshaw), 55

Open-ended questions, 208, 212

Operating inefficiencies, 156–157. *See also* Efficiency

Operational definition: concept of, 9; developing, for performance consulting, 8–19, 30; field example of, 17–19; job description and, 122, 133; worksheet for, 15–16, 179

Organization: characteristics of, 117; interventions related to, 176, 183, 210–211; people performance and, 116, 117; social system of, 127–132

Organizational development, 12

Organizational dynamics: background on, 116; competencies related to, 12; group norms and, 116, 127–132; work environment and, 115–127

Organizational effectiveness theories, 171–174

Organizational structures: evolution and theories of, 171–172; hierarchy tool assessment of, 149, 155

Outcasts, 128

Outcomes, job, 226–229, 236–238, 241

Outputs, job, 226–229, 234–236, 241

Outsourcing, 172

Outsourcing Training and Development (Hale), 197

Overhead. *See* Indirect costs

Ownership, sustaining, 108–109

P

Paradigms, creating new, 186–187

Payne, S., 167

Peace Corps service, 90

Peer pressure, 188, 189, 190

People characteristics: behavior and, 128; isolating changes in, 126–127; performance and, 116, 118, 126–127

People performance measurement. *See* Performance measurement

People performance worksheets, 221, 222, 223–226, 239

Performance: group norms and, 116, 127–132; organizational dynamics and, 116; personal causes of, 126–127; work environment and, 116–127

Performance and Instruction Quarterly, 86

Performance appraisal process, measuring the results of, 202. *See also* Merit reviews; Performance measurement

Performance-Based Certification (Hale), 197

Performance-Based Evaluation (Hale), 76, 167

Performance-Based Management (Hale), 111

Performance consultants: barriers for, 164–166, 195–196; certification of, 5, 13–14; characteristics of, 6–8; credibility and influence for, 79–101; determining costs of, 21; group norms for, 133; hierarchy tool applied to, 164–166; image management for, 31, 35, 80, 92–93, 94–96, 101; impartiality of, 80, 93, 94–96; information sources for, 86–87; internal *versus* external, 132; interventions for, 195–196; job description for, 133–135; language of, 94, 170, 200; *versus* other consultants, 6–8, 29; performance measurement of, 239; professional and academic backgrounds of, 116; roles of, 4–5, 6–8, 9–14, 174; status of, 80, 90–91, 100; work environment of, 132–133. *See also* Consultants

Performance consulting: competencies related to, 11–13, 30, 31, 134–135; cost management for, 70–75; defining a process for, 19–28, 30; measurement of, 36–40, 41, 212–214, 239; operational defining of, 8–19, 29, 33–34;

organizational dynamics and, 116; phases of, 19–23; products and services alignment for, 40–54; professional definitions of, 9–14; standards for evaluating, 4–5, 13–14, 36–40, 41, 54; transition to, 33–55; vision and mission for, 23, 28–29, 30, 33–34. *See also* Transition to performance consulting

Performance Consulting (Robinson and Robinson), 31

Performance consulting continuums, 6–8, 29

Performance gap: discussing, with clients, 143; scorecard tool assessment of, 140, 141–142, 143

Performance improvement: approaches to, 4, 5–6, 170–174, 175; interventions for, 169–197; measurement of, 212–214; sustaining change and, 104–111. *See also* Interventions

Performance Improvement, 81

Performance Improvement Interventions (Van Tiem, Moseley, and Dessinger), 31

Performance management competencies, 31

Performance measurement (people performance), 217–242; books on, 241–242; criteria and metrics for, 209, 217–242; criteria selection techniques for, 220–226; hidden criteria in, 218–220, 221; importance of, 217; inadequate criteria and measures in, 217–220; job evaluation and, 226–238; in logic chain, 106; of performance consultants, 239; reasons for, 220–226; worksheets for, 221–222,

223–226, 239. *See also* Measurement; Results measurement

Performance-observation competency, 11

Performance problems: diagnosing, 137–167; group norms and, 127–132; hierarchy tool for analyzing, 139, 145–166; isolating environmental changes and, 120–121; isolating job changes and, 121–125; isolating people changes and, 126–127; scorecard tool for analyzing, 139–144

Performance shaping, 18

Performance technology, 94

Performance Technology Handbook (Pershing), 101

Pershing, J., 31, 101

Personal power: evaluating, 84–85, 100; position power and, 79, 82, 100; sources of, 82. *See also* Credibility and influence

Personal problems: counseling for, 176, 186, 187; health and, 126–127, 150, 173, 187

Petroleum logistics case study, 119–120

Phases: of interventions and measurement, 204–206; of performance consulting process, 19–23

Physical space: hierarchy tool assessment of, 150, 158, 159; interventions in, 185, 210–211; research and theories of, 173–174; work environment and, 120, 130

Physicians, measurement criteria for, 232–238

Plain Talk (Iverson), 101

Plan: for credibility and influence, 100; transition, 33–36, 54–55

Political savvy, 17–18, 31; in acquiring information, 88; for action-focused interventions, 188; for credibility and influence, 80, 88–89, 90–91, 100; for information-focused interventions, 177; techniques for developing, 90–91

Position power, 79, 100; personal power and, 82

Power. *See* Credibility and influence; Personal power; Position power; Social power

Preretirement planning, 174

Presence, establishing a, 31, 80, 92–93, 94–96

Price components, 63–64

Principles of Speech (Monroe), 173

Proactivity, 31

Process improvement, 70–76

Process mapping and analysis, 68, 70–76

Process or task performance worksheet, 71, 72, 179

Processes: cost management and, 68, 70–76; describing, 70; evaluating and measuring, 71, 232–234, 239; hierarchy tool assessment of, 149, 156; practices *versus*, 70; systems *versus*, 13

Processing costs, 60

Product managers case study: group norms and expense reduction in, 131–132; hierarchy tool in, 159; job outputs evaluation in, 235–236; job redefinition in, 124–125

Product performance: improvement of, 144; measures of, 209

Product portfolio worksheets: modifying, 54–55; purposes of, 42–43;

using, to evaluate processes, 73; using, with clients, 54, 179

Product Portfolio Worksheet 1: field example of using, 47–50; instructions for using, 45–47; modifying, 54–55; purposes of, 42–45; template for, 43; using, to evaluate processes, 73

Product Portfolio Worksheet 2: instructions for using, 51–53; modifying, 54–55; purposes of, 42–43, 51; template for, 44–45

Product pricing, 63–64

Product support programs, 42

Production costs, 59–61, 62

Production line errors, 120–121

Productivity measures, 209

Products and services: alignment of, with performance consulting role, 40–55; business drivers and, 41–42; describing, 42–50; describing clients', 54; evaluating, 51–53; practicing new, with willing clients, 53

Professional demeanor, 218

Professional organizations, 86

Profit margin, 63–64

Promotion criteria, 221

Psychological appeals, 188

Q

Qualification of clients, 96–99

Qualitative measures, 221, 224–226. *See also* Measures

Quality movement, 174

Quantitative measures, 221, 224. *See also* Measures

Questioning, 12, 200, 208, 212

Questioning error, 163

Questions, for merit reviews, 238–239, 240–241

Quick Show Me Your Value (Seagrave), 76

R

Random sampling, 163

Ranking, 189

Ranshaw, J., 55, 101

Ratings, 51

Raw materials costs, 59–60, 62

Readiness, client, 96–99

Reagan, R., 174

Reasoning competencies, 12, 31

Reciprocity, 31

Recognition, 181–183, 193. *See also* Rewards and consequences

Red Cross, 191

Reddy, W. B., 55

Redesign interventions, 184, 185, 196, 210–211

Redundancy, 155

Reengineering, 174

Reframing, interventions of, 176, 186–188, 196, 210–211

Regulatory requirements, programs driven by, 42

Reilly, R., 166

Relationships: competency in, 12, 218; for credibility and influence, 80, 82, 83, 84, 85, 100; job requirements for, 122; as performance criteria, 218; professional, 86; reframing, 187–188; working conditions and, 123

Reporting: of adoption, 104, 107; as intervention, 181; ongoing measurement and, 110–111

Reputation, 80, 90–91, 100, 101, 238. *See also* Credibility and influence

Request for services, defining and understanding, 20–23, 26, 38–39

Research and development (R&D) costs, 62

Research journals, 86

Researchers, performance consultants as, 11

Resiliency and capability: data collection methods for, 150–151; hierarchy tool assessment of, 146, 150–151, 157–160; hypotheses for, 150–151, 157–160; interventions related to, 176

Resource efficiency, 233

Resource identification, for transition to performance consulting, 34, 35, 46, 52

Resources, organizational: deficient, 159–160; excess, 158; hierarchy tool assessment of, 151, 157–158; people performance and, 116, 117; for performance consultant, 132

Response time, 232

Responsiveness standards, 37

Results: documentation of, 95; evidence of, 208–212; focus on, in performance consulting, 8, 13; reporting, 110–111; scorecard tool assessment of, 140, 142; tracking adoption and, 104, 107, 110–111, 207, 214

Results measurement, 22, 199–216; books on, 215–216; criteria in, 200–201, 202–203; criteria selection for, 206–207, 208, 209, 212–214; definitions related to, 200–201; evidence and data collection for, 204–206, 208–212; inappropriate criteria and metrics in, 203; insufficient criteria in, 202; job aid for, 208, 209; in logic chain, 106; metrics in, 201, 203, 208, 209; multiple sources of

measures for, 203–204; ongoing, 110–111; for performance consulting, 36–40, 41, 212–214; in phases of intervention, 204–206; problems in, 202–203; reasons for, 199–200, 201–202. *See also* Measurement; Performance measurement

Retail promotion campaign, measurement of, 201, 202

Retention. *See* Turnover and retention

Return on investment (ROI), 21, 58; results measurement and, 199

Rewards and consequences: group norms and, 128, 130; hierarchy tool assessment of, 148–149, 151, 154; interventions focused on, 176, 179–183, 193, 195, 210–211; performance measurement and, 217, 238–241

Rigor, 21, 161–162

Risk taking, 82–83, 132

Rituals, analysis of, 12

Robinson, D. G., 31

Robinson, J., 31

ROI of Human Capital, The (Fitzenz), 241

Rossett, A., 167

S

Safety performance criteria, 218

Salaries and benefits costs, 62

Sales costs, 57–58, 61, 67

Sales job variability, 121

Sales performance improvement, 143–144, 182–183, 219–220

Sales representative evaluation, 219–220, 223–226, 231

Sampling error, 163

Satisfaction criteria and metrics, 207, 209, 214, 236–237

Schaller, L. E., 82, 101

Scientific management, 171

Scorecard tool, 139–144; guidelines for using, 142–144; job aid version of, 139–140, 142–144; for measures, criteria, and metrics, 209; uses of, 139–140; worksheet version of, 140–142

Seagrave, T., 76

Self-assessment, 30, 31

Self-confidence, 31, 35, 85

Self-discipline, 31

Self-esteem, employee, 115

Self-management competencies, 31

Self-reporting, 104

Senge, P., 82

Senior managers case study: advocacy intervention in, 190; behavior change in, 103–104, 106–107, 109, 110; business case development in, 206

Service costs, 61

Service economy, 172

Service interventions, 176, 189, 191, 196, 210–211

Service organizations, cost components of, 59

Service pricing, 63–64

Shipping costs, 61

Shrock, S., 242

Signage, 150, 156, 181

Six Sigma, 174

Skepticism, 146, 158

Skill-building programs, drivers of, 42

Slogans, for performance consultants, 94, 95

Smallwood, N., 242

Smith, M., 111

Social competencies, 31. *See also* Interpersonal skills

Social power, 31

Social sensitivity, 83

Social systems: analysis and management of, 12, 127–132; elements of, 127–128; organizational dynamics and, 115; research on, 136

Society for Human Resource Management, 86

Solutions: biases for, 4–5, 7–8, 84, 145; designing, 22; development of, 14, 22; dramatizing causality and, 104–108; "flavor of the month," 105; logic chains for, 105–108. *See also* Interventions

Space race, 174

Speaking up: courage for, 80, 82–83, 100; staying focused and, 93–94

Spectators, performance consultants as, 7–8

Sponsors and sponsorship: identification of, 91; sustaining, 21, 108–109

Spontaneity, 31

Stack, J., 77

Stakeholder buy-in, 21

Stalk, G., 77

Standardization, interventions for, 176, 183–185, 193, 196, 210–211

Standards: enforcement of, 181–182; hierarchy tool assessment of, 150, 156; for performance consulting, 4–5, 13–14, 36–40, 41, 54; scorecard assessment of, 140, 141–142

Standards for the Training Function (Hale), 167

Standards movement, 174

Statistical process control (SPC), 68

Status: in organizations, 128, 130–131; of performance consultant, 80, 90–91, 100, 183

Steinbeck, J., 173

Stewart, C., 167

Stock, B., 81

Stock brokers, 86

Strategy development, for transition to performance consulting, 34, 35

Stratton, A., 76

Stress reduction case study: advocacy intervention used in, 190; behavior change in, 103–104, 106–107, 109, 111; business case development in, 206

Succession planning, 108–109

Suicide, 111, 190

Summative evaluation, 205. *See also* Evaluation

Supplier relationships, 177, 187–188

Sustaining change: books on, 111; problem of, 103–104; techniques for, 104–111

Symbols, analysis of, 12

Synthetics, 173

System, process *versus*, 13

Systematic Interviewing (Dillard and Reilly), 166

Systematic processes: approach of, 14; evaluation of, 40

Systems view, 13, 136

T

Target population, 163

Task characteristics, performance and, 116, 118

Task design, 183

Task performance worksheet, 71, 72

Taylor, F., 171, 197

Team charters, 177

Technical competencies, 11

Technology: changes in job characteristics and, 119–120; changes in social system and, 127, 129–130, 131–132; evaluating, for value, 75; hierarchy tool assessment of, 150; impact of, on organizations, 172, 173

Thiagarajan, S., 30

36-Hour Course in Finance for Nonfinancial Managers (Cooke), 76

Time: respecting clients', 92–93, 95; tracking, 37, 38–39, 74–75; valuing, 65–66, 74–75

Time and motion studies, 171

Time zones, 122

Timetable, for reporting progress, 111

Tosti, D., 83–84

Total Quality Management (TQM), 174

Tracking: of adoption, 104, 107, 110–111, 207, 214; for ongoing measurement and reporting, 110–111; of time, 37, 38–39, 74–75

Training and development: budget for, 158; costs of, 62; evaluation of, 76; hierarchy tool assessment of, 150–151, 158, 160; historical evolution of, 174; interventions using, 176, 186, 187, 196, 210–211; measurement of, 76, 199, 203–204, 215

Training departments: cost reduction in, 74–75; in information chain, 81; transition of, to performance consulting, 33, 36, 47–50, 74, 213

Transition to performance consulting, 33–55; books on, 30–31, 55; false starts in, 33; hierarchy tool assessment for, 164–166; interventions for, 195–196; measurement of, 213–214; plan for, 33–36, 54–55; products/services portfolio assessment for, 42–54; standards and evaluation development for, 36–40, 41, 54

Trust: integrity and, 83–84; verification and, 80, 87–88, 90–91, 100

Tsunami relief efforts, 191

Turning Research into Results (Clark and Estes), 197

Turnover and retention, 48, 160, 199, 214

U

Ukens, L., 31, 55

Ulrich, D., 215, 242

Uncertainty, ability to handle, 218

Understanding Financial Statements and Financial Analysis (Gill), 77

Unintended consequences, 205, 228, 229, 237, 241

U.S. Department of Labor, Dictionary of Occupational Titles, 9–11

User councils, 189

V

Values: hierarchy tool assessment of, 148–149, 151, 154; merit reviews and, 238–239; scorecard tool assessment of, 140

Van de Ven, A. H., 241

Van Tiem, D., 31

Variable costs, 62–63, 214

Variable direct costs, 62–63

Variance, 68

Vendors, 84

Vertical integration, 171, 172

Vision, client's: alignment with, 192; hierarchy tool analysis of, 146, 147, 148; interventions that define, 176, 177–178

Vision statements: evaluating clients', 146, 147, 148; for performance consulting, 28–29, 30, 33–34

Visioning: competency of, 12; of performance consulting role, 23, 28–29, 30, 33–34

Volume criterion, 229–230

W

Wall Street Journal, 86

War stories, 106

Warehousing costs, 61

Watzlawick, P., 101

Weakland, J., 101

Web-based training, 203–204

Web sites, as information source, 86

Western Electric Company, 172

Westgaard, O., 216

What Smart Trainers Know (Ukens), 31, 55

Why the Bottom Line Isn't (Ulrich and Smallwood), 242

Work environment: books on, 136; components of, 116–120; hierarchy tool assessment of, 150, 158; importance of, 115; interventions for, 185, 210–211; isolating changes in, 120–121; job conditions and,

121–125, 229–232; of perfor-
mance consultants, 132–133; re-
search and theories on, 173–174
Work processes. *See* Processes
Work quantity, 234
Work rule assessment, 149, 156. *See
also* Processes
Working conditions, 121, 123–125

Workplace characteristics and
changes, 120, 127, 130
World War II, 173
Worth, 235

Z

Zero defects, 174

About the Author

Judith Hale has dedicated her professional career to helping management develop effective and practical ways to improve individual and organizational performance. She is known for making sense out of confusion and helping others stay focused on what matters. She is able to explain complex ideas so people understand their relevance and how to apply them. She has developed useful models for implementing new programs, identifying organizational needs, defining and assessing competencies, and developing performance management systems.

Her consulting firm, Hale Associates, was started in 1974 and enjoys long-term relationships with a variety of major corporations. The services the firm provides include consultation on implementation strategies, certification, and evaluation. Judith is currently working with a task force to develop models for deploying performance improvement initiatives worldwide on quality, process improvement, training, standards, certification, and technology.

Judith is the author of *Outsourcing Training and Development* (2006), *Performance-Based Management* (2003), *Performance-Based Evaluation* (2002), *Performance-Based Certification* (2000), *Performance Consultant's Fieldbook* (1998), *The Training Manager's Competencies* (1989), and coauthor of *Achieving a Leadership Role for Training* (1995).

She has served on the Illinois Occupational Skills Standards Credentialing Council. She is a past president of the International Society of Performance and Improvement (ISPI), has served on its President's Advisory Council, received the Outstanding Member of the Year Award in 1987, and became a member for life in 2006. She was nominated for ASTD's Gordon Bliss Award in 1995. She was president of the International Board of Standards for Performance and

Instruction. She served as president of the Chicago Chapter of the Industrial Relations Research Association and was a commercial arbitrator with the American Arbitration Association. She taught graduate courses in management for fourteen years for the Insurance School of Chicago and received the school's Outstanding Educator award in 1986. Judith speaks regularly at international and national conferences on subjects related to deployment, evaluation, needs assessment, certification, and performance improvement.

She received a B.A. from Ohio State University, an M.A. from Miami University, and a Ph.D. from Purdue University.

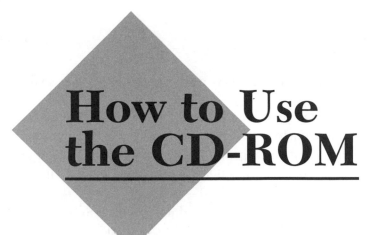

How to Use the CD-ROM

SYSTEM REQUIREMENTS

PC with Microsoft Windows 98SE or later
Mac with Apple OS version 8.6 or later

USING THE CD WITH WINDOWS

To view the items located on the CD, follow these steps:

1. Insert the CD into your computer's CD-ROM drive.
2. A window appears with the following options:

    Contents: Allows you to view the files included on the CD-ROM.

    Software: Allows you to install useful software from the CD-ROM.

    Links: Displays a hyperlinked page of websites.

    Author: Displays a page with information about the author(s).

    Contact Us: Displays a page with information on contacting the publisher or author.

    Help: Displays a page with information on using the CD.

    Exit: Closes the interface window.

If you do not have autorun enabled, or if the autorun window does not appear, follow these steps to access the CD:

1. Click Start -> Run.
2. In the dialog box that appears, type d:\start.exe, where d is the letter of your CD-ROM drive. This brings up the autorun window described in the preceding set of steps.
3. Choose the desired option from the menu. (See Step 2 in the preceding list for a description of these options.)

**IN CASE OF
TROUBLE**

If you experience difficulty using the CD-ROM, please follow these steps:

1. Make sure your hardware and systems configurations conform to the systems requirements noted under "System Requirements" above.

2. Review the installation procedure for your type of hardware and operating system. It is possible to reinstall the software if necessary.

To speak with someone in Product Technical Support, call 800-762-2974 or 317-572-3994 Monday through Friday from 8:30 a.m. to 5:00 p.m. EST. You can also contact Product Technical Support and get support information through our website at www.wiley.com/techsupport.

Before calling or writing, please have the following information available:

- Type of computer and operating system.
- Any error messages displayed.
- Complete description of the problem.

It is best if you are sitting at your computer when making the call.

Pfeiffer Publications Guide

This guide is designed to familiarize you with the various types of Pfeiffer publications. The formats section describes the various types of products that we publish; the methodologies section describes the many different ways that content might be provided within a product. We also provide a list of the topic areas in which we publish.

FORMATS

In addition to its extensive book-publishing program, Pfeiffer offers content in an array of formats, from fieldbooks for the practitioner to complete, ready-to-use training packages that support group learning.

FIELDBOOK Designed to provide information and guidance to practitioners in the midst of action. Most fieldbooks are companions to another, sometimes earlier, work, from which its ideas are derived; the fieldbook makes practical what was theoretical in the original text. Fieldbooks can certainly be read from cover to cover. More likely, though, you'll find yourself bouncing around following a particular theme, or dipping in as the mood, and the situation, dictate.

HANDBOOK A contributed volume of work on a single topic, comprising an eclectic mix of ideas, case studies, and best practices sourced by practitioners and experts in the field.

An editor or team of editors usually is appointed to seek out contributors and to evaluate content for relevance to the topic. Think of a handbook not as a ready-to-eat meal, but as a cookbook of ingredients that enables you to create the most fitting experience for the occasion.

RESOURCE Materials designed to support group learning. They come in many forms: a complete, ready-to-use exercise (such as a game); a comprehensive resource on one topic (such as conflict management) containing a variety of methods and approaches; or a collection of likeminded activities (such as icebreakers) on multiple subjects and situations.

TRAINING PACKAGE An entire, ready-to-use learning program that focuses on a particular topic or skill. All packages comprise a guide for the facilitator/trainer and a workbook for the participants. Some packages are supported with additional media—such as video—or learning aids, instruments, or other devices to help participants understand concepts or practice and develop skills.

- *Facilitator/trainer's guide* Contains an introduction to the program, advice on how to organize and facilitate the learning event, and step-by-step instructor notes. The guide also contains copies of presentation materials—handouts, presentations, and overhead designs, for example—used in the program.

• *Participant's workbook* Contains exercises and reading materials that support the learning goal and serves as a valuable reference and support guide for participants in the weeks and months that follow the learning event. Typically, each participant will require his or her own workbook.

ELECTRONIC CD-ROMs and web-based products transform static Pfeiffer content into dynamic, interactive experiences. Designed to take advantage of the searchability, automation, and ease-of-use that technology provides, our e-products bring convenience and immediate accessibility to your workspace.

METHODOLOGIES

CASE STUDY A presentation, in narrative form, of an actual event that has occurred inside an organization. Case studies are not prescriptive, nor are they used to prove a point; they are designed to develop critical analysis and decision-making skills. A case study has a specific time frame, specifies a sequence of events, is narrative in structure, and contains a plot structure—an issue (what should be/have been done?). Use case studies when the goal is to enable participants to apply previously learned theories to the circumstances in the case, decide what is pertinent, identify the real issues, decide what should have been done, and develop a plan of action.

ENERGIZER A short activity that develops readiness for the next session or learning event. Energizers are most commonly used after a break or lunch to stimulate or refocus the group. Many involve some form of physical activity, so they are a useful way to counter post-lunch lethargy. Other uses include transitioning from one topic to another, where "mental" distancing is important.

EXPERIENTIAL LEARNING ACTIVITY (ELA) A facilitator-led intervention that moves participants through the learning cycle from experience to application (also known as a Structured Experience). ELAs are carefully thought-out designs in which there is a definite learning purpose and intended outcome. Each step—everything that participants do during the activity—facilitates the accomplishment of the stated goal. Each ELA includes complete instructions for facilitating the intervention and a clear statement of goals, suggested group size and timing, materials required, an explanation of the process, and, where appropriate, possible variations to the activity. (For more detail on Experiential Learning Activities, see the Introduction to the *Reference Guide to Handbooks and Annuals*, 1999 edition, Pfeiffer, San Francisco.)

GAME A group activity that has the purpose of fostering team spirit and togetherness in addition to the achievement of a pre-stated goal. Usually contrived—undertaking a desert expedition, for example—this type of learning method offers an engaging means for participants to demonstrate and practice business and interpersonal skills. Games are effective for team building and personal development mainly because the goal is subordinate to the process—the means through which participants reach decisions, collaborate, communicate, and generate trust and understanding. Games often engage teams in "friendly" competition.

ICEBREAKER A (usually) short activity designed to help participants overcome initial anxiety in a training session and/or to acquaint the participants with one another. An icebreaker can be a fun activity or can be tied to specific topics or training goals. While a useful tool in itself, the icebreaker comes into its own in situations where tension or resistance exists within a group.

INSTRUMENT A device used to assess, appraise, evaluate, describe, classify, and summarize various aspects of human behavior. The term used to describe an instrument depends primarily on its format and purpose. These terms include survey, questionnaire, inventory, diagnostic, survey, and poll. Some uses of instruments include providing instrumental feedback to group members, studying here-and-now processes or functioning within a group, manipulating group composition, and evaluating outcomes of training and other interventions.

Instruments are popular in the training and HR field because, in general, more growth can occur if an individual is provided with a method for focusing specifically on his or her own behavior. Instruments also are used to obtain information that will serve as a basis for change and to assist in workforce planning efforts.

Paper-and-pencil tests still dominate the instrument landscape with a typical package comprising a facilitator's guide, which offers advice on administering the instrument and interpreting the collected data, and an initial set of instruments. Additional instruments are available separately. Pfeiffer, though, is investing heavily in e-instruments. Electronic instrumentation provides effortless distribution and, for larger groups particularly, offers advantages over paper-and-pencil tests in the time it takes to analyze data and provide feedback.

LECTURETTE A short talk that provides an explanation of a principle, model, or process that is pertinent to the participants' current learning needs. A lecturette is intended to establish a common language bond between the trainer and the participants by providing a mutual frame of reference. Use a lecturette as an introduction to a group activity or event, as an interjection during an event, or as a handout.

MODEL A graphic depiction of a system or process and the relationship among its elements. Models provide a frame of reference and something more tangible, and more easily remembered, than a verbal explanation. They also give participants something to "go on," enabling them to track their own progress as they experience the dynamics, processes, and relationships being depicted in the model.

ROLE PLAY A technique in which people assume a role in a situation/scenario: a customer service rep in an angry-customer exchange, for example. The way in which the role is approached is then discussed and feedback is offered. The role play is often repeated using a different approach and/or incorporating changes made based on feedback received. In other words, role playing is a spontaneous interaction involving realistic behavior under artificial (and safe) conditions.

SIMULATION A methodology for understanding the interrelationships among components of a system or process. Simulations differ from games in that they test or use a model that depicts or mirrors some aspect of reality in form, if not necessarily in content. Learning occurs by studying the effects of change on one or more factors of the model. Simulations are commonly used to test hypotheses about what happens in a system—often referred to as "what if?" analysis—or to examine best-case/worst-case scenarios.

THEORY A presentation of an idea from a conjectural perspective. Theories are useful because they encourage us to examine behavior and phenomena through a different lens.

TOPICS

The twin goals of providing effective and practical solutions for workforce training and organization development and meeting the educational needs of training and human resource professionals shape Pfeiffer's publishing program. Core topics include the following:

> Leadership & Management
> Communication & Presentation
> Coaching & Mentoring
> Training & Development
> E-Learning
> Teams & Collaboration
> OD & Strategic Planning
> Human Resources
> Consulting

What will you find on pfeiffer.com?

• The best in workplace performance solutions for training and HR professionals

• Downloadable training tools, exercises, and content

• Web-exclusive offers

• Training tips, articles, and news

• Seamless on-line ordering

• Author guidelines, information on becoming a Pfeiffer Affiliate, and much more

Discover more at www.pfeiffer.com